Decision Making
for Business

RENEWALS 458-4574

Decision Making for Business: A Reader

This book – *Decision Making for Business: A Reader* – is one of a series of three readers which constitute the main teaching texts of the Open University course Business Behaviour in a Changing World (B300). The other titles are *Strategy for Business: A Reader*, edited by Marianna Mazzucato and *Policy Issues for Business: A Reader*, edited by Vivek Suneja.

This course is one of three core courses which are compulsory elements in the Open University's BA in Business Studies. In addition to the compulsory courses, students who intend to gain this degree also study courses which include topics such as Economics, Organizational Change, Design and Innovation, Quantitative Methods.

Business Behaviour in a Changing World (B300) is innovative in terms of the breadth of material studied. The course covers decision-making, strategy and policy from a variety of different theoretical stances supplemented by a range of empirical findings. In this way B300 provides a synthesis of each of the fields while at the same time considering the important linkages between them.

As with all Open University courses, students are not only supplied with teaching texts; they also receive comprehensive guidance on how to study and work through these texts. In the case of B300, this guidance is contained in three Study Guides which are supplied to students separately. These guides explain the choice of readings, identify key points and guide the students' work and understanding. A core feature of the guides is an explicit focus on the identification, development, deployment and testing of a series of business graduate skills. These include study skills, cognitive skills of analysis and assessment, IT and numeracy.

Each student is allocated a local tutor and is encouraged to participate in a strategically integrated set of tutorials which are held during the course.

Details of this and other Open University courses can be obtained from the Course Reservations Centre, PO Box 724, The Open University, Milton Keynes MK7 6ZS, United Kingdom. Tel.: +44 (0)1908 653231, e-mail: ces-gen@open.ac.uk. Alternatively, you may visit the Open University website at http://www.open.ac.uk where you can learn more about the wide range of courses and packs offered at all levels by the Open University.

For information about the purchase of Open University course components, contact Open University Worldwide Ltd, The Berrill Building, Walton Hall, Milton Keynes MK7 6AA, United Kingdom. Tel.: +44 (0)1908 858785; fax: +44 (0)1908 858787; e-mail: ouwenq@open.ac.uk; website: http://www.ouw.co.uk.

Decision Making
for Business
A READER

EDITED BY GRAEME SALAMAN
AT THE OPEN UNIVERSITY

SAGE Publications
London · Thousand Oaks · New Delhi
www.sagepub.co.uk

in association with

The Open University

www.open.ac.uk

WITHDRAWN
UTSA Libraries

© Compilation, original and editorial material, The Open University 2002
All rights reserved.

First Published 2002

Apart from any fair dealing for the purposes of research or private study, or criticism or review, as permitted under the Copyright, Designs and Patents Act, 1988, this publication may be reproduced, stored or transmitted in any form, or by any means, only with the prior permission in writing of the publishers, or in the case of reprographic reproduction, in accordance with the terms of licences issued by the Copyright Licensing Agency. Inquiries concerning reproduction outside those terms should be sent to the publishers.

SAGE Publications Ltd
6 Bonhill Street
London EC2A 4PU

SAGE Publications Inc
2455 Teller Road
Thousand Oaks, California 91320

SAGE Publications India Pvt Ltd
32, M-Block Market
Greater Kailash – I
New Delhi 110 048

British Library Cataloguing in Publication data

A catalogue record for this book is available from the British Library

ISBN 0–7619–7410–5
ISBN 0–7619–7411–3 (pbk)

Library of Congress control number available

Typeset by Keystroke, Jacaranda Lodge, Wolverhampton
Printed in Great Britain by The Alden Press, Oxford

Library
University of Texas
at San Antonio

SERIES INTRODUCTION

The importance and influence of business in the modern world has been widely recognized. For us as citizens, consumers, employees, managers, voters and so on, understanding how firms, and indeed all forms of organization work, is therefore of direct relevance. The way that businesses conduct themselves affects us all. As a consequence it is vital for us to understand how they make decisions, for example to invest in some products or services rather than others. The variety of factors that are taken into account, the way in which conclusions are reached, all help us get to grips with these sorts of issues. This involves developing an understanding of how decisions in organizations are made. We also should understand the strategies that businesses pursue, the development of their core competencies as well as how organizations innovate. Finally, the range of policy issues from regulation of competition to environment and the developing world provide a rich contextual seam within which strategies and decisions are made in a world where the norm is change.

This book is one in a series of three readers which bring together classic and seminal materials, many of them summaries and reviews, which are designed to achieve the teaching objectives of the Open University course Business Behaviour in a Changing World (B300) – a core course in the Open University's BA in Business Studies. The volumes are organized in an innovative way around three important themes: decision-making, strategy and policy. The volumes have been designed to supply a selection of articles, theoretical and empirical, in each of these areas. They are supported by study guides so that together they allow the identification, development, deployment and practice of a range of skills required by the Business Studies courses in general. Therefore while they constitute the core teaching resources of this Open University course, the volumes would also make admirable selections for any course concerned with these areas. They are not intended to be cutting edge or fashionable. They are designed as a resource for anyone seeking an understanding of the changing nature of organizations and of the world of business.

Each of these volumes has been edited by members of the course team. But in a very real sense they are collective products of the course team as a whole. That is why all the members of the course team deserve recognition and acknowledgement for their contribution to the course and to these collections.

CONTENTS

ACKNOWLEDGEMENTS

Chapter 1: Houghton Mifflin for Janis, Irving L. 'A perfect failure: the Bay of Pigs', *Victims of Groupthink*, pp. 14–49. Copyright © 1972 by Houghton Mifflin Company. Used with permission.

Chapter 2: Blackwell publishers for Valentin, Erhard K. 'Anatomy of a fatal business strategy', *Journal of Management Studies*, 31 (1994). Copyright © Blackwell Publishers 1994.

Chapter 3: Blackwell Publishers for Cyert, R.M. and March, J.G. 'A summary of basic concepts in the behavioural theory of the firm', in *A Behavioural Theory of the Firm*. Copyright © Blackwell Publishers 1965.

Chapter 4: Sage Publications Ltd. for Miller, S., Hickson, D. and Wilson, D. 'Decision-making in organisations', in S. Clegg et al. (eds), *Handbook of Organisation Studies*. Copyright © Susan J. Millar, David J. Hickson and David C. Wilson 1996.

Chapter 5: Tavistock for Pettigrew, A. 'Decision-making as a political process', in A. Pettigrew, *The Politics of Organisational Decision-Making*. Copyright © Andrew Pettigrew 1973.

Chapter 6: Blackwell Publishers for an extract from Brunsson, N. 'The irrationality of action and action rationality: decisions, ideologies and organizational actions', *Journal of Management Studies*, 19(1) (1982). Copyright © Blackwell Publishers 1982.

Chapter 7: Macmillan (New York) for Strauss, A. et al. 'The hospital and its negotiated order', in E. Friedson et al. (eds), *The Hospital in Modern Society*. Copyright © Macmillan NY 1963.

Chapter 8: Routledge & Keegan and Paul and Aldine Press for Zimmerman, D. (1971) 'The practicalities of rule use', in J. Douglas (ed.), *Understanding Everyday Life*.

Chapter 9: The Academy of Management for Smircich, L. and Stubbart, C. 'Strategic Management in an Enacted World', *Academy of Management Review*, 10(4). Copyright © 1985 by the Academy of Management. Reproduced with the permission of the Academy of Management in the format textbook via Copyright Clearance Center.

Chapter 10: John Wiley and Sons for Lant, T. K. et al. (1992) 'The role of managerial learning and interpretation in strategic persistence and reorientation', *Strategic Management Journal*, 13(8). Copyright © *Strategic Management Journal* 1992. Reprinted with permission of John Wiley and Sons Limited.

Chapter 11: Blackwell Publishers for Schwenk, C. 'The cognitive perspective on strategic decision-making', *Journal of Management Studies*, 25(1). Copyright © Blackwell Publishers 1988.

Chapter 12: Bate, P. (1984) 'The impact of organisational culture on approaches to organisational problem solving', *Organisation Studies*, 5(1). Copyright © Paul Bate 1984.

Chapter 13: Routledge for Brunsson, N. and Olsen, J. P. 'Organisational forms: can we choose them?', *The Reforming Organisation* (1993). Copyright © Routledge 1993.

Chapter 14: Blackwell Publishers for du Gay, P. and Salaman, G. 'The cult(ure) of the customer', *Journal of Management Studies*, 29(5). Copyright © Blackwell Publishers 1992.

Chapter 15: Routledge and The Open University for Newman, J. 'Managerialism and social welfare', in G. Hughes and G. Lewis (eds), *Unsettling Welfare: Reconstruction of Social Policy*. Copyright © The Open University 1998.

Chapter 16: From Laroche, H. 'From decision to action in organizations', *Organizational Science*, 6(1) (1995).

Decision-making is central to an understanding of organizations and of business. Organizations which are in so many respects incredibly efficient and reasonable sometimes seem to do such daft or dangerous things. Businesses which are successful for many years suddenly get it wrong and seem unable to correct. We notice these things and we wonder. Was it stupidity? Almost certainly not. Was it indifference? Possibly. It's certainly worth looking at the objectives and priorities the decision-makers were pursuing. Was it some sort of incompetence – that is, were decision-makers concerned with the right priorities but unable for some reason to gather sufficient data, analyse it sensibly and thoroughly in order to come to a sensible answer? Or was it a result of splits and divisions within and between the organizations concerned. Again, very probably.

This book is concerned with the importance of decisions, processes of decision-making and the implications of 'flawed' decision-making. It will suggest that patterns of decision-making can be described and explained. It will suggest that understanding patterns of decision-making requires reference to, and use of, theories and that these theories differ. Understanding decision-making raises questions about our understanding of how organizations work. Theories of decision-making are also variants of theories of how organizations as a whole work. As the authors of Chapter 4 point out: 'the area of organizational decision-making is part of the broader field of organization studies and organization theory. It has therefore followed a similar pattern of evolution, drawing on a variety of paradigms and perspectives and being characterized by a multiplicity of theories, models and methodologies' (Miller et al.: 74).

The book will identify some of the sources and consequences of limited decision-making. And it will suggest that understanding patterns of decision-making may require an understanding of sources of 'distortion' and 'irrationality', and references to the forms of rationality – the dominant logics – which establish the taken-for-granted assumptions underlying decision-making.

Why look at processes of organizational decision-making? There are a number of answers, and Chapter 4 discusses some of them. One reason is that decision-making is central to organizations since decisions underpin and direct organizational activity. Much of this volume is concerned with exploring the relationships between organizational decision-making and the structure and functioning of the organization. But the main reason for studying decision-making is because the decisions taken in organizations are important because they determine (or justify) organizational action; and because they reveal how organizations think.

Now that is a contentious statement. Surely *organizations* don't think: only people think. There are two points to be made here. First, increasingly organizations do 'think', at least in a rudimentary and mechanical way in that computers and systems can be programmed to respond to incoming data automatically, and this tendency – for decisions to be enshrined in computer systems – will increase. However these are still examples of human thinking embedded in automatic systems.

But there is a more serious sense in which it is possible to talk of organizations thinking. Of course all thinking within organizations is done by people. But the way in which people within an organization think is a product of forces within (and without) the organization itself, not just of their individual personalities and intellects. Organizations influence – in ways which will be discussed in this book – the ways members think on behalf of or as members of, the organization. The way the organization is structured, the way information flows (or is obstructed), the values people hold, the way power is exercised, and many other factors discussed in this book influence how people think (and when they think and even *if* they think). As one authority has put it: 'Organizations have cognitive systems and memories. Individuals come and go, but organizations preserve knowledge, behaviours, mental maps, norms and values over time. The distinctive feature of organization level information activity is sharing' (March, 1999: 243).

Within organizations there may well exist shared ways of thinking, shared sets of assumptions – often known as cognitive routines – which are historically based but which have become irrelevant for future success. As one commentator has observed (Van de Ven, 1986: 596), this can result in a potentially dangerous paradox: size, success, age of organizations can result in the development of habitual ways of thinking which threaten adaptation and innovation: 'the older, larger, and more successful organizations become, the more likely they are to have a large repertoire of structures and systems which discourage innovation while encouraging tinkering.'

So to this extent it is possible to talk of organizations thinking, not in the sense that there is a supra human entity with its own organizational mind, and not in the sense that decision-makers are mere puppets, but in the sense that being a member of an organization and being exposed to its systems and culture and history will significantly influence how members think. Individual employees while retaining their own judgement and discretion will nevertheless tend to think in a way that is subtly informed by their organizational membership.

Central to any understanding of decision-making is the notion of rationality. Rationality refers to the quality of thinking and decision-making. Rationality is where we begin. We expect decision-making – at least organizational decision-making (we are less demanding about individual decision-making) – to be rational. This is the norm against which we judge the actual realities of decision-making. If we attribute rationality to a decision or a decision-making process we are saying that it follows various steps which we consider to be thorough, logical, systematic, reflecting what we believe to be the proper and necessary stages and elements of an efficient process. (Rationality in decision-making is discussed by Miller et al. in Chapter 4. It is also discussed by numerous other contributors to this volume.) This book explores the nature and determinants of forms of rationality within organizations. However there are some important distinctions and qualifications that need to be made. Some important clarifying points on rationality and its role within the modern organization have been made by Max Weber who as well as noting the central value and role of rationality in modern thinking also defined the modern organization precisely in terms of its 'rationality', i.e. the way in which decisions are made. The passage is worth quoting because it establishes a major theme of this book.

> Experience tends universally to show that the purely bureaucratic type of administrative organization . . . is, from a purely technical point of view, capable of attaining the highest degree of efficiency and is in this sense formally the most rational known means of carrying out imperative control over human beings. It is superior to any other form in precision, in stability, in the stringency of its discipline, and in its reliability. It thus makes possible a particularly high degree of calculability of results for the heads of the organization and for those acting in relation to it. It is finally superior both in intensive efficiency and in the scope of its operations, and is formally capable of application to all kinds of administrative tasks. (Weber, 1964: 24)

This passage positions rationality at the heart of the modern organization. But what does Weber mean by rationality? Weber distinguishes three different forms of rationality, all and each of which are still apparent, and these distinctions are still important. First, Weber distinguishes what he calls *formal* rationality. This rationality is concerned less with reality and more with appearance. It is based on the use of or reference to, means of calculation. The application of calculation, particularly accounting type calculation and measurement to organizational processes and decision-making. This is a form of rationality that has nothing necessarily to do with the efficiency of the process involved: it concerns the language in which the issue is expressed: the extent to which the decision or choice or assessment is ' . . . capable of being expressed in numerical, calculable terms' (Weber, 1964: 185). So according to Weber – and this usage is still very much with us – a decision could be 'formally' rational in that it was dressed up in the language of calculation (accountancy-speak, for example, or statistics) but be by other measures irrational, or questionable.

Secondly, Weber distinguishes what he calls *substantive* rationality. This comes in two variants. As he notes this:

> . . . conveys only one element common to all the possible empirical situations; namely that it is not sufficient to consider only the purely formal fact that calculations are being made on grounds of expediency by the methods which are,

among those available, technically the most nearly adequate. It addition, *it is necessary to take account of the fact that economic activity is oriented to ultimate ends of some kind, whether they be ethical, political, utilitarian, hedonistic, the attainment of social distinction, of social equality, or of anything else. Substantive rationality cannot be measured in terms of formal calculation alone, but also involves a relation to the absolute values or to the content of the particular given ends to which it is oriented. In principle there is an indefinite number of possible standards of value which are 'rational' in this sense.* (Weber, 1964: 185, emphasis added)

Weber offers two types of substantive rationality which are still current in commonsense reactions to decisions taken by organizations. One sense of Weber's substantive rationality refers to *the appropriateness of means to the achievement of chosen ends* – i.e. the degree to which the 'methods are, among those available, technically the most nearly adequate'. Secondly it refers to the nature, even the rationality of the ends themselves. This is a sensible and commonsense distinction. It is a classic sense of rationality: that the method someone chooses is clearly sensible and 'rational' given the end they are pursuing. If one wishes to pursue a certain end then we can judge the various means available in terms of their likelihood of achieving the desired end. If someone wants to own a car it is a rational strategy to get a job and save money, or to seek a better paid job. It is less rational to spend the day in prayer, or to write to car manufacturers asking them to give you one. This means/ends link is one key form of rationality. It is obviously contextually limited by the prevailing state of knowledge and theory. What counts as an acceptable method of ensuring an outcome depends on the prevailing beliefs and theories about causation. It made total sense in the context of available knowledge for the eighteenth century barber surgeon to bleed his consumptive patient. It doesn't make sense to us, but it is a great mistake to think that while we can see the fallacies and errors of our predecessors (or our contemporaries in other belief systems), our own beliefs about the appropriate means to achieve ends are beyond dispute: that we (uniquely) are free from error, that our knowledge alone is complete, our truth absolute. One of the objectives of this book is to point out how many of the currently widely accepted assumptions about appropriate means for achieving organizational ends are extremely specific to our period: they reflect not rationality *per se* but today's limited version of it.

The second type of rationality refers not to the suitability of means to ends but *the choice of ends themselves*. This too is open to dispute and difference. These ends are personally and culturally fixed. No end is intrinsically more rational than another, despite the different values placed on different ends in different societies and periods and belief systems. Some ends – often those that derive from value systems different from our own – may seem 'irrational' to us. This sort of attributed irrationality is particularly prone to spatial, temporal, or cultural distance and difference. The ends pursued by people far away or different often seem strange. It is a small step to then judge them irrational. Of course there are no absolutely rational ends since any way of attributing or assessing the rationality of ends is ultimately value-based. Even widely accepted and pervasive ends can be seen as irrational. By what standards for example, is the pursuit of profit rational? What are the obvious irrationalities of an emphasis on profit?

Weber's distinctions establish the basis for the analysis of this book. We will look at the ways in which certain procedures, or frameworks or types of information symbolically come to represent rationality within particular epochs, cultures or ways of thinking. We will also consider how the means that decision-makers deem appropriate for the achievement of certain ends reflect not a neutral detached analysis and assessment of available options but an unthinking commitment to certain established, shared and powerful values or cognitive systems. And we will consider how the processes of decision-making and shared cognitive structures may themselves have an impact on the quality and rationality of thinking and on the choice of means used to achieve desired ends. Finally we shall consider how the ends that organizations pursue are not natural, neutral or given, but chosen (if subconsciously) and chosen within certain cultural regimes which establish their strength and value.

References

March, James (1999) *The Pursuit of Organisational Intelligence*. Oxford: Blackwell.

Van de Ven, A. (1986) 'Central problems in the management of innovation', *Management Science*, 32(5): 590–607.

Weber, M. (1964) *The Theory of Social and Economic Organisation* (edited with a foreword by Talcott Parsons). New York: Free Press.

The Anatomy of Decision-making

This section is concerned with the questions: what happens when people in organizations make decisions, and in particular what happens when organizations make a disastrous decision – what forces and dynamics cause things to 'go wrong'? It looks at the ways in which decision-making can and does deviate from the ideal, and idealized, rational model. A major question addressed in this section is: 'What are the limitations of the rational choice model of decision-making?'. Chapter 1 offers an overview of the literature which identifies the problems with and limitations of the rational decision-making model. There are a number of classic books and articles that have contributed enormously to our understanding of what happens when people actually make decisions and how this differs from the formal rational process. This literature shows the various ways in which managers actually behave when making decisions. Although some of these models of decision-making include some level of explanation, on the whole most of the literature summarized in this section is descriptive.

Of the four chapters, two look at examples of seriously defective decision-making. The other two offer frameworks for understanding why things went wrong or review a number of such frameworks. Every now and again things go badly wrong, sometimes with obvious and public consequences. These occasions are worth studying but although extreme and unusual they usefully reveal the dynamics and features of flawed decision-making. There are two cases explored in Section 1, one a commercial example, the other a governmental one. They reveal some of the key pathologies of decision-making, particularly group dynamics, the role of authority, organizational ideological and cognitive factors which will be explored in greater detail and depth in this module. This first section also contains a comprehensive review of many theories of flawed organizational decision-making.

The key objective of Section 1 is to 'problematize' the process of decision-making: to make the normal strange, to suggest that what we sometimes accept as everyday and normal in fact does merit attention and does merit explanation. So to problematize is to defamiliarize – to renew our perception of things: to analyse by what processes and assumptions we have come to see these events as not requiring explanation or analysis. The first section argues that the reality of decision-making processes differs considerably from the idealized systematic rational model and that these dynamics and features require attention and explanation.

Section 1 also contains two important chapters – by Cyert and March, and Miller et al. – which overview the different ways in which decision-making deviates from the rational model and also offers some overview and mapping of the different sorts of theories researchers have used to predict and understand the nature of decision-making.

A Perfect Failure: The Bay of Pigs

IRVING L. JANIS*

The Kennedy administration's Bay of Pigs decision ranks among the worst fiascoes ever perpetrated by a responsible government. Planned by an over-ambitious, eager group of American intelligence officers who had little background or experience in military matters, the attempt to place a small brigade of Cuban exiles secretly on a beachhead in Cuba with the ultimate aim of over-throwing the government of Fidel Castro proved to be a 'perfect failure' (T. Draper, cited in Meyer and Szule, 1962: 146). The group that made the basic decision to approve the invasion plan included some of the most intelligent men ever to participate in the councils of government. Yet all the major assumptions supporting the plan were so completely wrong that the venture began to founder at the outset and failed in its earliest stages.

The 'ill-starred adventure'

Ironically, the idea for the invasion was first suggested by John F. Kennedy's main political opponent, Richard M. Nixon. As Vice President during the Eisenhower administration, Nixon had proposed that the United States government secretly send a trained group of Cuban exiles to Cuba to fight against Castro. In March 1960, acting on Nixon's suggestion, President Dwight D. Eisenhower directed the Central Intelligence Agency to organize Cuban exiles in the United States into a unified political movement against the Castro regime and to give military training to those who were willing to return to their homeland to engage in guerrilla warfare. The CIA put a large number of its agents to work on this clandestine operation, and they soon evolved an elaborate plan for a military invasion. Apparently without informing President Eisenhower, the CIA began to assume in late 1960 that they could land a brigade of Cuban exiles not as a band of guerrilla infiltrators but as an armed force to carry out a full-scale invasion.

* Houghton Mifflin for Janis, Irving L. 'A perfect failure: the Bay of Pigs', *Victims of Groupthink*, pp. 14–49. Copyright © 1972 by Houghton Mifflin Company. Used with permission.

Two days after his inauguration in January 1961, President John F. Kennedy and several leading members of his new administration were given a detailed briefing about the proposed invasion by Allen Dulles, Head of the CIA, and General Lyman Lemnitzer, Chairman of the Joint Chiefs of Staff. During the next 80 days, a core group of presidential advisers repeatedly discussed this inherited plan informally and in the meetings of an advisory committee that included the three Joint Chiefs of Staff. In early April 1961, at one of the meetings with the President, all the key advisers gave their approval to the CIA's invasion plan. Their deliberations led to a few modifications of details, such as the choice of the invasion site.

On 17 April 1961, the brigade of about 1400 hundred Cuban exiles, aided by the United States Navy, Air Force, and the CIA, invaded the swampy coast of Cuba at the Bay of Pigs. Nothing went as planned. On the first day, not one of the four ships containing reserve ammunition and supplies arrived; the first two were sunk by a few planes in Castro's air force, and the other two promptly fled. By the second day, the brigade was completely surrounded by 20,000 troops of Castro's well-equipped army. By the third day, about 1200 members of the brigade, comprising almost all who had not been killed, were captured and ignominiously led off to prison camps.

In giving their full approval, President Kennedy, Dean Rusk, Robert McNamara, and other high-level policy-makers in the United States government had assumed that 'use of the exile brigade would make possible the toppling of Castro without actual aggression by the United States' (Sorensen, 1966: 332). The President's main advisers certainly did not expect such an overwhelming military disaster. Nor did they anticipate that the United States government's attempts to disclaim responsibility for the initial air assault would be thoroughly discredited, that friendly Latin American countries would be outraged, that protest meetings would be held in the United States and throughout the world to denounce the United States for its illegal acts of aggression against a tiny neighbor, that intellectuals who had regarded the new administration with bright hopes would express disaffection in sarcastic telegrams ('Nixon or Kennedy: Does it make any difference?'), or that European allies and United Nations statesmen would join in condemnation. None of them guessed that the abortive invasion would encourage a military rapprochement between Castro and the Soviet leaders, culminating in a deal to set up installations only 90 miles from United States' shores equipped with nuclear bombs and missiles and manned by more than 5000 Soviet troops, transforming Cuba within 18 months into a powerful military base as a satellite of the Soviet Union. Had the President and his policy advisers imagined that this nightmarish scenario would materialize (or had they even considered such an outcome to be a calculated risk), they undoubtedly would have rejected the CIA's invasion plan.

We are given a vivid picture of the President's reactions in Sorensen's *Kennedy*, described by a *New York Times* reviewer as 'the nearest thing we will ever have to the memoirs Kennedy intended to write.' When the first news reports revealed how wrong his expectations had been, President Kennedy was stunned. As the news grew worse during the next three days, he became angry and sick at heart.

He realized that the plan he thought he had approved had little in common with the one he had in fact approved. 'How could I have been so stupid to let them go ahead?' he asked. Sorensen wrote, 'His anguish was doubly deepened by the knowledge that the rest of the world was asking the same question' (Sorensen, 1966: 346).

Arthur Schlesinger, Jr., in his authoritative history of the Kennedy administration, recalled that 'Kennedy would sometimes refer incredulously to the Bay of Pigs, wondering how a rational and responsible government could ever have become involved in so ill-starred an adventure' (Schlesinger, 1965: 292). The policy advisers who participated in the deliberations felt much the same way, if not worse. Allen Dulles, for example. was 'still troubled and haggard' (Schlesinger, 1965: 295) several days later and offered to resign as chief of the CIA. Secretary of Defense McNamara, when he left the government seven years later, publicly stated that he still felt personally responsible for having misadvised President Kennedy on the Bay of Pigs (*New York Times*, 5 February 1968). All who participated in the Bay of Pigs decision were perturbed about the dangerous gap between their expectations and the realities they should have anticipated. which resulted, as Sorensen put it, in 'a shocking number of errors in the whole decision-making process' (Sorensen, 1966: 338).

Qualifications of the core members of the advisory group

It seems improbable that the shocking number of errors can be attributed to lack of intellectual capability for making policy judgements. The core members of Kennedy's team who were briefed on the Cuban invasion plan included four cabinet members and three men on the White House staff, all of whom were well qualified to make objective analyses of the pros and cons of alternative courses of action on vital issues of government policy.

Dean Rusk, Secretary of State, had been recruited by John F. Kennedy from his high-level position as head of the Rockefeller Foundation because of his solid reputation as an experienced administrator who could be counted on to have good ideas and sound judgement. He had served in policy-making positions in the State Department under Dean Acheson, first Head of the Office of Political Affairs and later as Deputy Undersecretary in charge of policy co-ordination. During the Truman administration, Rusk became a veteran policy-maker and exerted a strong influence on a variety of important decisions concerning United States foreign policy in Asia.

Robert McNamara, the Secretary of Defense, was an expert statistician who had worked his way up to the presidency of the Ford Motor Company. He enjoyed a towering reputation for his intellectual brilliance and cold logic combined with personal integrity. Early in his career he had been on the faculty of the Harvard Business School. Later he developed his expertise in the statistical control unit of the United States Air Force, where he helped to work out a successful system for surveillance and control to facilitate decision-making about the flow of materials and production. During his years at Ford Motor Company, McNamara had also devised new techniques for improving rational methods of decision-making.

Douglas Dillon, Secretary of the Treasury, was asked to attend all White House meetings on the plans to invade Cuba because he was valued as an objective and analytic thinker. The only Republican member of Kennedy's cabinet, Dillon was selected because of the 'superior ability' and 'wisdom' he had displayed as Undersecretary of State during the Eisenhower administration. He soon became a respected member of the Kennedy team and a personal friend of the Kennedy family.

Then, too, there was Robert Kennedy, the Attorney General, one of the most influential members of the President's team. According to his close associates in the government, the President's brother was a bright young man whose strengths far outweighed his weaknesses. The Attorney General had been fully briefed on the invasion plan from the beginning. He did not attend the subsequent formal meetings of the advisory committee but was kept informed. On at least one occasion he used his personal influence to suppress opposition to the CIA plan.

Also on hand was McGeorge Bundy, the President's Special Assistant for National Security Affairs, who had the rank of a cabinet member. A key man on Kennedy's White House team, Bundy was one of the leading intellectuals imported to Washington from Harvard University, where he had been Dean of Arts and Sciences. His background in decision-making was not limited to the problems of a great university; earlier in his career, as a scholar, he had made a close study of Secretary of State Acheson's decisions.

The White House staff also included Arthur Schlesinger, Jr., an outstanding Harvard historian whom the President asked to attend all the White House meetings on the invasion plan, and Richard Goodwin, another Harvard man 'of uncommon intelligence.' Goodwin did not attend the policy-making meetings but was informed about the invasion plan, discussed it frequently with Schlesinger, and conferred with Rusk and others during the weeks preceding the final decision.

The President asked five of the seven members of this core group to join him at the White House meetings of the ad hoc advisory committee on the Cuban invasion plan. At these meetings, Kennedy's advisers found themselves face-to-face with the three Joint Chiefs of Staff, in full, medaled regalia. These military men were carry-overs from the Eisenhower administration; throughout the deliberations, they remained quite detached from the Kennedy team. Also present at the meetings of the advisory committee were five others who had fairly close ties to the President and his main advisers. Two of the most active participants were the Director and Deputy Director of the CIA, Allen Dulles and Richard Bissell. They, too, were carry-overs from the Eisenhower administration, but President Kennedy and his inner circle welcomed them as members of the new administration's team. According to Roger Hilsman (Director of the Intelligence branch of the State Department), Bissell 'was a brilliant economist and government executive whom President Kennedy had known for years and so admired and respected that he would very probably have made him Director of the CIA when Dulles eventually retired' (Hilsman, 1967: 30). Bissell was the most active advocate of the CIA plan; his eloquent presentations did the main job of convincing the conferees to accept it.

Three others who participated in the White House meetings as members of the advisory committee were exceptionally well qualified to appraise the political consequences of the invasion: Thomas C. Mann, Assistant Secretary of State for Inter-American affairs; Adolph A. Berle, Jr., Chairman of the Latin American task force; and Paul Nitze, Assistant Secretary of Defense, who had formerly been the Director of the policy planning staff in the State Department.

The group that deliberated on the Bay of Pigs decision included men of considerable intellectual talent. Like the President, all the main advisers were shrewd thinkers, capable of objective, rational analysis, and accustomed to speaking their minds. But collectively they failed to detect the serious flaws in the invasion plan.

Six major miscalculations

The President and his key advisers approved the Bay of Pigs invasion plan on the basis of six assumptions, each of which was wrong. In retrospect, the President's advisers could see that even when they first began to discuss the plan, sufficient information was available to indicate that their assumptions were much too shaky. They could have obtained and used the crucial information beforehand to correct their false assumptions if at the group meetings they had been more critical and probing in fulfilling their advisory roles.

Assumption 1: No will know that the United States was responsible for the invasion of Cuba. Most people will believe the CIA story, and skeptics can easily be refuted.

When President Kennedy was first told about the plan by the CIA representatives, he laid down one firm stipulation: the United States armed forces would not overtly participate in an invasion of Cuba. He repeated this essential condition each time the matter was discussed. He would not consider accepting the CIA's plan to use the armed Cuban brigade unless it could be safely assumed that the United States government would not be held responsible for initiating a military attack against its small neighbor. On the assumption that this requirement could be met, the plan was seen as a golden opportunity to overthrow Castro. The Castro regime had been a source of irritation to the United States government, even though the President and his advisers did not consider it a direct threat to American security.

In response to the President's questions about the plan, Allen Dulles and Richard Bissell assured Kennedy and his advisory group that all the world would believe that Cuban dissidents were the sole initiators and executors of the invasion. They said that highly effective precautions would mask completely the fact that the United States was engineering the invasion. The brigade of Cuban exiles would be quietly and unspectacularly landed in their homeland. The only noisy part would be the preliminary air attacks against Cuban airfields, but these would be handled by a clever cover story. The United States would be able to deny all complicity in the bombing of Cuban bases. The planes used in the bombing raids would be B-26s of Second World War vintage, without any United States markings. They would look like planes in Castro's air force and could plausibly be claimed to belong to Cuban defectors.

During the weeks preceding the invasion, it became increasingly apparent that the cover story would not work. The President's Press Secretary. Pierre Salinger, has called the plan 'the least covert military operation in history.' A week before the invasion, President Kennedy complained heatedly, 'I can't believe what I'm reading! Castro doesn't need agents over here. All he has to do is read our papers. It's all laid out for him' (Salinger, 1966: 194). American newsmen had gotten wind of the invasion plan. They were reporting 'secret' details about what was going on in United States military training camps in Guatemala, where the Cubans were being readied for the invasion, and describing efforts being made in Miami to recruit more Cuban volunteers. Yet, according to Schlesinger, 'somehow the idea took hold around the cabinet table that this would not much matter so long as United States soldiers did not take part in the actual fighting (Schlesinger, 1965: 249).

Thus, despite evidence at hand, the policy-makers ignored the old adage that one must expect any secret known to a large number of people to leak out. Apparently they never discussed the obvious danger that a secret act of military aggression against a neighboring country might be revealed by one or more insiders, particularly when the invasion plan was known to hundreds of Cuban exiles who were being recruited and trained to carry it out. It was also known to a large number of foreign politicians, who might have had their own reasons for revealing it. Leaders of the Cuban exiles' political movements (each of whom had his own ideas about what should be done), government officials in Guatemala (who had allowed the CIA to set up camps to train the Cuban brigade), and officials in Nicaragua (who had agreed to allow the United States to use Nicaraguan air bases to launch air attacks against Cuba) – all knew what was being planned. Furthermore, members of the policy-making group were warned on several occasions by Senator J. William Fulbright, Chairman of the Foreign Relations Committee, and by other prestigious men that an invasion attempt would probably be attributed directly to the United States and would seriously damage United States relations with Latin American countries and European allies. Despite all warnings, the members of Kennedy's advisory group failed to question the assumption that the secret would not be revealed. President Kennedy was so confident that he publicly promised at a press conference on 12 April 1961 (five days before the invasion), that 'there will not be, under any conditions, any intervention in Cuba by United States armed forces, and this Government will do everything it possibly can . . . to make sure that there are no Americans involved in actions inside Cuba' (Sorensen, 1966: 334).

The world did not immediately learn that the first invaders to land on Cuban soil were in fact United States Navy frogmen (in violation of the President's orders), but the United States nevertheless was blamed for the invasion from the outset. The CIA's cover story was quickly torn to pieces by the world press. The credibility of Adlai Stevenson, the United States representative to the United Nations, was also sacrificed, despite President Kennedy's solemn statement to his intimates only a few days earlier that 'the integrity and credibility of Adlai Stevenson constitute one of our great national assets. I don't want anything to be done [in handling the cover story] which might jeopardize that' (Sorensen, 1966: 271). The truth having been carefully withheld from him, Stevenson solemnly denied United States complicity in the bombings at a meeting of the United Nations General Assembly. His statements were immediately seen by foreign observers as inconsistent with news reports about the air attacks and were soon labeled outright lies when some of his alleged facts were disproved 24 hours later by authentic photographs. Stevenson later said that this was the most humiliating experience of his long years of public service.

Assumption 2: The Cuban air force is so ineffectual that it can be knocked out completely just before the invasion begins.

The invasion plan called for a surprise attack by American bombers, which would destroy Castro's air force on the ground before the invaders moved in. The conferees at the White House thought that the obsolete B-26s used to do the job would be able to destroy Cuba's military planes. They did not make sufficient inquiries to find out that these lumbering old planes would have limited capabilities and would frequently develop engine trouble. The first attack was a surprise, but only a small percentage of Cuba's planes was destroyed. Consequently, the invasion plan went awry at the outset because the Cuban air force was able to assert air control over the landing site. Cuban jet training planes, which were fast and efficient, prevented the freighters containing ammunition and supplies from reaching their destination. The supposedly ineffective Cuban air force shot down half of the American B-26s attempting to protect the invaders and repeatedly bombed the ground troops as they arrived on shore.

A second air strike by United States planes was called off by President Kennedy because it would have revealed too clearly that the planes belonged to the United States and that the entire invasion was an unprovoked attack by the United States. But even if the second air strike had been carried out, it would probably have been even less effective than the first, because there was no longer any element of surprise and the Cuban air force was well dispersed in hidden airfields.

Assumption 3: The 1400 men in the brigade of Cuban exiles have high morale and are willing to carry out the invasion without any support from United States ground troops.

In line with his firm policy of no direct intervention by the United States, President Kennedy explicitly asked the CIA planners if the members of the Cuban exile brigade were willing to risk their lives without United States military participation. The President and his advisers were given a strong affirmative answer, and Dulles and Bissell repeatedly assured them that morale in the brigade was superb. Had the conferees asked the CIA representatives to present evidence supporting this assurance, they might have discovered that they were relying on biased information. CIA agents in Guatemala were sending reports conveying a rosy overall picture to Dulles and Bissell without informing them about exactly what was going on. In order to build morale, the agents deliberately misled the men in the exile brigade by assuring them that they were only a small part of the invading force, that other Cuban brigades were being trained elsewhere for the same mission, that diversionary landings would draw most of Castro's troops away from their invasion site, and that the United States Marines would be participating in the invasion. Furthermore, one month before the invasion, when the policy-making group in Washington was being assured about the magnificent morale of the exile brigade, the men were actually bitterly discontent and beginning to revolt. They objected to being saddled with officers who had been in the army of the reactionary Batista regime and had been recruited and promoted because of their willingness to take order from CIA agents. When discontent finally broke out in a full-scale mutiny, the CIA agents arrested a dozen of the ringleaders and confined them in a prison camp deep in the Guatemala jungle. Such was the high morale of the exile brigade.

Ironically, one of the most convincing 'demonstrations' of high morale to President Kennedy and his advisers was the fact that sons of the political leaders of the Cuban exiles volunteered for the brigade. But both the fathers and the sons had been hoaxed by CIA agents into believing that the invasion would not be allowed to fail, that the United States government was committed to using armed forces to back them up.

When the invasion took place, the men in the brigade fought well, and their morale was sustained for a time by false hope. They thought that despite all the official 'propaganda' put out by the United States government to the contrary, a large number of American troops would land to reinforce them. They had also been led to expect that American ships would bring them the supplies they so urgently needed and would remain offshore to rescue them if necessary.

Assumption 4: Castro's army is so weak that the small Cuban brigade will be able to establish a well-protected beachhead.

Another question frequently discussed by President Kennedy and his advisers was whether the small exile brigade could achieve its initial goal of establishing a firm beachhead without United States military participation. Again, without looking into the evidence, the conferees accepted the optimistic picture presented by Dulles and Bissell, who described Castro's army as poorly equipped, poorly trained, riddled with dissension, and unable to cope with even a small-scale invasion. These assurances happened to be directly contrary to reports of Castro's military strength by experts in the State Department and in the British Intelligence

Service. The CIA planners chose to ignore the experts' reports, and Kennedy's policy advisers did not pursue their questions far enough to become aware of the contradictory estimates, which would have revealed the shakiness of the CIA's assumptions.

As it turned out, Castro's army responded promptly and vigorously to the invasion, even though the invaders fought well. A militia patrol, guarding the coastline because of the invasion alert, was on hand to shoot at the vanguard of the invading force, the Navy frogmen sent out to mark the landing site. Soon large numbers of well-equipped Cuban troops were shelling the beachhead with 122 mm howitzers, 37 mm cannons, and rocket-throwers. Cuban armored tanks began moving in within one day after the invaders landed. By the following day, the exile brigade was surrounded by 20,000 well-equipped Cuban troops, backed up by more than 200,000 troops and militiamen who could have been brought to bear if needed.

Having grossly underestimated Castro's military capabilities, President Kennedy and his advisers belatedly realized that a successful beachhead could not be established in Cuba without a military force at least ten times larger than the one they had agreed to send in. According to Sorensen: 'The President thought he was approving a plan rushed into execution on the grounds that Castro would later acquire the military capability to defeat it. Castro, in fact, already possessed that capability' (Sorensen, 1996: 340).

Assumption 5: The invasion by the exile brigade will touch off sabotage by the Cuban underground and armed uprisings behind the lines that will effectively support the invaders and probably lead to the toppling of the Castro regime.

When first asked by President Kennedy to appraise the CIA's invasion plans, the Joint Chiefs of Staff asserted that the chances for successfully establishing a beachhead were favorable but that 'ultimate success would depend on either a sizeable uprising inside the island or sizeable support from outside' (Schlesinger, 1965: 238). Since American intervention was ruled out by the President, victory would depend on anti-Castro resistance and uprisings behind the lines. A second appraisal by the Joint Chiefs of Staff, just one month before the invasion, made this assumption explicit. Without the support of the Cuban resistance, they reported, there would be no way to overcome the hundreds of thousands of men in Castro's army and militia.

Although skeptical at first about relying on mass insurrection against the Castro regime, President Kennedy was encouraged by his advisory group to set his doubts aside, and he ended up accepting the assumption (Sorensen, 1966: 332). Shortly after the Bay of Pigs debacle, he told Sorensen that he had really thought there was a good chance that the landing of the exile brigade, without overt United States participation, would rally the Cuban people to revolt and oust Castro. According to Schlesinger, this view was shared by Kennedy's closest advisers: 'We all in the White House considered uprisings behind the lines essential to the success of the operation; so, too, did the Joint Chiefs of Staff; and so, we thought, did the CIA' (Schlesinger, 1965: 247).

Once again the CIA spokesmen had misled the other conferees in the White House by neglecting to say that they were aware of strong reasons for not going along with this assumption. As advocates of the CIA plan, Allen Dulles and Richard Bissell confined their remarks almost entirely to the positive side of the picture. They relayed the unsubstantiated reports of their secret agents claiming that more than 2500 people were in the resistance organization in Cuba, that at least 20,000 more were sympathizers, and that CIA contacts inside Cuba were requesting a large number of arms drops.

Long after events had shown that the assumption of a Cuban uprising was completely mistaken, Allen Dulles revealed that from the beginning the CIA had not expected much support from the Cuban resistance. In fact, the CIA had no intelligence estimates that the landing would touch off widespread revolt in Cuba. The intelligence branch of the agency had not been asked to estimate the chances of an invasion being supported by the resistance movement or by popular uprisings behind the lines. Nor were any of the experts on the Cuban desk of the State Department, who kept a daily surveillance of political activities in Cuba, asked for their judgements. Most of the participants in the White House meetings did not know this and simply assumed that the estimates mentioned by Dulles and Bissell had the full authority of the government's intelligence agency behind them.

Had the policy advisers asked more penetrating questions, some of the excluded expert might have been consulted. In the absence of impartial briefings by non-partisan experts on Cuba, no one reminded the group of the results of a carefully conducted poll, reported in the preceding year, that had shown that the overwhelming majority of Cubans supported the Castro regime. These poll results had been circulated throughout the United States government and were generally believed to indicate relatively little hope of inducing widespread action against Castro inside Cuba. This evidence was either forgotten or ignored by the political experts in the advisory group.

Even a few skeptical questions put to Dulles or Bissell might have corrected gross misconceptions. The President and his advisers might have learned that the CIA planners realized (without mentioning it in their briefings) that the pre-invasion air strike would allow Castro plenty of time to move against the underground and to round up political dissidents. This was a necessary sacrifice, the CIA men had decided, in order to knock out Castro's air force.

The lack of detailed questioning about these matters is remarkable when we consider that President Kennedy started off with strong misgivings about the amount of anti-Castro support that could be mustered on the island. His misgivings were shared by at least one other member of his White House staff. Arthur Schlesinger, Jr., in the memorandum he gave the President during the crucial week of decision, stated his doubts about uprisings behind the lines and argued that there was no convincing evidence that mass revolt would be touched off or that Castro's regime was so weak that it could be toppled by the exiles' landing. He warned that if the brigade established a secure foothold in Cuba, the operation would at best lead to a protracted civil war and then Congressmen and other influential politicians in the United States would demand that we intervene by sending in the Marines. Others, including a well-informed journalist just returned from Cuba who was invited to the White House, made similar pessimistic forecasts. Apparently none of these dissenting views was taken seriously enough by the President or his advisers to lead them to ask the intelligence community for an objective assessment of the effectiveness of the Cuban resistance.

Within 24 hours of the first air strikes, it became apparent that there would be no sabotage or rebellion and that Castro's regime had the domestic situation firmly in hand. Just as had been expected by the CIA (but not by the main body of the policy-making group), the Cuban police force was alerted by the initial air strike and moved swiftly against internal sources of resistance. In Havana alone, some 200,000 political suspects were promptly rounded up. Elsewhere in Cuba anyone suspected of having underground connections was jailed. Even organized resistance units that were already armed and waiting for a favorable opportunity to strike out against Castro's regime were ineffective, initiating only sporadic incidents of token resistance.

The Revolutionary Council composed of exiled political leaders of the Cuban resistance movement, who were supposed to set up the new democratic government after the beachhead was established, complained bitterly after the invasion that no effort had been made to co-ordinate the invasion with underground activities. They said that the CIA in Cuba had failed to provide supplies for organized resistance units, thus preventing them from executing long-standing plans to cut power lines and blow up factories. The CIA was also charged with gross negligence for ignoring the armed guerrillas in the Escambray Mountains, for not using the channels available for contacting underground groups throughout the island, and for sending in their own unknown agents, who succeeded only in confusing the entire underground movement. Sorensen concludes that there was no co-operation between the planners and the Cuban underground because the CIA mistrusted the exiled left-wing leaders, just as the right-wing leaders supported by the CIA were mistrusted by most members of the underground. Consequently, 'No coordinated uprising or underground effort was really planned or possible' (Sorensen, 1966: 339). The members of the White House advisory group might have found all this out in advance if they had been sufficiently vigilant to require the CIA representatives to present full details about their plans (or lack of plans) for mobilizing the resistance movement in Cuba.

Assumption 6: If the Cuban brigade does not succeed in its prime military objective, the men can retreat to the Escambray Mountains and reinforce the guerrilla units holding out against the Castro regime.

A major reason for approving the CIA's plan was the decision-makers' expectation that even if the invasion failed to establish a new government in Cuba, there would

Figure 1.1 *Map of Cuba showing location of the Bay of Pigs*

still be a net gain. At worst, the invaders would join up with the rebels in the Escambray Mountains and strengthen the anti-Castro forces on the island; so in one way or another the Cuban exiles, who were already showing signs of unrest about getting back to their homeland in order to fight against the Castro regime, supposedly would be put to good use. Dulles and Bissell, when summarizing the CIA's plan, told the advisory group on more than one occasion that the entire operation was safe because the invaders could, if necessary, escape from the beaches into the mountains. President Kennedy and others in the group were greatly reassured by this argument.

Toward the end of their deliberations, any qualms the policy advisers may have had about the mission were put to rest. They believed the CIA was planning a small invasion (rather than a large-scale amphibious assault) that would enable the brigade of exiles to infiltrate the mountains. But they never had the most relevant information, which they could have obtained. The essential facts contradicted the reassuring view that was being conveyed to the group. Evidently none of the policy-makers at the White House meetings asked to be fully briefed.

After the fiasco was over, President Kennedy and his advisers learned for the first time that the CIA officers in charge of the operation in Guatemala had not planned for an escape to the mountains and had discontinued training for guerrilla warfare long before most of the Cuban exiles in the brigade had started their training. In any case, the escape to the Escambray Mountains was a realistic backstop only as long as the plan called for landing at Trinidad, near the foothills of the mountains. When, as a result of the deliberations of the White House advisory group, Trinidad was judged too conspicuous and was replaced by the Bay of Pigs, there was no possibility that the invaders could retreat to the mountains. Schlesinger acknowledges that he and the others attending the White House meetings simply overlooked the geography of Cuba: 'I don't think we fully realized that the Escambray Mountains lay 80 miles from the Bay of Pigs, across a hopeless tangle of swamps and jungle' (Schlesinger, 1965: 250). This oversight might have been corrected if someone in the advisory group had taken the trouble to look at a map of Cuba, available in any atlas.

The cost of sending an invading force without an escape route soon became measurable in human lives as well as in dollars and cents. Within two days after landing on the shores of Cuba, the men in the brigade found themselves completely surrounded and learned for the first time that they had no option but to be killed or captured. Seven months later, Castro struck a hard bargain with the United States State Department and allowed the 1200 men who had been imprisoned to be released for the ransom price of $53 million in food and drugs (*New York Times*, 1964: 238).

The suffering of the 1200 imprisoned men and the ransom money were only part of the losses sustained because of the policy-makers' false assumption that the invaders could easily join guerrillas in the mountains. Had they learned beforehand that there would be no way of escaping from the beaches, President Kennedy's advisers might not have been so complacent about the net gain they were expecting, and they might have decided to drop the entire invasion plan.

Why did the advisory group fail?

Why so many miscalculations? Couldn't the six false assumptions have been avoided if the advisory group had sought fuller information and had taken it into account? Some of the grossest errors resulted from faulty planning and communication within the CIA. The agency obviously had its own serious defects, but they do not concern us in the present inquiry. Nor are we going to try to unravel the complicated reasons for the Joint Chiefs' willingness to endorse the CIA's plan. The central question is: Why did the President's main advisers, whom he had selected as core members of his team, fail to pursue the issues sufficiently to discover the shaky ground on which the six assumptions rested? Why didn't they pose a barrage of penetrating and embarrassing questions to the representatives of the CIA and the Joint Chiefs of Staff? Why were these men taken in by the incomplete and inconsistent answers they were given in response to the relatively few critical questions they raised? Schlesinger says that 'for all the utter irrationality with which retrospect endowed the project, it had a certain queer logic at the time as it emerged from the bowels of government' (Schlesinger, 1965: 295). Why did the

President's policy advisers fail to evaluate the plan carefully enough to become aware of 'its utter irrationality'? What was the source of the 'queer logic' with which the plan was endowed?

Even with the apparently unqualified endorsement of the military sector of the United States government, the six assumptions behind the Bay of Pigs invasion were not so abstruse that military expertise was needed to evaluate them realistically. Sorensen points out that a communication gap between the military and civilian sectors of Kennedy's administration led to a gap between the concept of the Cuban invasion and actuality:

> With hindsight it is clear that what in fact [the President] had approved was diplomatically unwise and militarily doomed from the outset. What he thought he was approving appeared at the time to have diplomatic acceptability and little chance of outright failure. That so great a gap between concept and actuality should exist at so high a level on so dangerous a matter reflected a shocking number of errors in the whole decision-making process. (Sorensen, 1966: 338)

But why did the *civilian* policy advisers – especially the core group of key cabinet members and White House staff – fail to close the gaps by picking to pieces the faulty assumptions? They did not put Dulles and Bissell through the kind of cross-examination that would have required the two men to reveal the inadequacies of their estimates and to go back to their agency to seek out better information. They did not make adequate use of the military and political experts who sat with them on the advisory committee. The Joint Chiefs of Staff could have been encouraged to spell out the military pros and cons of the invasion plan and to state their misgivings; the three State Department officials could have been encouraged to do the same about the chances for armed uprisings inside Cuba and the prospects of a provisional government's mobilizing popular support for the overthrow of the Castro regime.

Schlesinger acknowledges that because no one voiced any opposition at the meetings of the advisory committee, the members of the White House staff – himself included – 'failed in their job of protecting the President,' and 'The representatives of the State Department failed in defending the diplomatic interests of the nation' (Schlesinger, 1965: 256).

The official explanation

Why did the brilliant, conscientious men on the Kennedy team fail so dismally? The answers given by Schlesinger, Sorensen, Salinger, Hilsman, and other knowledgeable insiders include four major factors, which evidently correspond closely with the reasons John F. Kennedy mentioned in post-mortem discussions with leading members of the government.

Political calculations

When presenting the invasion plan, the representatives of the CIA, knowingly or unknowingly, used a strong political appeal to persuade the Kennedy administration to take aggressive action against the Castro regime. The President was asked, in effect, whether he was as willing as the Republicans to help the Cuban exiles fight against the Communist leadership in Cuba. If he did nothing, the implication was that Castro was free to spread his brand of communism throughout Latin America.

The political consequences were especially obvious when the CIA representatives called attention to the so-called disposal question: What can we do with a trained brigade of Cuban exiles who are clamoring to get back to Cuba? The problem seemed particularly acute because the Guatemalan government had become embarrassed about the publicity the exiles were receiving and had asked that the men be removed. If we don't send them to invade Cuba, Allen Dulles in effect told the advisory committee, we will have to transfer them to the United States. He declared, 'We can't have them wandering around the country telling everyone what they have been doing' (Schlesinger, 1965: 242). Obviously they would spread the word, loud and clear, that Kennedy had prevented them from trying to overthrow Castro's dictatorship, and Kennedy might be accused of being soft on communism when it became known that he scuttled an anti-Castro operation. Furthermore, Castro would soon receive jets from the Soviet Union, and Cuban pilots were being trained in Czechoslovakia to fly them. Once the new planes arrived, a successful amphibious landing by the exile brigade would no longer be possible. After 1 June 1961, according to the CIA, the massive power of the United States Marines and Air Force would be required for a successful invasion of Cuba. Anyhow, the invasion could not be postponed for long because the rainy season was coming. This was the last chance for a purely Cuban invasion, and if Kennedy postponed it he would be seen as hampering the anti-Communist exiles who wanted to return to their homeland to fight for a democratic Cuba.

A new administration bottled in an old bureaucracy

Slightly less than three months elapsed between the day the ill-fated CIA plan was presented to leading members of the new administration and the day the CIA operatives tried to carry it out. The pressures to arrive at a decision during those early months of the Kennedy administration came when the President and his senior advisers were still developing their decision-making procedures, before they were fully familiar with each other, with their respective roles, and with the ways of circumventing bureaucratic obstacles that make obtaining relevant information difficult. The new cabinet members and the White House staff had high esprit de corps but had not reached the point where they could talk frankly with each other without constant concern about protocol and deferential soft-pedaling of criticism. Kennedy himself did not yet know the strengths and weaknesses of his newly appointed advisers. For example, the President did not realize, as he did later, that the new Secretary of State was inclined to defer to the military experts and to withhold his objections to Defense Department toughness in order to avoid charges of State Department softness (Sorensen, 1966: 303). Nor had he yet learned that it was wrong to assume, as he put it later, 'that the military and intelligence people have some secret skill not available to ordinary mortals' (Schlesinger, 1965: 258).

Secrecy – to the point of excluding the experts

As happens with many other vital decisions involving military action, the clandestine nature of the plan to invade Cuba precluded using the usual government channels for shaping a foreign policy decision. Ordinarily, all relevant agencies would have been allowed to study the proposed course of action, suggest alternatives, and evaluate the pros and cons of each alternative. Bureaucratic requirements of secrecy are likely to exclude from decision-making many of the most relevant experts. When the Bay of Pigs invasion was being planned, at least two groups of experts in the United States government were not consulted – those in the intelligence branch of the CIA and on the Cuban desk in the State Department. Schlesinger commented:

> The same men . . . both planned the operation and judged its chances of success. . . . The 'need-to-know' standard – i.e. that no one should be told about a project unless it becomes operationally necessary – thus had the idiotic effect of excluding much of the expertise of government at a time when every alert newspaper man knew something was afoot. (Schlesinger, 1965: 248).

The requirements of secrecy even extended to the printed matter distributed to the inner circle of policy-makers. The memoranda handed out by the CIA and Joint Chiefs of Staff at the beginning of each session were collected at the end. This made it impossible for the participants to ponder over the arguments and to check out details by collecting information from resources available in their own offices. In short, the expert judgement of the policy-makers who participated in the Bay of Pigs decision was impaired by the secrecy imposed.

Threats to personal reputation and status

Government policy-makers, like most executives in other organizations, hesitate to object to a policy if they think their forthright stand might damage their personal status and political effectiveness. This is sometimes referred to as the effectiveness trap. In his account of the Bay of Pigs fiasco, Schlesinger admits that he hesitated to bring up his objections while attending the White House meetings for fear that others would regard it as presumptuous for him, a college professor, to take issue with august heads of major government institutions.

Is the official explanation complete?

Do these four factors fully explain the miscalculations that produced the invasion decision? It seems to me that they do not. Because of a sense of incompleteness about the explanation, I looked for other causal factors in the sphere of group dynamics. After studying Schlesinger's analysis of the Bay of Pigs fiasco and other authoritative accounts, I still felt that even all four factors operating at full force simultaneously could hardly have given rise to such a faulty decision. Perhaps the four-factor explanation would be plausible if the policy advisers had met hurriedly only once or twice and had had only a few days to make their decision. But they had the opportunity to meet many times and to think about the decision for almost three months.

Here are the main reasons for this judgement: firstly, the political pressures mainly stemmed from the realization that the Kennedy administration might be accused of having prevented the Cuban exiles from carrying out an invasion against the pro-Communist government of Cuba. But if Kennedy and his advisers had examined the six assumptions carefully enough to see how faulty they were, wouldn't they have realized that permitting the Bay of Pigs fiasco to materialize would be at least as embarrassing, both at home and abroad? Moreover, even if the political pressure centering on disposing of the trained exile brigade was an overriding consideration, we are still left with a puzzling question: Why didn't the policy-makers explore some of the obvious alternatives for solving the disposal question without resorting to a full-scale invasion? They might have negotiated for another camp elsewhere in central America and allowed the exile brigade to infiltrate Cuba in small groups, going to landing places where they could easily join up with the guerrilla units in the mountains. Evidently this solution to the disposal problem. which would have had less damaging political repercussions than the all-out versus all-off alternatives that were considered, was never seriously examined.

Secondly, although the Kennedy administration was indeed new, most of the men who participated in the decision were old hands at policy-making. How probable is it that Bundy, McNamara, Rusk, Dillon, Mann, Berle, and Nitze would suppress their objections and risk allowing the nation to suffer a grave setback merely because they were uncertain about the proper way to behave? Moreover, isn't it improbable that all these men would share Kennedy's naive assumption – which he undoubtedly was expressing in greatly exaggerated form – that the military had special skill unavailable to other assessors of the invasion plan? Some of the false assumptions on which the plan was based such as keeping United States involvement a secret – were more political than military, and the advisers knew that in these matters they had more expertise than the military men. Probably, Bundy, McNamara, Dillon, and the top State Department officials all concluded that nothing really important was wrong with the invasion plan. Otherwise, regardless of their new roles and other considerations that might have made them hesitate to communicate their objections, at one of the many sessions in which the invasion plan was discussed they would undoubtedly have managed to call attention to the unacceptable grounds for the assumptions on which it rested.

Thirdly, many experts in the government were certainly excluded in a futile effort to keep the plan secret. But wouldn't the President's key advisers have insisted on consulting their own experts if they had carefully inspected the shaky grounds on which the CIA planners were basing their judgements? A few incisive questions about the evidence for the CIA planners' estimates of Castro's military and political strength might have quickly revealed that they were relaying uninformed estimates made without consulting the intelligence experts in their own agency or in the State Department. Wouldn't the President and his advisers then have realized that there was 'a need for them to know,' and wouldn't experts have been asked to provide the policy-makers with an objective appraisal? With the experts excluded, outside criticism of the CIA's plan was kept to a minimum. But why was there so little criticism from inside the group of high-level government officials who were sufficiently expert to evaluate at least some, if not all, of the assumptions?

Finally, even the highest government officials may become concerned about potential damage to their status and future effectiveness that might result from criticizing a plan proposed by the military. Still, it was by no means clear that agreeing to the plan would be more advantageous than calling attention to gaps in the CIA's rationale and raising valid objections. If any advisers had realized that the invasion was going to be a fiasco, wouldn't they also have realized that acquiescing would be much more damaging to their reputation than raising critical questions to force the others, however reluctantly, to re-examine their assumptions? Would the policy advisers remain silent at meeting after meeting if they thought the President was being misled into making a stupid decision, damaging to his administration and to the country as a whole? When given the responsibility of forming a judgement about vital matters of national policy, such men are not likely to be intimidated by vague threats of damage to their careers. Moreover, the four members of the Kennedy team who had worked with the President before and during the election campaign – Bundy, Schlesinger, Goodwin and Robert Kennedy – would not have felt such constraints when they talked among themselves about the plan to invade Cuba. They knew the President well enough to realize that he valued fresh viewpoints and independent thinking, that he was ready to change his mind in response to strong arguments, and that he would support them against backbiting from anyone in the executive branch on whose toes they might be stepping.

Sensitized by my dissatisfaction with the four-factor explanation, I noticed in Schlesinger's account of what the policy-makers said to each other during and after the crucial sessions numerous signs of group dynamics in full operation. From studying this material I arrived at the groupthink hypothesis.

Groupthink does not replace the four-factor explanation of the faulty decision; rather, it supplements the four factors and perhaps gives each of them added cogency in the light of group dynamics. It seems to me that if groupthink had not been operating, the other four factors would not have been sufficiently powerful to hold sway during the months when the invasion decision was being discussed.

Symptoms of groupthink among President Kennedy's advisers

According to the groupthink hypothesis, members of any small cohesive group tend to maintain esprit de corps by unconsciously developing a number of shared illusions and related norms that interfere with critical thinking and reality testing. If the available accounts describe the deliberations accurately, typical illusions can be discerned among the members of the Kennedy team during the period when they were deciding whether to approve the CIA's invasion plan.

The illusion of invulnerability

An important symptom of groupthink is the illusion of being invulnerable to the main dangers that might arise from a risky action in which the group is strongly tempted to engage. Essentially, the notion is that 'If our leader and everyone else in our group decides that it is okay, the plan is bound to succeed. Even if it is quite risky, luck will be on our side.' A sense of 'unlimited confidence' was widespread among the 'New Frontiersmen' as soon as they took over their high government posts, according to a Justice Department confidant, with whom Robert Kennedy discussed the secret CIA plan on the day it was launched:

> It seemed that, with John Kennedy leading us and with all the talent he had assembled, *nothing could stop us*. We believed that if we faced up to the nations problems and applied bold, new ideas with common sense and hard work, we would overcome whatever challenged us. (Guthman, 1971: 88, italics added)

That this attitude was shared by the members of the President's inner circle is indicated by Schlesinger's statement that the men around Kennedy had enormous confidence in his ability and luck: 'Everything had broken right for him since 1956. He had won the nomination and the election against all the odds in the book. Everyone around him thought he had the Midas touch and could not lose' (Schlesinger, 1965: 259). Kennedy and his principal advisers were sophisticated and skeptical men, but they were, nevertheless, 'affected by the euphoria of the new day' (Schlesinger, 1965: 259). During the first three months after he took office – despite growing concerns created by the emerging crisis in Southeast Asia, the gold drain, and the Cuban exiles who were awaiting the go-ahead signal to invade Cuba – the dominant mood in the White House, according to Schlesinger, was 'buoyant optimism.' It was centered on the 'promise of hope' held out by the President: *'Euphoria reigned; we thought for a moment that the world was plastic and the future unlimited'* (Schlesinger, 1965: 214, italics added).

All the characteristic manifestations of grand euphoria – the buoyant optimism, the leader's great promise of hope, and the shared belief that the group's accomplishments could make 'the future unlimited' – are strongly reminiscent of the thoughts and feelings that arise among members of many different types of groups during the phase when the members become cohesive. At such a time, the members become somewhat euphoric about their newly acquired 'we-feeling'; they share a sense of belonging to a powerful, protective group that in some vague way opens up new potentials for each of them. Often, there is boundless admiration of the group leader.

Once this euphoric phase takes hold, decision-making for everyday activities, as well as long-range planning, is likely to be seriously impaired. The members of a cohesive group become very reluctant to carry put the unpleasant task of critically assessing the limits of their power and the real losses that could arise if their luck does not hold. They tend to examine each risk in black and white terms. If it does not seem overwhelmingly dangerous, they are inclined simply to forget about it, instead of developing contingency plans in case it materializes. The group members know that no one among them is a superman, but they feel that somehow the group is a supergroup, capable of surmounting all risks that stand in the way of carrying out any desired course of action: 'Nothing can stop us!' Athletic teams and military combat units may often benefit from members' enthusiastic confidence in the power and luck of their group. But policy-making committees usually do not.

We would not expect sober government officials to experience such exuberant esprit de corps, but a subdued form of the same tendency may have been operating – inclining the President's advisers to become reluctant about examining the drawbacks of the invasion plan. In group meetings, this groupthink tendency can operate like a low-level noise that prevents warning signals from being heeded. Everyone becomes somewhat biased in the direction of selectively attending to the messages that feed into the members' shared feelings of confidence and optimism, disregarding those that do not.

When a cohesive group of executives is planning a campaign directed against a rival or enemy group, their discussions are likely to contain two themes, which embody the groupthink tendency to regard the group as invulnerable: 'We are a strong group of good guys who will win in the end' and 'Our opponents are stupid, weak, bad guys.' It is impressive to see how closely the six false assumptions fit these two themes. The notion running through the assumptions is the over-optimistic expectation that 'we can pull off this invasion, even though it is a long-shot gamble.' The policy advisers were probably unaware of how much they were relying on shared rationalizations in order to appraise the highly risky venture as a safe one. Their over-optimistic outlook would have been rudely shaken if they had allowed their deliberations to focus on the potentially devastating consequences of the obvious drawbacks of the plan, such as the disparity in size between Castro's military forces of 200,000 and the small brigade of 1400 exiles. In a sense, this difference made the odds against their long-shot gamble 200,000 to 1400 (over 140 to 1).

When discussing the misconceptions that led to the decision to approve the CIA's plan, Schlesinger emphasizes the gross underestimation of the enemy. Castro was regarded as a weak 'hysteric' leader whose army was ready to defect; he was considered so stupid that 'although warned by air strikes he would do nothing to neutralize the Cuban underground' (Schlesinger, 1965: 293). This is a stunning example of the classical stereotype of the enemy as weak and ineffectual.

In a concurrence-seeking group, there is relatively little healthy skepticism of the glib ideological formulas on which rational policy-makers, like many other people who share their nationalistic goals, generally rely in order to maintain self-confidence and cognitive mastery over the complexities of international politics. One of the symptoms of groupthink is the members' persistence in conveying to each other the cliche and oversimplified images of political enemies embodied in long-standing ideological stereotypes. Throughout their deliberations they use the same old stereotypes, instead of developing differentiated concepts derived from an open-minded inquiry enabling them to discern which of their original ideological assumptions, if any, apply to the foreign policy issue at hand. Except in unusual circumstances of crisis, the members of a concurrence-seeking group tend to view any antagonistic out-group against whom they are plotting not only as immoral but also as weak and stupid. These wishful beliefs continue to dominate their thinking until an unequivical defeat proves otherwise, whereupon – like Kennedy and his advisers – they are shocked at the discrepancy between their stereotyped conceptions and actuality.

A subsidiary theme, which also involved a strong dose of wishful thinking, was contained in the Kennedy group's notion that 'we can get away with our clever cover story.' When the daily newspapers were already demonstrating that this certainly was not so, the undaunted members of the group evidently replaced the original assumption with the equally over-optimistic expectation that 'anyhow, the non-Communist nations of the world will side with us. After all, we *are* the good guys.'

Over-optimistic expectations about the power of their side and the weakness of the opponents probably enable members of a group to enjoy a sense of low vulnerability to the effects of any decision that entails risky action against an enemy. In order to maintain this complacent outlook, each member must think that everyone else in the group agrees that the risks can be safely ignored.

The illusion of unanimity

When a group of people who respect each other's opinions arrive at a unanimous view, each member is likely to feel that the belief must be true. This reliance on consensual validation tends to replace individual critical thinking and reality testing, unless there are clear-cut disagreements among the members. The members of a face-to-face group often become inclined, without quite realizing it, to prevent latent disagreements from surfacing when they are about to initiate a risky course of action. The group leader and the members support each other, playing up the areas of convergence in their thinking, at the expense of fully exploring divergences that might disrupt the apparent unity of the group. Better to share a pleasant, balmy group atmosphere than to be battered in a storm.

This brings us to the second outstanding symptom of groupthink manifested by the Kennedy team – a shared illusion of unanimity. In the formal sessions dealing with the Cuban invasion plan, the group's consensus that the basic features of the CIA plan should be adopted was relatively free of disagreement.

According to Sorensen, 'No strong voice of opposition was raised in any of the key meetings, and no realistic alternatives were presented' (Sorensen, 1966: 341). According to Schlesinger, 'the massed and caparisoned authority of his senior officials in the realm of foreign policy and defense was unanimous for going ahead. . . . Had one senior advisor opposed the adventure, I believe that Kennedy would have canceled it. No one spoke against it' (Schlesinger, 1965: 258–9).

Perhaps the most crucial of Schlesinger's observations is, 'Our meetings took place in a *curious atmosphere of assumed consensus*' (Schlesinger, 1965: 250, italics added). His additional comments clearly show that the assumed consensus was an illusion that could be maintained only because the major participants did not reveal their own reasoning or discuss their idiosyncratic assumptions and vague reservations. President Kennedy thought that prime consideration was being given to his prohibition of direct military intervention by the United States. He assumed that the operation had been pared down to a kind of unobtrusive infiltration that, if reported in the newspapers, would be buried in the inside pages. Rusk was certainly not on the same wavelength as the President, for at one point he suggested that it might be better to have the invaders fan out from the United States naval base at Guantánamo, rather than land at the Bay of Pigs, so that they could readily retreat to the base if necessary. Implicit in his suggestion was a lack of concern about revealing United States military support as well as implicit distrust in the assumption made by the others about the ease of escaping from the Bay of Pigs. But discussion of Rusk's strange proposal was evidently dropped long before he was induced to reveal whatever vague misgivings he may have had about the Bay of Pigs plan. At meetings in the State Department, according to Roger Hilsman, who worked closely with him, 'Rusk asked penetrating questions that frequently caused us to re-examine our position' (Hilsman, 1967: 58). But at the White House meetings Rusk said little except to offer gentle warnings about avoiding excesses.

As usually happens in cohesive groups, the members assumed that 'silence gives consent.' Kennedy and the others supposed that Rusk was in substantial agreement with what the CIA representatives were saying about the soundness of the invasion plan. But about one week before the invasion was scheduled, when Schlesinger told Rusk in private about his objections to the plan, Rusk, surprisingly, offered no arguments against Schlesinger's objections. He said that he had been wanting for some time to draw up a balance sheet of the pros and cons and that he was annoyed at the Joint Chiefs because 'they are perfectly willing to put the President's head on the block, but they recoil at doing anything which might risk Guantánamo' (Schlesinger, 1965: 257). At that late date, he evidently still preferred his suggestion to launch the invasion from the United States naval base in Cuba, even though doing so would violate President Kennedy's stricture against involving America's armed forces.

McNamara's assumptions about the invasion were quite different from both Rusk's and Kennedy's. McNamara thought that the main objective was to touch off a revolt of the Cuban people to overthrow Castro. The members of the group who knew something about Cuban politics and Castro's popular support must have had strong doubts about this assumption. Why did they fail to convey their misgivings at any of the meetings?

Suppression of personal doubts

The sense of group unity concerning the advisability of going ahead with the CIA's invasion plan appears to have been based on superficial appearances of complete concurrence, achieved at the cost of self-censorship of misgivings by several of the members. From post-mortem discussions with participants, Sorensen concluded that among the men in the State Department, as well as those on the White House staff, 'doubts were entertained but never pressed, partly out of a fear of being labelled "soft" or undaring in the eyes of their colleagues' (Sorensen, 1966: 343). Schlesinger was not at all hesitant about presenting his strong objections in a memorandum he gave to the President and the Secretary of State. But he became keenly aware of his tendency to suppress objections when he attended the White House meetings of the Kennedy team, with their atmosphere of assumed consensus:

> In the months after the Bay of Pigs I bitterly reproached myself for having kept so silent during those crucial discussions in the Cabinet Room, though my feelings of guilt were tempered by the knowledge that a course of objection would have accomplished little save to *gain me a name as a nuisance*. I can only explain my failure to do more than raise a few timid questions by reporting that one's impulse to blow the whistle on this nonsense was simply undone by the *circumstances of the discussion*. (Schlesinger, 1965: 255, italics added)

Whether or not his retrospective explanation includes all his real reasons for having remained silent, Schlesinger appears to have been quite aware of the need to refrain from saying anything that would create a nuisance by breaking down the assumed consensus.

Participants in the White House meetings, like members of many other discussion groups, evidently felt reluctant to raise questions that might cast doubt on a plan that they thought was accepted by the consensus of the group, for fear of evoking disapproval from their associates. This type of fear is probably not the same as fear of losing one's effectiveness or damaging one's career. Many forthright men who are quite willing to speak their piece despite risks to their career become silent when faced with the possibility of losing the approval of fellow members of their primary work group. The discrepancy between Schlesinger's critical memoranda and his silent acquiescence during the meetings might be an example of this.

Schlesinger says that when the Cuban invasion plan was being presented to the group, 'virile poses' were conveyed in the rhetoric used by the representatives of the CIA and the Joint Chiefs of Staff (1965: 256). He thought the State Department representatives and others responded by becoming anxious to show that they were not softheaded idealists but really were just as tough as the military men. Schlesinger's references to the 'virile' stance of the militant advocates of the invasion plan suggest that the members of Kennedy's in-group may have been concerned about protecting the leader from being embarrassed by their voicing 'unvirile' concerns about the high risks of the venture.

At the meetings, the members of Kennedy's inner circle who wondered whether the military venture might prove to be a failure or whether the political consequences might be damaging to the United States must have had only mild misgivings, not strong enough to overcome the social obstacles that would make arguing openly against the plan slightly uncomfortable. By and large, each of them must have felt reasonably sure that the plan was a safe one, that at worst the United States would not lose anything from trying it. They contributed, by their silence, to the lack of critical thinking in the group's deliberations.

Self-appointed mindguards

Among the well-known phenomena of group dynamics is the alacrity with which members of a cohesive in-group suppress deviational points of view by putting social pressure on any member who begins to express a view that deviates from the dominant beliefs of the group, to make sure that he will not disrupt the consensus of the group as a whole. This pressure often takes the form of urging the dissident member to remain silent if he cannot match up his own beliefs with those of the rest of the group. At least one dramatic instance of this type of pressure occurred a few days after President Kennedy had said, 'we seem now destined to go ahead on a quasi-minimum basis' (Schlesinger, 1965: 256). This was still several days before the final decision was made.

At a large birthday party for his wife, Robert Kennedy, who had been constantly informed about the Cuban invasion plan, took Schlesinger aside and asked him why he was opposed. The President's brother listened coldly and then said, 'You may be right or you may be wrong, but the President has made his mind up. Don't push it any further. Now is the time for everyone to help him all they can.' Here is another symptom of groupthink, displayed by a highly intelligent man whose ethical code committed him to freedom of dissent. What he was saying, in effect, was, 'You may well be right about the dangerous risks, but I don't give a damn about that; all of us should help our leader right now by not sounding any discordant notes that would interfere with the harmonious support he should have.'

When Robert Kennedy told Schlesinger to lay off, he was functioning in a self-appointed role that I call being a 'mindguard.' Just as a bodyguard protects the

President and other high officials from injurious physical assaults, a mindguard protects them from thoughts that might damage their confidence in the soundness of the policies to which they are committed or to which they are about to commit themselves.

At least one other member of the Kennedy team, Secretary of State Rusk, also effectively functioned as a mindguard, protecting the leader and the members from unwelcome ideas that might set them to thinking about unfavorable consequences of their preferred course of action and that might lead to dissension instead of a comfortable consensus. Undersecretary of State Chester Bowles, who had attended a White House meeting at which he was given no opportunity to express his dissenting views, decided not to continue to remain silent about such a vital matter. He prepared a strong memorandum for Secretary Rusk opposing the CIA plan and, keeping well within the prescribed bureaucratic channels, requested Rusk's permission to present his case to the President. Rusk told Bowles that there was no need for any concern, that the invasion plan would be dropped in favor of a quiet little guerrilla infiltration. Rusk may have believed this at the time, but at subsequent White House meetings he must soon have learned otherwise. Had Rusk transmitted the Undersecretary's memorandum, the urgent warnings it contained might have reinforced Schlesinger's memorandum and jolted some of Kennedy's in-group, if not Kennedy himself, to reconsider the decision. But Rusk kept Bowles' memorandum firmly buried in the State Department files.

Rusk may also have played a similar role in preventing Kennedy and the others from learning about the strong objections raised by Edward R. Murrow, whom the President had just appointed director of the United States Information Agency. In yet another instance, Rusk appears to have functioned as a dogged mindguard, protecting the group from the opposing ideas of a government official with access to information that could have enabled him to assess the political consequences of the Cuban invasion better than anyone present at the White House meetings could. As Director of Intelligence and Research in the State Department, Roger Hilsman got wind of the invasion plan from his colleague Allen Dulles and strongly warned Secretary Rusk of the dangers. He asked Rusk for permission to allow the Cuban experts in his department to scrutinize thoroughly the assumptions relevant to their expertise. 'I'm sorry,' Rusk told him, 'but I can't let you. This is being too tightly held' (Hilsman, 1967: 31). Rusk's reaction struck Hilsman as strange because all the relevant men in his department already had top security clearance. Hilsman assumed that Rusk turned down his urgent request because of pressure from Dulles and Bissell to adhere to the CIA's special security restrictions. But if so, why, when so much was at stake, did the Secretary of State fail to communicate to the President or to anyone else in the core group that his most trusted intelligence expert had grave doubts about the invasion plan and felt that it should be appraised by the Cuban specialists? As a result of Rusk's handling of Hilsman's request, the President and his advisers remained in the curious position, as Hilsman put it, of making an important political judgement without the benefit of advice from the government's most relevant intelligence experts (Hilsman, 1967: 31).

Taking account of the mindguard functions performed by the Attorney General and the Secretary of State, together with the President's failure to allow time for discussion of the few oppositional viewpoints that occasionally did filter into the meetings, we surmise that some form of collusion was going on. That is to say, it seems plausible to infer that the leading civilian members of the Kennedy team colluded – perhaps unwittingly – to protect the proposed plan from critical scrutiny by themselves and by any of the government's experts.

Docility fostered by suave leadership

The group pressures that help to maintain a group's illusions are sometimes fostered by various leadership practices, some of which involve subtle ways of making it difficult for those who question the initial consensus to suggest alternatives and to raise critical issues. The group's agenda can readily be manipulated by a suave leader, often with the tacit approval of the members, so that there is simply no opportunity to discuss the drawbacks of a seemingly satisfactory plan of action. This is one of the conditions that fosters groupthink.

President Kennedy, as leader at the meetings in the White House, was probably more active than anyone else in raising skeptical questions; yet he seems to have encouraged the group's docility and uncritical acceptance of the defective arguments in favor of the CIA's plan. At each meeting, instead of opening up the agenda to permit a full airing of the opposing considerations, he allowed the CIA representatives to dominate the entire discussion. The President permitted them to refute immediately each tentative doubt that one of the others might express, instead of asking whether anyone else had the same doubt or wanted to pursue the implications of the new worrisome issue that had been raised.

Moreover, although the President went out of his way to bring to a crucial meeting an outsider who was an eloquent opponent of the invasion plan, his style of conducting the meeting presented no opportunity for discussion of the controversial issues that were raised. The visitor was Senator J. William Fulbright. The occasion was the climactic meeting of 4 April 1961, held at the State Department, at which the apparent consensus that had emerged in earlier meetings was seemingly confirmed by an open straw vote. The President invited Senator Fulbright after the Senator had made known his concern about newspaper stories forecasting a United States invasion of Cuba. At the meeting, Fulbright was given an opportunity to present his opposing views. In a 'sensible and strong' speech Fulbright correctly predicted many of the damaging effects the invasion would have on United States foreign relations (Schlesinger, 1965: 252). The President did not open the floor to discussion of the questions raised in Fulbright's rousing speech. Instead, he returned to the procedure he had initiated earlier in the meeting; he had asked each person around the table to state his final judgement and after Fulbright had taken his turn, he continued the straw vote around the table. McNamara said he approved the plan. Berle was also for it; his advice was to 'let her rip.' Mann, who had been on the fence, also spoke in favor of it.

Picking up a point mentioned by Berle, who had said he approved but did not insist on 'a major production,' President Kennedy changed the agenda by asking what could be done to make the infiltration more quiet. Following discussion of this question – quite remote from the fundamental moral and political issues raised by Senator Fulbright – the meeting ended. Schlesinger mentions that the meeting broke up before completion of the intended straw vote around the table. Thus, wittingly or unwittingly, the President conducted the meeting in such a way that not only was there no time to discuss the potential dangers to United States foreign relations raised by Senator Fulbright, but there was also no time to call upon Schlesinger, the one man present who the President knew strongly shared Senator Fulbright's misgivings.

Of course, one or more members of the group could have prevented this by-passing by suggesting that the group discuss Senator Fulbright's arguments and requesting that Schlesinger and the others who had not been called upon be given the opportunity to state their views. But no one made such a request.

The President's demand that each person, in turn, state his overall judgement, especially after having just heard an outsider oppose the group consensus, must have put the members on their mettle. These are exactly the conditions that most strongly foster docile conformity to a group's norms. After listening to an opinion leader (McNamara, for example) express his unequivocal acceptance, it becomes more difficult than ever for other members to state a different view. Open straw votes generally put pressure on each individual to agree with the apparent group consensus, as has been shown by well-known social psychological experiments (See Elms, 1972: 136–46 for a review of research by S. Asch, R. Crutchfield, S. Milgram, M. Sherif, and other social psychologists).

A few days before the crucial meeting of 4 April, another outsider who might have challenged some of the group's illusions attended one of the meetings but was never given the opportunity to speak his piece. At the earlier meeting, the outsider was the acting Secretary of State, Chester Bowles, attending in place of Secretary Rusk, who was abroad at a SEATO conference. Like Senator Fulbright, Bowles was incredulous and at times even 'horrified' at the group's complacent acceptance of the CIA's invasion plans. However, President Kennedy had no idea what Bowles was thinking about the plan, and he probably felt that Bowles was there more in the role of a reporter to keep Rusk up to date on the deliberations than as a participant in the discussion. In any case, the President neglected to give the group the opportunity to hear the reactions of a fresh mind; he did not call upon Bowles at any time. Bowles sat through the meeting in complete silence. He felt he could not break with formal bureaucratic protocol, which prevents an Undersecretary from volunteering his opinion unless directed to do so by his chief or by the President (Schlesinger, 1965: 250). Bowles behaved in the prescribed way and confined his protestations to a State Department memorandum addressed to Rusk, which, as we have seen, was not communicated to the President.

An additional bit of information about Bowles' subsequent career seems to fit in with all of this, from the standpoint of group psychology. During the bitter weeks following the Bay of Pigs fiasco, Chester Bowles was the first man in the new administration to be fired by President Kennedy. Some of Bowles' friends had told the press that he had opposed the Cuban venture and had been right in his forecasts about the outcome. Evidently this news annoyed the President greatly. Bowles' opponents in the administration pointed out that even if Bowles had not leaked the story to the press, he had discussed the matter with his friends at a time when it would embarrass the White House. This may have contributed to the President's solution to the problem of what to do about the inept leadership of the inefficient State Department bureaucracy. He decided to shift Bowles out of his position as second-in-command, instead of replacing Rusk, whom he liked personally and wanted to keep as a central member of his team. 'I can't do that to Rusk,' Kennedy later said when someone suggested shifting Rusk to the United Nations: 'He is such a *nice* man' (Schlesinger, 1965: 436).

During the Bay of Pigs planning sessions, President Kennedy, probably unwittingly, allowed the one-sided CIA memoranda to monopolize the attention of the group by failing to circulate opposing statements that might have stimulated an intensive discussion of the drawbacks and might therefore have revealed the illusory nature of the group's consensus. Although the President read and privately discussed the strongly opposing memoranda prepared by Schlesinger and Senator Fulbright, he never distributed them to the policy-makers whose critical judgement he was seeking. Kennedy also knew that Joseph Newman, a foreign correspondent who had just visited Cuba, had written a series of incisive articles that disagreed with forecasts concerning the ease of generating a revolt against Castro. But although he invited Newman to the White House for a chat, he did not distribute Newman's impressive writings to the advisory group.

The members themselves, however, were partially responsible for the President's biased way of handling the meetings. They need not have been so acquiescent about it. Had anyone suggested to the President that it might be a good idea for the group to gain more perspective by studying statements of opposing points of view, Kennedy probably would have welcomed the suggestion and taken steps to correct his own-sided way of running the meetings.

The taboo against antagonizing valuable new members

It seems likely that one of the reasons the members of the core group accepted the President's restricted agenda and his extraordinarily indulgent treatment of the CIA representatives was that a kind of informal group norm had developed, producing a desire to avoid saying anything that could be construed as an attack on the CIA's plan. The group apparently accepted a kind of taboo against voicing damaging criticisms. This may have been another important factor contributing to the group's tendency to indulge in groupthink.

How could such a norm come into being? Why would President Kennedy give preferential treatment to the two CIA representatives? Why would Bundy, McNamara, Rusk, and the others on his team fail to challenge this preferential treatment and accept a taboo against voicing critical opposition? A few clues permit some conjectures to be made, although we have much less evidence to go on than for delineating the pattern of preferential treatment itself.

It seems that Allen Dulles and Richard Bissell, despite being holdovers from the Eisenhower administration, were not considered outsiders by the inner core of the Kennedy team. President Kennedy and his closest associates did not place these two men in the same category as the Joint Chiefs of Staff, who were seen as members of an outside military clique established during the earlier administration, men whose primary loyalties belonged elsewhere and whose presence at the White House meetings was tolerated as a necessary requirement of governmental protocol. (Witness Secretary Rusk's unfriendly comments about the Joint Chiefs being more loyal to their military group in the Pentagon than to the President, when he was conversing privately with fellow in-group member Schlesinger.) President Kennedy and those in his inner circle admired Dulles and Bissell, regarded them as valuable new members of the Kennedy team, and were pleased to have them on board. Everyone in the group was keenly aware of the fact that Bissell had been devoting his talents with great intensity for over a year to developing the Cuban invasion project and that Dulles was also deeply committed to it. Whenever Bissell presented his arguments, 'we all listened transfixed,' Schlesinger informs us, 'fascinated by the workings of this superbly clear, organized and articulate intelligence.' Schlesinger reports that Bissell was regarded by the group as 'a man of high character and remarkable intellectual gifts' (Schlesinger, 1965: 241). In short, he was accepted as a highly prized member.

The sense of power of the core group was probably enhanced by the realization that the two potent bureaucrats who were in control of America's extensive intelligence network were affiliated with the Kennedy team. The core members of the team would certainly want to avoid antagonizing or alienating them. They would be inclined, therefore, to soft-pedal their criticisms of the CIA plan and perhaps even to suspend their critical judgement in evaluating it.

The way Dulles and Bissell were treated by President Kennedy and his associates after their plan had failed strongly suggests that both men continued to be fully accepted as members of the Kennedy team during the period of crisis generated by their unfortunate errors. According to Sorensen, Kennedy's regard for Richard Bissell did not change after the Bay of Pigs disaster, and he regretted having to accept Bissell's resignation. When Dulles submitted his resignation, President Kennedy urged him to postpone it and asked him to join a special commission to investigate the causes of the fiasco. During the days following the defeat, Kennedy refrained from openly criticizing either Bissell or Dulles (this must have required considerable restraint). On one occasion when a mutual friend of Dulles and Kennedy told the President self-righteously that he was deliberately going to avoid seeing the CIA director, Kennedy went out of his way to support Dulles by inviting him for a drink and ostentatiously putting his arm around him in the presence of the would-be ostracizer. This is a typical way for a leader of a cohesive group to treat one of the members who is temporarily 'in the dog house.'

The picture we get, therefore, is that the two CIA representatives, both highly esteemed men who had recently joined the Kennedy team, were presenting their 'baby' to the rest of the team. As protagonists, they had a big head start toward eliciting a favorable consensus. New in-group members would be listened to much more sympathetically and much less critically than outsiders representing an agency that might be trying to sell one of its own pet projects to the new President.

Hilsman, who also respected the two men, says that Dulles and Bissell 'had become emotionally involved . . . so deeply involved in the development of the Cuban invasion plans that they were no longer able to see clearly or to judge soundly.' He adds, 'There was so deep a commitment, indeed, that there was an unconscious effort to confine consideration of the proposed operation to as small a number of people as possible, so as to avoid too harsh or thorough a scrutiny of the plans' (Hilsman, 1967: 31). If Hilsman is correct, it is reasonable to assume that the two men managed to convey to the other members of the Kennedy team their strong desire 'to avoid too harsh or thorough a scrutiny.'

Whatever may have been the political or psychological reasons that motivated President Kennedy to give preferential treatment to the two CIA chiefs, he evidently succeeded in conveying to the other members of the core group, perhaps without realizing it, that the CIA's 'baby' should not be treated harshly. His way of handling the meetings, particularly his adherence to the extraordinary procedure of allowing every critical comment to be immediately refuted by Dulles or Bissell without allowing the group a chance to mull over the potential objections, probably set the norm of going easy on the plan. which the two new members of the group obviously wanted the new administration to accept. Evidently the members of the group adopted this norm and sought concurrence by continually patching the original CIA plan, trying to find a better version, without looking too closely into the basic arguments for such a plan and without debating the questionable estimates sufficiently to discover that the whole idea ought to be thrown out.

Conclusion

Although the available evidence consists of fragmentary and somewhat biased accounts of the deliberations of the White House group, it nevertheless reveals gross miscalculations and converges on the symptoms of group think. My tentative conclusion is that President Kennedy and the policy advisers who decided to accept the CIA's plan were victims of groupthink. If the facts I have culled from the accounts given by Schlesinger, Sorensen, and other observers are essentially accurate, the groupthink hypothesis makes more understandable the deficiencies in the government's decision-making that led to the enormous gap between conception and actuality.

The failure of Kennedy's inner circle to detect any of the false assumptions behind the Bay of Pigs invasion plan can be at least partially accounted for by the group's tendency to seek concurrence at the expense of seeking information, critical appraisal, and debate. The concurrence-seeking tendency was manifested by shared illusions and other symptoms, which helped the members to maintain a sense of group solidarity. Most crucial were the symptoms that contributed to complacent overconfidence in the face of vague uncertainties and explicit warnings that should have alerted the members to the risks of the clandestine military operation – an operation so ill conceived that among literate people all over the world the name of the invasion site has become the very symbol of perfect failure.

Note

The main reference used in preparing this chapter was Arthur M. Schlesinger Jr.'s *A Thousand Days*, which presents a detailed account of the meetings at which President Kennedy and his advisers discussed and approved the Bay of Pigs invasion plan. In addition to having access to official records, Schlesinger was able to draw on his personal observations as an insider. He attended most of the meetings of the advisory committee and frequently discussed the issues with the President and with fellow members of the White House staff. Another major source of information was Theodore Sorensen's *Kennedy*. Although Sorensen did not participate in any of the meetings, he had extensive discussions with the President and with other participants during the weeks immediately following the Cuban fiasco. Additional details were obtained from books by Hilsman, Guthman, Meyer and Szule, and Salinger, cited in the references. I have also drawn heavily from an unpublished paper by my daughter, Charlotte Janis, prepared partly under my supervision, which presented an analysis of the group processes that entered into the Bay of Pigs decision on the basis of material culled from the above-mentioned references.

References

Elms, A. (1972) *Social Psychology and Social Relevant*. Boston: Little, Brown.

Guthman, E. (1971) *We Band of Brothers*. New York: Harper & Row.

Hilsman, R.(1967) *To Move a Nation*. New York: Doubleday.

Meyer, K. B. and Szule, T. (1962) *The Cuban Invasion*. New York: Praeger.

The New York Times, (1964) *The Kennedy Years*. New York: Viking.

Salinger, P. (1966) *With Kennedy*. New York: Avon Books.

Schlesinger, A. M., Jr. (1965) *A Thousand Days*. Boston: Houghton Mifflin. Reprinted by permission of the publisher.

Sorensen, T. C. (1966) *Kennedy*. New York: Bantam edition. Reprinted by permission of Harper & Row, Publishers.

Anatomy of a Fatal Business Strategy

ERHARD K. VALENTIN*

In the early 1970s, the Boise Cascade Corporation launched an ambitious venture that in little more than two years increased the number of building materials outlets operated by its Building Materials Distribution Division (BMD) from 24 to more than 120. Yet, by 1982, this undertaking had turned into a nightmare. All but the most essential BMD staff positions were eliminated in May of 1982, as operating losses mounted; and by mid-1987, all stores had been sold or closed.

BMD's strategic miscues are identified in this article via comparative analysis; then they are examined within the behavioural and the organizational context in which they emerged. This interpretive study furthers understanding organizational phenomena, particularly the intra-organizational dynamics of failure. [. . .]

Method

Ethnographic data were collected using the participant–observer approach. [. . .]. To collect such data and understand its meaning, the researcher must live among his subjects and perhaps, as some authorities contend, participate directly in the affairs of the social group under study [. . .]. This participant–observer was employed by Boise Cascade while BMD's fatal expansion plan was formulated and implemented. As an administrative assistant to BMD's general manager and other top division-level executives, I attended many planning sessions and participated extensively in drafting proposals and memoranda that reflected the thoughts and concerns of BMD's key executives. I had access to all pertinent planning documents and to much of the correspondence between division- and higher-level management. Furthermore, I kept extensive notes and maintained an invaluable file of planning documents and inter-office memoranda. [. . .]

* Blackwell publishers for Valentin, Erhard K. 'Anatomy of a fatal business strategy', *Journal of Management Studies*, 31 (1994). Copyright © Blackwell Publishers 1994.

Some further aspects of the methodology are intertwined with the conceptual underpinnings, delineated in the next section, that guided the interpretation of data.

Conceptual underpinnings

Business failures, such as that of BMD, can be studied profitably from two complementary perspectives, the strategic and the behavioural points of view. While strategic diagnosis can be instrumental in identifying which decisions and actions were flawed, behavioural diagnosis sheds light on how and why flawed decisions and actions materialized. [. . .]

The behavioural perspective

From a behavioural vantage point, business strategies are neither developed nor unimplemented in direct relation to objective reality, but in relation to various inferences about the world as 'viewed through the lenses of decision-makers and . . . coloured by their beliefs and political interests' (Fahey and Narayanan, 1989: 362). The quality of such inferences, Stubbart (1989) maintains, depends significantly on the context-specific expertise of the decision-makers who generate them. Accordingly, some businesses fail not because resources or systems needed to cope effectively with the real external environment cannot be acquired or implemented economically and expeditiously, but because various behavioural factors impair strategic problem-sensing or effective strategy development and implementation (Kiesler and Sproull, 1982). This assertion is well-supported by an expansive stream of research. Inquiries into the limits of human information processing, the effects of group dynamics and organizational culture on decision-making, and the structure of the managerial decision-making process are among its most prominent tributaries.

INFORMATION PROCESSING Because human information processing capacity is bounded (Cyert and March, 1963; Simon, 1955, 1956), people rely extensively on heuristics, such as reasoning by analogy [. . .]. In BMD's case, for instance, wishful thinking, availability, vividness, simulation, confirmation) and other biases seemingly afflicted decision-making and coalesced to make implausible prospects seem imminent.

Wishful thinking occurs when the probability of a specified event is over-estimated because the event seems desirable [. . .], whereas availability bias refers to the inflationary effect of the ease with which an event can be recalled or imagined on estimates of the frequency with which similar events have occurred in the past or are likely to occur in the future. Recency and vividness enhance availability (Nisbett and Ross, 1980); therefore, events that have been experienced recently or that have been described in colourful detail tend to be perceived as more prevalent or likely to recur than they are in fact. Simulation entails visualizing hypothetical scenarios and, typically, attendant causal associations between actions and consequences. The more a scenario is simulated, the more vivid and available it and its underlying premises usually become [. . .].

Planning of any sort entails simulation, as does conveying those plans in detail to others. A spiral of self-delusion, therefore, may be triggered as a seemingly bright strategic prospect is discussed repeatedly in planning sessions or during the course of casual conversation. Specifically, behavioural decision theory implies that, because attractiveness promotes wishful thinking and articulation enhances vividness and availability, the more a strategic option is discussed, the more certain the anticipated results are likely to appear. In turn, the option itself is apt to appear increasingly attractive and to raise the aspirations of executives considering it. Some executives, therefore, may become over-eager to implement a beguiling, but hastily selected, alternative and may eventually frame the prospect of not implementing an enticing and much-discussed course of action as a loss [. . .]. Their judgements may be distorted further by confirmation bias, which entails seeking out data that supports emerging or firmly entrenched commitments and beliefs while avoiding contrary information [. . .].

GROUP DYNAMICS AND ORGANIZATIONAL CULTURE Interactions among individuals, particularly in group contexts, tend either to dampen or to intensify biases (Bazerman, 1990: 150–3; Whyte, 1989). Therefore, group-consensus decisions may be better than individual decisions on many occasions; however, at other times, especially when they are exacted by cajoling or political pressure, they may be much worse, as the groupthink literature suggests [. . .]. Furthermore, a cohesive *organizational culture*, especially when coupled with undue confidence, may engender esprit de corps; but it may also promote 'tunnel vision', the illusion of control, and perilous inertia [. . .]. Organizational culture, including organizational ideology, develops as if organizations had memories and, accordingly, is a product of the experiences and perspectives of past and present members of the organization, especially its key executives [. . .].

THE STRUCTURE OF MANAGERIAL DECISION-MAKING Because rationality is bounded and typical strategic issues are vague and ill-structured, executives operating individually or in groups commonly reduce the realm of possibility unwittingly and, perhaps, inevitably to a few partially evaluated and ranked alternatives before they have learned enough to formulate lucid problem statements or formal decision-making, such as strategic planning, is initiated [. . .]. Such filtering or pre-selection occurs because deriving meaning from the manifold signals emitted by the manager's vibrant world entails simulating scenarios in which environmental signals are juxtaposed with prospective courses of actions, competitors' reactions, prospective results, organizational goals, personal aspirations, and the like (Sherman and Corty, 1984: 218–24). Often, only a single alternative emerges from pre-selection processes (Alexander, 1979). Moreover, as

Pettigrew (1985: 659) has observed, actual managerial decisions are commonly 'shaped by political/cultural considerations, though often expressed in rational/analytical terms'.

A behavioural framework for studying organizational phenomena

Pettigrew (1985a, 1985b, 1987) has outlined an integrative approach to exploring the behavioural dimension of organizational phenomena, such as economic failure, that he labelled *contextualist inquiry*. The contextualist research paradigm [. . .] requires viewing organizations as complex continuing systems driven by multifarious circumstances and processes, some of which induce change while others foster continuity or even rigidity [. . .]. It also involves, in an eclectic fashion, developing linkages among political, psychosocial, or other conceptual frameworks capable of explaining the researcher's data [. . .].

A central tenet of the contextualist framework is that, at any point in time, an organization's capabilities, prospects, decisions, and actions are rooted substantially in the preceding events, choices, and experiences that comprise its history and shaped its culture. Accordingly, contextualists expect firms to be 'stamped with the character of their inheritance and early development', as Child and Smith (1987: 568) have noted, not only in terms of physical systems and distinctive competencies, but also in terms of beliefs, vested interest, and power structures. Such roots to the past frequently enable firms to prosper for a time; but eventually, they are apt to foster rigidities that prevent the organization from responding effectively to inevitable environmental change (Zucker, 1987). Contextualist explanations of economic failure, therefore, must address not only recent circumstances, but also distant organizational and environmental antecedents.

The rise and fall of BMD: a descriptive contextual account

The history of BMD is unfolded in this section. Particular attention is focused on the dynamic *corporate context* in which BMD developed and eventually perished, changes in the competitive *sectoral context* to which BMD would not or could not adapt, and the leadership, ideologies, parochial interests, and conflicts that characterized BMD's *inner context*.

The origin and evolution of Boise Cascade

In 1956, at the age of 36, Robert V. Hansberger was named President of the Boise Payette Lumber Company, an obscure American forest products firm. [. . .] Shortly after taking the helm at Boise Payette, Hansberger began to transform his minute enterprise into a powerful international conglomerate, the Boise Cascade

Corporation, which he managed for 16 years. At the outset, he recruited bright and ambitious MBAs from Harvard and Stanford; then he asked these 'young tigers', as he called them, to acquire undervalued companies with the understanding that they would manage what they amassed in an atmosphere unencumbered by bureaucracy (Hartley, 1992: 46–54). Their innate abilities and highly developed skills, Hansberger often intimated, comprised Boise Cascade's most significant competitive advantage.

Acquisitions were financed largely by exchanging fractions of Boise Cascade's stock for the targeted firm's outstanding shares or by borrowing against acquired timber lands and other marketable assets. Moreover, crafty accounting was used to the extent permitted at the time by law to inflate reported earnings (Steiner, 1976). Hence, the more firms Boise Cascade acquired, the greater its rate of growth appeared to be, and until 1970, the more valuable its common stock became. Until 1970, Boise Cascade was among the darlings of Wall Street; and appropriately, Bob Hansberger was among the most admired financial 'wizards' of the 1960s (Hartley, l992: 46).

Boise Cascade's earliest acquisitions were confined largely to the forest products industry; however, related expansion increasingly gave way to diversification. By 1970, the firm had made approximately 35 significant acquisitions, and had branched out from manufacturing and distributing lumber and paper products into on-site home construction, recreational land development, mobile home and recreational vehicle production, pleasure cruises, engineering and heavy construction, electrical utilities, urban redevelopment, publishing, and composite can manufacturing. When the business press began referring to Boise Cascade as an unwieldy conglomerate, Hansberger rebuffed his critics and labelled his enterprise an 'idea company' dedicated to synergistic growth (Hartley, l992: 48). 'We try to keep a wet edge around the perimeter of all our operating groups and divisions', he said: 'Where the wet edge touches some field with which we have a very distinctive relationship . . . this could be a field we might move into' (Hansberger, 1969). He professed to realize that synergy could not be created simply by acquiring businesses at bargain prices; however, he also acknowledged that rapid earnings-per-share growth was his prime objective. Moreover, synergies that revealed themselves to Bob Hansberger and, perhaps, to some of his cadre were largely invisible to security analysts and other outside observers, who increasingly concluded that Boise Cascade was indeed a far-flung conglomerate driven much more by opportunistic financial criteria than by sound strategic product-market objectives (Boschken, 1974: 20–5). By the early 1970s they had noted, for instance, that Boise Cascade had not secured a dominant position in any specific product market even though it had equalled or surpassed other firms classified as forest product companies in terms of sales revenue (Hartley, 1992: 47). Moreover, as if bargain prices magnified the 'distinctive relationships' that purportedly comprised the fabric of Hansberger's wet-edge expansion ideology, one 'young tiger' advised this researcher that 'Any acquisition is a good deal at the right price'.

The origin and early helmsmen of BMD

Companies that owned saw mills and timber lands were among Boise Cascade's earliest acquisitions. However, many of the acquired firms also owned lumber yards, which seemed unprofitable and were seen as prospective sources of cash and leverage that could be used to finance new ventures. In the late 1960s, Pete O'Neill, one of Hansberger's young protégés, was put in charge of selling more than 100 such unwanted yards. However, he convinced Bob Hansberger to prune rather than liquidate, and quickly turned what he retained into a profitable enterprise, BMD. Like its parent company, BMD was headquartered in Boise, Idaho.

In 1968, BMD consisted of two dozen Northwestern lumber yards, which catered predominantly to professional housing contractors, farmers, and ranchers, and of six wholesaling facilities, which served captive as well as independent lumber yards. Then, early in 1970, O'Neill acquired the Western Lumber Company of San Diego, California. It was the first and the most prosperous of four major BMD acquisitions consummated during 1970 and 1971. Two of the four acquisitions, located in the Midwest and the South Atlantic states, turned out to be unprofitable and were sold within six years.

O'Neill was promoted to Senior Vice President in 1972 and placed in charge of the Building Materials Group, which consisted of BMD and three other divisions. He chose Dan Hogan to head BMD. Hogan had managed for many years a wholesale outlet that was eventually acquired by Boise Cascade, and he had served briefly as general manager of the dozen or so lumber yards and the four wholesale branches that once comprised BMD's Northwest Region. His gruff manner, coarse charm, and pragmatic wisdom endeared him to Pete O'Neill and to his subordinates, who saw Hogan much as he saw himself – tough, fair, earthy, and practical. Although Hogan had earned a college degree, he was essentially a stereotypical lumberman and the antithesis of Hansberger's 'young tigers'. Moreover, once his mind was made up about an issue, Hogan shunned even constructive questioning and equated disagreement with disloyalty.

Corporate retrenchment and the expansion of BMD

CORPORATE RETRENCHMENT 1970 marked the end of a decade of steady US economic growth; and by 1971, Boise Cascade's real estate ventures and several other undertakings unrelated to forest products were in very serious financial trouble. As write-offs that eventually approached $500 million mounted, the firm's common stock began to plummet toward 10 per cent of its 1969 value. Hansberger, under pressure from stockholders, vowed to retrench by transforming his diverse ventures into a focused and highly integrated forest products company. Operations not directly involved in manufacturing or selling lumber or paper products were to be sold, and proceeds from these troublesome ventures were to be invested in core businesses.

Stockholders welcomed retrenchment, yet in 1972, replaced the very enterprising and likeable Bob Hansberger with his long-time right-hand man, the very polished, Stanford-educated John B. Fery. The new CEO, who had joined Boise Cascade early in 1957, fully endorsed retrenchment and in 1973 hired a prestigious consulting firm to identify vertical integration opportunities and to assess the strategic fit and growth potential of every business unit.

EMERGENCE OF THE DUAL EXPANSION PLAN By 1974, the consultants had begun to study BMD intensively; however, its status was never in doubt. The CEO and the consultants recognized that, although BMD's earnings fluctuated with the housing cycle, on average, the division had been very profitable. Furthermore, BMD was a readily expandable pipeline for building products manufactured by Boise Cascade's lumber, plywood, and particleboard mills. They also realized do-it-yourself (DIY) home improvement sales had begun to surge throughout the USA and that industry experts generally expected home improvement retailers to experience unprecedented prosperity throughout the 1980s. Accordingly, targeting the DIY segment in addition to contractors promised to enhance profit margins. Moreover, it seemed reasonable to assume that people who could not afford new homes would refurbish or expand older homes and, therefore, that DIY retailing could smooth BMD's cyclical earnings.

By 1975 the consultants had confirmed the attractiveness of DIY retailing and, in several reports submitted over the next three years, claimed substantial operating economies could be realized if contractors and DIY consumers were served from common facilities and merchandise inventories. BMD's operations in the San Diego vicinity suggested this possibility. They included five building materials centres, acquired in 1970, that were designed to serve not only con-tractors, but also consumers whose DIY projects ranged from minor repairs to adding rooms and finishing basements. These facilities were centrally managed, were situated along shopping strips near residential areas, and were laid out to look much more like DIY building materials retail stores than contractor supply outlets. However, near a side entrance, each of these stores had a sales counter reserved exclusively for contractors. Therefore, regardless of where their offices or their construction sites were located, contractors were never more than a few minutes from a Boise Cascade building materials centre where they could place orders on account and pick up sundry items. Inventories of bulky products, such as lumber and plywood, were kept at low levels at these outlets because shipments to construction sites were made from a large central facility rather than from the stores. This *satellite system* was immensely profitable because it achieved efficiency without compromising service to either of the two targeted market segments.

THE CONSULTANTS' FINAL REPORT In April of 1978, the consultants formally presented their final recommendations, which had been preceded by an ample series of interim reports and, therefore, contained no surprises. The consultants offered the following advice:

1 Modify existing contractor yards so as to turn them into dual-segment building materials centres capable of attracting DIY customers in addition to contractors.

2 Initiate an accelerated expansion programme. Specific growth targets were not stated; however, outlets were to be built, acquired, and refurbished as necessary to increase revenue attributable to DIY sales from 5 to approximately 40 per cent and gross profit to more than 50 per cent.

3 Hire a division retailing manager to take charge of purchasing, merchandising, pricing, promotion, and refurbishing contractor outlets.

4 In the interest of effectiveness and efficiency, develop a higher degree of uniformity among stores in terms of layouts, displays, product assortments, prices, and advertising.

5 Develop a modern computerized retailing information system.

Other sections of the consultants' report cautioned against locating outlets near competitors' stores. However, so-called home centres were not considered rivals. Vis-à-vis building materials centres, home centres offered narrower selections of basic building products and did not cater to contractors. Moreover, unlike building materials centres, they usually carried household, lawn and garden, and automotive goods. On the surface, the report stated, DIY building materials centres and home centres appear to compete directly, but in fact, they coexist profitably in many places; and the three BMD outlets with the most competition from home centres (all located in the San Diego vicinity) recorded the highest returns on investment for 1977. BMD's managers generally agreed with the consultants' assessment. Home centres, they believed, were capable of selling 'a few sticks and light bulbs', but posed no serious threat because, in their estimation, such outlets offered neither the range of products nor the technical help provided by 'real' building materials retailers.

Although every store in the San Diego satellite configuration consistently generated a much larger return than any other BMD outlet, the report recommended concentrating on acquiring and building facilities in metropolitan areas of moderate size with solid contractor and DIY sales potential. This recommendation clearly reflected the predilections of BMD's general manager, Dan Hogan, who was very apprehensive about entering large cities capable of supporting satellite configurations.

IMPLEMENTATION OF THE DUAL-EXPANSION PLAN: THE SECTORAL CONTEXT Between 1971 and 1973, US housing starts stayed well above the 2 million mark, and lumber production and distribution capacity increased accordingly. Then, in 1974, housing starts fell to 1.3 million, and BMD's net income before taxes declined from $17 million in 1973 to $7 million. Housing

·starts and BMD's profits deteriorated further in 1975, but they recovered significantly in 1976 and peaked in 1977 and 1978. Nevertheless, the latter 1970s were plagued by uncertainty. On the bright side, US demographics, in conjunction with housing demolition statistics were interpreted by some economists as suggesting that as many as 2.3 million starts per year would be needed on average throughout the 1980s to satisfy demand. However, other forecasters warned that housing prices, which nearly tripled during the 1970s, and rising mortgage rates would curtail private investment in multi-unit housing and allow only high-income families to qualify for loans on single-family dwellings (Dean, 1982; Goldfarb, 1982). They believed a sharp decline in housing starts was imminent and that housing and related industries would not recover until new homes became affordable again. The dual-expansion venture was launched during these uncertain times with the acquisition of the 18-store Independent Lumber Company of Colorado early in 1978. The following year, BMD gained a foothold in the 'Sunbelt' region by acquiring 61 units – 46 in Texas, 10 in Oklahoma, and 5 in Kansas – from Lone Star Industries. Approximately 120 building materials centres and a dozen wholesaling facilities comprised BMD by mid-1980. However, some retail sales areas were as small as 2000 square feet while others were 15 times as large; and although a few stores were located near prime shopping strips, others were situated far from the beaten path. This admixture clearly reflected BMD's opportunistic acquisition ideology.

IMPLEMENTATION OF THE DUAL-EXPANSION PLAN: THE ORGANIZATIONAL CONTEXT By the late 1970s, Hogan was firmly in charge of BMD. Pete O'Neill, BMD's founder, had left the company in 1976; and his successors, who had no expertise in building materials manufacturing or distribution, were largely figureheads whose impact on BMD was inconsequential. Hogan never asked for their advice, never developed close relationships with them, and for all practical purposes, interacted directly with top management (i.e. the CEO and the president). However, Hogan was very close to his hand-picked region and area managers, who grew in number as the dual expansion plan was implemented. By 1980 BMD's governing inner circle consisted of three region managers, who oversaw the Northwest/Rocky Mountain Region, the West Coast Region, and the South Central Region, and 10 area managers, each of whom reported to one of the three region managers.

In the interest of vertical integration, BMD's purchases of Boise Cascade wood products were monitored very closely, and local managers were strongly encouraged, but not required, to buy 'in-house'. Otherwise, BMD was extremely decentralized. Nearly all operating decisions, including merchandising, pricing, promotion, and vendor decisions, were made autonomously at the store level. Only the San Diego satellite system and nine DIY retail stores located in Houston, Texas, which had been acquired from Lone Star Industries, were centrally managed insofar as each of these clusters was supervised directly by a retailing manager who reported to an area or a region manager. Extreme decentralization might have been appropriate for a contractor supply chain, but DIY retailing required much tighter co-ordination. Accordingly, the consultants (who were well-schooled, but not specifically in retailing) soon discovered that successful retailing chains generally were much more standardized and operated under much more centralized administrative structures than BMD. By 1977 they had begun to recommend centralizing the DIY retailing operations and turning them over to an experienced retailing manager.

At that juncture, Hogan and his inner circle, which had considered DIY retailing a potentially lucrative sideline, became apprehensive. They had no confidence in the proposed measures and sensed that retailing experts would become BMD's kingpins if a highly centralized structure were imposed. Moreover, they seemed firmly convinced and maintained steadfastly that local autonomy accounted for the division's past successes and would give BMD a competitive edge in DIY retailing. Standardization and centralized control, especially in the hands of a newcomer unfamiliar with BMD's ways, they argued, would destroy the very foundation on which BMD was built. In sum, they favoured dual expansion, but only if they could maintain their sovereignty.

The centralization issue had smouldered for months when, in 1978, Hogan agreed to hire a retailing manager and a three-man staff. However, Hogan's pact with higher management was such that the new retailing manager became little more than an adviser who was expected to make DIY retailing successful by 'selling' his programme piece by piece to Dan Hogan and his line managers. Accordingly, the retailing manager was held accountable for retailing operations and was expected to cement vendor relations, negotiate volume discounts, and recommend items, vendors, and merchandising plans to store managers. However, he could not impose his ideas on anyone. Large purchases, for example, could seldom be finalized until a sufficient number of store managers could be coaxed into accepting a portion of the tentatively negotiated volume at the tentatively negotiated price; and products and brands favoured by one store manager were often rejected by another. Both vendors and the retailing staff were confused and frustrated by BMD's protocols; hence, relations between the retailing staff and line management were plagued by incessant squabbling. During the early 1980s, several area managers installed their own area retailing managers, who were to work closely with store-level personnel and the division retailing staff, yet reported to their respective area managers. Like the division retailing staff, area retailing managers were expected to 'sell' their ideas to store managers and were given no authority to impose them.

Bob Moutrie was BMD's first retailing manager. Region, area, and store managers typically found him likeable as a person, but tactless and inflexible in his professional capacity. In 1980, he was assigned other duties and exiled to BMD's operations in Houston. He left the company a few months later. BMD's search for a new division retailing manager lasted more than a year, but ended in 1981 with the hiring of Bill Van Note, who was assured of BMD's commitment to retailing and was offered a much higher salary than the one his predecessor had earned. Van Note was competent, advocated centralization and standardization, and, as Hogan learned to his chagrin, was direct and unafraid to speak out. Retailing personnel at all levels soon saw Van Note as the one executive who could and would champion their interests. He resigned abruptly, however, after five months on the job and after a particularly bitter disagreement with Dan Hogan. Hogan felt he had made enough concessions, whereas Van Note learned that neither Hogan nor his lieutenants had equated 'commitment to retailing' with implementing the very substantial changes he considered vital. For instance, Hogan believed he had supported Van Note's (and even Moutrie's) efforts to centralize and standardize insofar as he had encouraged his subordinates to work with the retailing staff and to come to some agreement with respect to vendors and merchandising. However, Van Note found himself engaged in endless haggling and unable to act without first obtaining approval from region, area, and sometimes store managers. By the time Van Note left, he had concluded that BMD was less interested in retailing than in promoting Boise Cascade's manufactured products and that BMD could not capitalize on its size because its stores were too dispersed (Caulfield, 1985: 89).

As if more money could buy an executive sufficiently ingenious to make retailing work on Hogan's terms the retailing manager's salary was raised substantially once more to allure Ed Savage, who joined BMD in May of 1982. He had been president of Moore's, a successful Eastern building materials chain, and was much more acquiescent than Van Note. Savage performed no miracles, however, and left Boise Cascade in 1985. After his departure, he explained to a reporter that even the vertical integration effort went awry since it was far more economical for many BMD outlets to buy local lumber in lieu of lumber produced by Boise Cascade's distant mills (Caulfield, 1985).

The decline of BMD

THE SECTORAL CONTEXT Nationally, housing starts began to decline sharply during the latter half of 1979 as housing prices skyrocketed and mortgage rates headed for levels well above 15 per cent. BMD, like many other businesses driven by residential construction, incurred substantial operating losses in 1980 that were not offset by DIY retailing. Consequently, BMD launched an internal re-examination of DIY retailing and its prospects, which was completed in May of 1981 while losses were still mounting. The chief analyst discovered that competition among DIY building materials stores had become much more intense and sophisticated than had been anticipated and that some metropolitan markets were already saturated with DIY stores. Furthermore, he found that, contrary to BMD's expectations, home centres had begun to compete directly and effectively with BMD's outlets. His report cautioned that BMD must rely on its 'strength in wood products' and its 'retail professionalism' to compete effectively. It seems doubtful, however, that BMD had any strengths in wood products that competitors, regardless of their size or degree of vertical integration, could not replicate at will; and clearly, BMD's retailing operations were managed much less proficiently than those of its more prosperous contemporaries. The report went on to reaffirm the soundness of the dual-expansion strategy, but asserted that the DIY facet could not be treated simply as an extension of the familiar contractor supply business. DIY retailing, it echoed, requires a high degree of standardization and centralization as well as readily accessible store sites. These conclusions sparked a quarrel between Dan Hogan and the chief analyst that precipitated the latter's dismissal from Boise Cascade after eight years of employment. Otherwise, the findings were ignored. Moreover, BMD's executives continued to maintain an extremely myopic and parochial conception of their sector insofar as only firms utilizing formats that were nearly identical to BMD's were considered truly relevant contemporaries. Consequently, all sectoral pace-setters, including Payless Cashways, Home Depot, and Lowe's, were deemed fringe rather than central sectoral constituents. Payless Cashways, for instance, was viewed as being closer in character to a home centre than to a true building materials outlet and, thus, was not recognized as a threat or as a pacesetter worthy of emulation.

THE CORPORATE AND THE INTERNAL CONTEXTS On the corporate front, the price of Boise Cascade's stock, which had been recovering, dropped rapidly in 1982 from 48¼ to 19¾ in response to poor earnings. Consequently, the CEO ordered personnel cuts throughout the firm; and BMD, which incurred very substantial losses in 1982 and 1983, was forced to eliminate most staff positions and to suspend the development of the retailing information system that top management had championed. A dozen or more information systems specialists, many of whom had been hired recently and moved to Boise at Boise Cascade's expense, were terminated in mid-1982, which signalled quite clearly that top management had suddenly lost confidence in the dual-expansion venture. Late in 1982, the price of Boise Cascade's stock began to recover just as dramatically as it has plunged; nevertheless, BMD was forced to make further personnel cuts from time to time and to sell or close various facilities under the guise of retrenching.

Boise Cascade's 1984 annual report depicted a strong corporation that had retrenched successfully; and BMD's fiscal year was described as 'modestly profitable'. However, the report noted that some BMD outlets had been sold or closed during the year and that Lowe's had agreed to buy 27 facilities in Texas and Oklahoma. Lowe's could have bought more stores, but found no others worth buying. Given the chance to 'cherry pick' from the nine Houston retail stores, Lowe's concluded BMD had 'no cherries in Houston . . . only the pits' (Perry, 1985: 86). The Lowe's deal was consummated in March of 1985 and was followed by the sale of BMD's California outlets. By the end of 1985, BMD consisted of only 22 building materials centres and nine wholesale yards. At that time, a Boise Cascade spokesman explained: 'Our commitment to our stores had really come down to determining which of our businesses held out the greatest long-range return on investment' (Caulfield, 1985: 89). By mid-1987, Dan Hogan had retired and all building materials centres had been sold or closed; only a few wholesale yards remained. Events chronicled in this section are summarized in Table 2.1.

Table 2.1 *Summary of events*

Corporate-level events	Year	Divison-level events
Phase I: Boise Cascade's and BMD's genesis		
R. V. Hansberger forms Boise Cascade (BC) and becomes CEO. Rapid concentric expansion follows, which increasingly gives way to conglomerate diversification; 130 unwanted lumber yards are amassed inadvertently as firms are acquired.	1956 1968	P. O'Neill forms BMD by intensively pruning Boise Cascade's agglomeration of unwanted lumber yards.
Boise Cascade's stock price peaks at 80¼	1969 1970 1971	Western Lumber and three other companies, which cater predominantly to contractors, are acquired.
	1972	D. B. Hogan becomes BMD's general manager, following O'Neill's promotion to head of the Building Materials Group.
Phase II: Boise Cascade's and BMD's transformation BC's stock price drops sharply as earnings decline and write-offs attributable to ventures not directly related to forest products mount. Top management announces its intent to retrench; yet, the CEO is replaced.	1972	
BC's stock price bottoms out at 8¼. New CEO J. Fery launches a full-scale retrenchment planning effort and hires consultants to assist. BMD is seen as an expandable pipeline for lumber products manufactured by BC's mills, and DIY retailing opportunities seem too good to pass up.	1973 1974	BMD begins to participate in formulating the dual-expansion plan, which most key BMD executives favour.
	1976	P. O'Neill, BMD's founder, leaves Boise Cascade.
	1977	The efficacy of BMD's extremely decentralized administrative structure is questioned; BMD's line managers vehemently oppose centralization. BMD withdraws from the South Atlantic states and from the St. Louis area.
	1978	The dual-expansion venture is launched. BMD hires a division retailing manager, but gives him very little authority because line managers fear centralization and

Table 2.1 *Continued*

Corporate-level events	Year	Divison-level events
		being displaced by retailing experts. As much contractor as DIY capacity is added between 1978 and 1980.
BC's stock price continues to fluctuate but exhibits a significant upward trend.	1981	
Phase III: BMD's decline BC's stock falls from 48¼ to 19¾ in response to poor corporate earnings. The CEO mandates deep personnel cuts throughout the firm and suspends the development of BMD's retailing information system. Stock prices recover dramatically after mid-year.	1982	BMD emerges as an unprofitable hodgepodge of 121 diverse outlets amid squabbling over centralization. Ordered personnel cuts are made, and further cost-cutting measures are implemented periodically.
	1984	The systematic liquidation of BMD begins under the guise of retrenchment.
The corporate retrenchment plan has been executed successfully, despite BMD's misfortunes.		
	1987	All building materials centres are sold or closed by mid-year.

Diagnosis

The strategic context

Why did BMD fail? The housing slump of 1980–2 and steadily intensifying competition are certainly among the uncontrollable contextual factors that affected BMD adversely. Had the housing market remained strong and had ambitious competitors not been aroused by surging DIY demand, BMD might not have folded. Controllable strategic factors that almost certainly contributed to BMD's extinction can be identified by comparing various elements of BMD's strategic recipe, e.g. its physical operations and managerial systems, to those of sectoral pacesetters, such as Payless Cashways, Home Depot, and Lowe's. Payless Cashways, which targeted only the DIY segment, was headed by David Stanley, an experienced investment broker hired in 1980 when the chain consisted of 68 scattered units. By the end of 1983, he had brought the number of facilities to 134 retail stores and eight distribution centres. Unlike BMD's Hogan, Stanley centralized the various retailing functions and hired experienced specialists to head purchasing, merchandising, promotion, site selection, and construction. Moreover, he realized that, as building materials retailing approached the mature stage of its life cycle, competition would intensify and operating economies would become critical. Accordingly, he endeavoured to dominate Payless Cashways' targeted metropolitan markets.

Payless Cashways continued to grow and to prosper after its decade of uninterrupted earnings growth ended in 1984. However, Home Depot, a chain of warehouse stores located mostly in large metropolitan areas, had become the new 'rising star' among DIY retailers by the mid-1980s. This chain was founded in 1978 by three executives who had been in the forefront of DIY building materials retailing for many years. Like Payless Cashways, Home Depot stressed service, merchandising, and pricing; but its retail sales floors exceeded 80,000 square feet and, on average, were more than three times as large as Payless Cashways'. Although in 1984 Home Depot consisted of only 31 centrally managed outlets with combined sales of $425 million, the chain had grown to 174 stores with sales exceeding $4 billion by 1992 (Loeb, l992).

In 1984, Lowe's 248 home improvement centres were located mainly in small towns and, therefore, were insulated substantially from major competitors, especially warehouse retailers. Although Lowe's targeted both the DIY and the contractor segments, its operations, too, were much more centralized than BMD's. Moreover, Lowe's had evolved as a dual-segment chain and, therefore, had acquired expertise in serving both contractors and DIY customers from common facilities for several decades.

Comparing BMD with the top building materials chains reveals that the following characteristics increasingly set BMD apart from them:

1 too many poor store sites;

2 diverse retailing floor sizes that, in conjunction with BMD ideology, impeded standardization;

3 lack of dominance in most of its metropolitan markets;

4 extreme decentralization;

5 an inadequate retailing information system.

These shortcomings seemingly reduced BMD's effectiveness and efficiency. Effectiveness refers to a firm's ability to gain the patronage of targeted customer segments, whereas efficiency pertains to revenue generated in relation to resources expended. In BMD's case, effectiveness surely was impaired by the division's primitive retailing information system; poor store sites; and extreme decentralization, which placed too many critical decisions in the hands of local 'Jacks of all trades' instead of retailing experts. Efficiency undoubtedly suffered from the lack of common store sizes, market penetration, standardization, centralization, and a modern retailing information system (Valentin, 1991).

Behavioural processes in context

From a strategic vantage point, it seems evident that BMD's recipe was inferior. But how did this strategic recipe emerge and persist?

The consultants whom Boise Cascade had hired in the early 1970s to assess each business unit's prospects quickly recognized that BMD's operations fell well within the scope of retrenchment and the new corporate mission. Therefore, using proceeds from divestitures to acquire more building materials outlets seemed perfectly appropriate. Moreover, factual information, when commingled with a few plausible assumptions, spawned conjectures that virtually mandated adding contractor-service capacity while extending BMD's market scope to encompass the DIY segment. Specifically:

1 *Fact*: Expanding BMD would increase Boise Cascade's captive distribution capacity for lumber, plywood, and other building products manufactured by its mills.

   Conjecture: Expanding BMD substantially would promote much tighter vertical integration.

2 *Fact*: DIY demand was growing rapidly and, according to industry experts, would continue to grow for many years; historically, DIY gross margins were much greater and DIY sales were much less cyclical than contractor sales; and BMD's dual-segment outlets, which were confined largely to the five-store San Diego satellite system at that time, were extremely profitable.

   Conjecture: BMD's San Diego operations were representative of the intrinsic potential of the dual-segment format, and DIY retailing would prove to be a natural and simple extension of the core (contractor) business.

3 *Fact*: In the mid-1970s, all but a few DIY and dual-segment chains were and unsophisticated.

   Conjecture: BMD would have no trouble competing.

In addition, faulty analogies were drawn between DIY retailing and the familiar contractor supply business. For instance, merchandising was equated with inventory control, which BMD had mastered, and DIY consumers were characterized as customers not very different from contractors, except that they knew less about construction and, individually, bought less than contractors. If BMD could serve professional home builders, it was argued, then surely BMD could deal with amateur handymen.

These speculative analogies and conjectures were soon assimilated into a beguiling shared vision that imparted a common sense of direction in advance of detailed planning. Moreover, it contained the rudiments of an economic rationale and a causal structure from which a detailed plan of action – the dual-expansion strategy – gradually emerged. Yet in essence, the dual-expansion alternative was pre-selected near the start of the planning process without systematically enumerating and evaluating other possibilities. As that plan was fleshed out, its rationale, causal structure, and cognitively simulated outcomes became increasingly vivid and available. Concomitantly, managerial aspirations rose to new levels since expansion promised an abundance of career opportunities.

Unfortunately, rising managerial aspirations and the scenario's vividness and availability seemed to blind decision-makers to its uncertainties and to the speculative nature of its central premises. As the fleshing-out process ran its course, speculative assumptions increasingly passed for solid facts, fanciful predictions were mistaken for realistic expectations, and data gathering was directed predominantly toward confirming predilections. Moreover, critical factors that accounted for the San Diego system's success were quickly forgotten; therefore, the dual-segment format soon appeared ideal regardless of whether stores were operated as a satellite system or autonomously, or whether stores were located along shopping strips or within industrial zones. Key executives hastily surmised that BMD could be turned into a major dual-segment chain largely by acquiring contractor yards opportunistically and refurbishing them so as to make them more appealing to consumers. Very little incremental investment would be required to convert each contractor yard to a dual-segment building materials centre, yet the payoff would be spectacular. Accordingly, the dual-expansion scheme was dubbed a 'no brainer' to accentuate its simplicity and the apparent certitude of the anticipated results.

Neither the desired level of vertical integration nor the anticipated profits were realized. The vertical integration objective was not achieved because price was the predominant acquisition criterion; therefore, many outlets were not located in markets that Boise Cascade's mills could serve economically or effectively (Caulfield, 1985). However, the dual-expansion plan had called for making opportunistic, price-driven acquisitions; and hence, it was expected from the outset that most stores would not be located near shopping areas and that retailing space would vary substantially among stores. Also, market penetration was never an objective, perhaps because Boise Cascade achieved nearly all of its successes without dominating markets, market share was not a source of significant competitive advantage in the contractor supply business, and lessons learned from serving contractors militated against placing outlets so close together that cannibalistic competition would ensue.

Extreme decentralization also was congruent with early visions of dual-expansion because it was taken for granted that the existing administrative structure would endure. After centralization and standardization issues surfaced, motivational, cognitive, and ideological forces militated against radical change since BMD's line managers believed that centralizing retailing would diminish their power and status and could precipitate their replacement by retailing experts. Nevertheless, their self-serving stance may have been rooted mainly in the sincere belief that centralization would ruin the division.

The histories of. BMD's more successful contemporaries suggest that the most constructive option available to BMD's incumbent line managers entailed relinquishing control over DIY retailing and concentrating on maintaining their dominion over contractor supply operations. Had they done so, BMD might have survived; and Dan Hogan and his cadre might have remained nominally in charge of the combined DIY-contractor operations, although they would have had little actual jurisdiction over DIY retailing. Unfortunately, heightened aspirations and inbred ideologies precluded them from acknowledging and, quite possibly, from sensing that, irrespective of higher-management's stance toward centralization, prior commitments to DIY retailing in view of a changing competitive climate mandated transformative organizational change. At some point, higher management should have abandoned tradition and imposed a centralized administrative structure. It should have given retailing experts significant authority and should have installed them in prominent positions. Unyielding incumbents should have been replaced. Apparently, however, top management, too, was blinded by chronic ideological biases against centralization, which had been a 'dirty word' since Bob Hansberger's era. Therefore, it was not completely swayed by evidence suggesting centralization was urgently required. Moreover, imposing a particular administrative structure on a division was not consistent with Boise Cascade tradition or ideology. Accordingly, top management supported centralization only halfheartedly and, even as time was running out, relied on comparatively slow and democratic *collaborative incremental orchestration* to effect change, which Dunphy and Stace (1988) consider appropriate only when minor adjustments are needed to align an organization with its external environment or when changes can be made gradually and key interest groups favour the new programme. When immediate radical change is vital, but is not supported by key stakeholders, Dunphy and Stace recommend *coercive transformative orchestration*.

Regarding BMD's retailing information system, the need for a sophisticated computerized network was not foreseen during the initial planning stages. However, by the late 1970s, a second consulting team had been hired to assess BMD's needs and to design templates of managerial reports to be generated. Yet even though the CEO urged BMD to develop and install the requisite system quickly, progress was extremely slow and did not advance beyond testing prototypes in one or two isolated stores because the division controller and his information systems manager, who were responsible for implementation, were afraid to make mistakes that BMD's line managers would blame on incompetence.

On the competitive front, several chains headed by executives with strong retailing backgrounds (e.g. Home Depot and Lowe's) or by executives who assembled expert staffs and used them effectively (e.g. Payless Cashways) grew into formidable adversaries during the late 1970s and the early 1980s. As such thriving chains expanded and became entrenched in various regions and prime metropolitan areas, BMD's performance deteriorated. Gradually, it became painfully evident that many BMD locations were poorly suited for DIY retailing; that serving DIY customers has little in common with serving contractors; and that little differences, such as dissimilar preferences for packaging, can quickly render anticipated economies unattainable. For instance, unlike contractors, many consumers prefer hardware items in plastic bubble packs, neatly displayed, even when the same items can be picked from bulk bins at substantial savings. Nevertheless, beyond changing or eliminating personnel at the store level, very little was done to identify controllable internal factors that might improve performance. In particular, BMD's line managers continued to denounce centralization and to reject evidence showing very clearly that successful retailers, including DIY chains, were far more centralized and standardized than BMD. BMD's line managers, apparently, failed to appreciate the significance of competitive changes and the inadequacies of the division's strategic recipe, but perceived centralization and standardization as serious threats to the division and to their personal aspirations. Research on cognitive processes suggests executives tend to find issues that portend loss of control or that cast doubt on their qualifications threatening (Jackson and Dutton, 1988); moreover, Zucker (1984: 671) found that 'organizations often resist change even when threatened with extinction'. As Boise Cascade regained its financial health, top management simply chose to abandon BMD before the division could jeopardize the firm's recovery.

Summary and concluding comments

The preceding interpretive account of the process that spawned and, for some time, sustained BMD's ill-fated venture illustrates how organizational and behavioural decision theory and related empirical findings facilitate understanding actual strategic miscues, lends further insight into departures of actual managerial decision-making from the tenets of economic rationality, and supports previous case research that suggests that past successes and ideological rigidities can foster dysfunctional inertia and mindsets. The study centred on a strategy rooted largely in speculative (and predominantly false) analogies and conjectures that became so vivid and available during the planning process that their verity was eventually taken for granted without the benefit of serious objective inquiry. Accordingly, further research might reveal that expansion in unfamiliar directions is particularly beguiling precisely because ambiguities abound – ambiguities that afford ample opportunities for drawing faulty analogies and for relying on self-serving conjectures in lieu of 'brutal' facts. Yet, controlled studies into the effects of ambiguity on individual decision-making suggest ambiguity invites caution rather than daring because individuals fear that, with the benefit of hindsight, others will accuse them of having acted unwisely (Frisch and Baron, 1988). Members of decision-making teams, however, are often judged mainly by one another. Consequently, being a 'team player' is frequently more important than being correct, collective folly is readily mistaken for wisdom, and adverse consequences are readily attributed to nothing worse than bad luck (Janis, 1982; Janis and Mann, 1977).

The particulars of this inquiry into BMD's demise when juxtaposed with Child and Smith's (1987) study of Cadbury Limited's successful transformation from an antiquated tradition-bound enterprise into a progressive confectioner also affords insights into problem-sensing and adaptive behaviour. Child and Smith asserted that a business unit's long-term viability hinges substantially on management's sensitivity to new sectoral requirements as they are spawned by new technologies or by intensified competition, for instance, and on its ability to adapt or to transform products, processes, and organizational structures accordingly. Deteriorating performance in absolute terms or in relation to industry leaders, they surmised, is likely to induce firms with solid earnings histories to contemplate revamping traditional strategic recipes and, as is often fitting, to emulate rivals that have emerged as sectoral exemplars. Usually, a company can gain at least a rudimentary understanding of prominent competitors' strategies from employees hired away from such firms, from business and trade journals, and from consultants and vendors who circulate among rival firms. When Cadbury's financial performance deteriorated as regional barriers gave way to global competition in the 1970s, its top management team came to realize that the firm's traditional strategic recipe was no longer viable; then it set out to reshape Cadbury largely in the image of Mars, the American competitor that had emerged as the confectionery sector's pacesetter. Cadbury's senior executives equated the firm's prospects as well as their personal fortunes with strategic change, infused expertise from Mars, and broke a long-standing tradition by using power when persuasion failed to overcome resistance to their new agenda.

BMD, in contrast, had been profitable, despite its parent company's ills, and the changing competitive climate had not yet threatened the division when corporate management first encouraged BMD to expand so as to become a prominent dual-segment chain. BMD's top executives, therefore, framed higher management's exhortation as an opportunity, but did not equate it with the division's or with their own economic survival. Therefore, when BMD's financial performance did degenerate, blame was cast on the most overt irritants, particularly slumping residential construction and 'those damned retailing people'. That competitive dynamics and other life-cycle forces were imposing new requirements for survival escaped their notice; and when the efficacy of BMD's extremely decentralized administrative structure was questioned, BMD's line managers deemed centralization, not changing competitive conditions or internal deficiencies, the most formidable threat to the division and to their personal aspirations. Had they felt less threatened by centralization, which they associated with inflexibility and the prospect of being displaced by retailing experts, BMD might have been just as successful as the top building materials chains, which were centrally managed by experienced retailing men or by CEOs who surrounded themselves with expert staffs.

The present study, then, alludes to a strong relationship between successful building materials distribution and the effective utilization of relevant domain-specific expertise. Such a relationship is also implied in more sweeping accounts of DIY building materials retailing in the 1980s (Shutt and O'Neill, 1990); moreover, a strong relations between success in any sort of business and domain-specific expertise (vis-à-vis native intelligence or mastery of analytical tools) has been hypothesized by Stubbart (1989) and others. However, mistaking dysfunctional mindsets for relevant expertise can be catastrophic. In BMD's case, the knowledge line managers had acquired from serving contractors for many years may have been more detrimental than helpful in transforming BMD. Research that reveals how the contextual relevance of knowledge can be assessed, especially before clear exemplars emerge within a sector, is direly needed. For instance, how could one know in advance that, in DIY building materials retailing, general retailing expertise would prove to be valuable while contractor sales expertise was apparently a source of dysfunctional mindsets? Further research into debiasing techniques, such as dialectical debate and devil's advocacy, is also needed (Schweiger et al., 1986; Schwenk, 1984).

[. . .]

References

Alexander, E. R. (1979) 'The design of alternatives in organizational contexts: a pilot study', *Administrative Science Quarterly*, 24: 382–404.

Bazerman, M. H. (1990) *Managerial Decision Making*. New York: Wiley.

Boschken, H. L. (1974) *Corporate Power and the Mismarketing of Urban Development: Boise Cascade Recreation Communities*. New York: Praeger.

Caulfield, J. (1985) 'Boise sells its California stores', *National Home Center News*, 1 Oct.

Child, J. and Smith, C. (1987) 'The context and process of organizational transformation – Cadbury Limited in its sector', *Journal of Management Studies*, 24(6): 565–93.

Cyert, R. M. and March, J. G. (1963) *A Behavioral Theory of the Firm*. Englewood Cliffs, NJ: Prentice-Hall.

Dean, W. (1982) *Housing and the Forest Products Markets in the '80s*. Eugene, Or: Random Lengths.

Dunphy, D. C. and Stace, D. A. (1988) 'Transformational and coercive strategies for planned organizational change: beyond the o.d. model', *Organizational Studies*, 9(3): 317–34.

Fahey, L. and Narayanan, V. K. (1989) 'Linking changes in revealed causal maps and environmental change: an empirical study', *Journal of Management Studies*, 26(4): 361–78.

Frisch, D. and Baron, J. (1988) 'Ambiguity and rationality', *Journal of Behavioral Decision Making, 1: 149–57.*

Goldfarb, J. (1982) Housing Industry. New York: Merrill Lynch Pierce Fenner & Smith, Inc.

Hansberger, R. V. (1969) 'Is Boise Cascade a conglomerate?', *Interface* (Boise Cascade's newsletter), 1(1): 1.

Hartley, R. F. (1992) *Marketing Mistakes*. Columbus, OH: Grid.

Jackson, S. and Dutton, J. (1988) 'Discerning threats and opportunities', *Administrative Science Quarterly*, 33: 370–87.

Janis, I. L. (1982) *Groupthink*. Boston: Houghton-Mifflin.

Janis, I. L. and Mann, L. (1977) *Decision Making*. New York: Free Press.

Kiesler, S. and Sproull, L. (1982) 'Managerial response to changing environments: perspectives on problem sensing from social cognition', *Administrative Science Quarterly*, 27: 548–70.

Loeb, W. F. (1992) 'Unbundle or centralize: what is the answer?' *Retailing Issues Letter*, 4(3): 1–4.

Nisbett, R. and Ross, L. (1980) *Human Inference: Strategies and Shortcomings of Social Judgment*. Englewood Cliffs, NJ: Prentice-Hall.

Perry, P. M. (1985) 'Boise retrenches', *National Home Center News*, February: 86.

Pettigrew, A. M. (1985a) *The Awakening Giant: Continuity and Change in Imperial Chemical Industries*. Oxford: Blackwell.

Pettigrew, A. M. (1985b) 'Contextualist research: a natural way to link theory and practice', in E. E. Lawler (ed.), *Doing Research that Is Useful in Theory and Practice*. San Francisco, CA: Jossey-Bass.

Pettigrew, A. M. (1987) 'Context and action in the transformation of the firm', *Journal of Management Studies*, 24(6): 649–70.

Schweiger, D. M., Sandberg, W. R. and Ragan, J. W. (1986) 'Group approaches for improving strategic decision making: a comparative analysis of dialectical inquiry, devil's advocacy, and consensus', *Academy of Management Journal*, 29(1): 51–71.

Schwenk, C. R. (1984) 'Devil's advocacy in managerial decision-making', *Journal of Management Studies*, 21(2): 153–68.

Sherman, S. J. and Corty, E. (1984) 'Cognitive heuristics', in R. S. Wyer and T. K. Srull (eds), *Handbook of Social Conditions*, vol. 1. Hillsdale, NJ: Erlbaum. pp. 189–286.

Shutt, C. A. and O'Neill, M. C. (1990) 'Whatever happened to the class of 80?', *Building Supply Home Centers*, November: 23–7.

Simon, H. A. (1955) 'A behavioral model of rational choice' *Quarter Journal of Economics*, 69: 99–118.

Simon, H. A. (1956) 'Rational choice and the structure of the environment', *Psychological Review*, 63: 129–38.

Steiner, P. O. (1976) *Mergers*, Arbor, MI: University of Michigan Press.

Stubbart, C. I. (1989) 'Managerial cognition: a missing link in strategic management research', *Journal of Management Studies* 26(4): 325–47.

Valentin, E. K. (1991) 'Retail market structure scenarios and their strategic applications', *International Review of Retail, Distribution and Consumer Research*, 1(3): 285–99.

Whyte, G. (1989) 'Groupthink reconsidered', *Academy of Management Review*, 14(1): 40–56.

Zucker, L. G. (1987) 'Normal change or risky business: institutional effects on the "hazard" of change in hospital organizations, 1959–79', *Journal of Management Studies*, 24(6): 671–700.

CHAPTER 3

A Summary of Basic Concepts in the Behavioral Theory of the Firm

RICHARD M. CYERT AND JAMES G. MARCH*

In its classic form, economic theory is simply a language designed to provide a systematic framework within which economic problems can be analysed. Such a role was assigned to theory by Marshall and is clearly implicit in contemporary theory. In this view theory performs two major functions. On the one hand, it is an exhaustive set of general concepts. Any variable observed in the system can be assigned to an appropriate niche. The theory is a set of filing cabinets with each drawer bearing the title of an economic concept. Within each file drawer there is a set of folders for each economic variable relevant to the concept. Within each folder there is a further breakdown in terms of the factors affecting the variable. At the same time, the theory is a statement of critical relations among system variables. These relations may be assumptions about interdependence among variables, about the functional form of the interdependences, or about broad structural attributes of the system.

[. . .]

One of the most important requirements for the usefulness of theory conceived in this general way is the requirement that all important variables in the system be conveniently represented within the concepts of the theory. The theory of the firm seems to meet this requirement reasonably well for the kinds of problems with which it has usually been faced (e.g. the perfectly competitive market). [. . .] The theory outlined in this volume specifies an alternative framework and an alternative set of key relations for dealing with the modern 'representative firm' – the large, multi-product firm operating under uncertainty in an imperfect market.

* Blackwell Publishers for Cyert, R.M. and March, J.G. 'A summary of basic concepts in the behavioural theory of the firm', in *A Behavioural Theory of the Firm*. Copyright © Blackwell Publishers 1965.

Goals, expectations and choice

The basic framework for analysis we have proposed, like the classic one, has two major organizing devices: It has a set of exhaustive variable categories; it has a set of relational concepts. [. . .] We have argued that we can analyse the process of decision-making in the modern firm in terms of the variables that affect organizational goals, the variables that affect organizational expectations, and the variables that affect organizational choice.

ORGANIZATIONAL GOALS Quite simply, we have identified two sets of variables affecting the goals of an organization. The first set influences the *dimensions* of the goals (what things are viewed as important). Within this set of variables, we can cite the composition of the organizational coalition, the organizational division of labor in decision-making, and the definition of problems facing the organization. Thus, we have argued that organizational goals change as new participants enter or old participants leave the coalition. We have argued that the operative goals for a particular decision are the goals of the sub-unit making that decision. Finally, we have argued that goals are evoked by problems.

The second set of variables influences the *aspiration level* on any particular goal dimension. Here we have identified essentially three variables: the organization's past goal, the organization's past performance, and the past performance of other 'comparable' organizations. The aspiration level is viewed as some weighted function of these three variables.

ORGANIZATIONAL EXPECTATIONS Expectations are seen as the result of drawing inferences from available information. Thus, we consider variables that affect either the process of drawing inferences or the process by which information is made available to the organization. With respect to inference drawing, we have not attempted to reflect all of the recent efforts in the psychology of individual choice. However, we have identified some simple pattern-recognition variables (e.g. linear extrapolation) and the effect of hopes on expectations. With respect to the process by which information is made available, we have cited particularly variables affecting search activity within the firm. Affecting the intensity and success of search are the extent to which goals are achieved and the amount of organizational slack in the firm. Affecting the direction of search are the nature of the problem stimulating search and the location in the organization at which search is focused.

ORGANIZATIONAL CHOICE Choice takes place in response to a problem, uses standard operating rules, and involves identifying an alternative that is acceptable from the point of view of evoked goals. Thus, the variables that affect choice are those that influence the definition of a problem within the organization, those that influence the standard decision rules, and those that affect the order of consideration of alternatives. The standard decision rules are affected primarily by the past experience of the organization and the past record of organizational slack. The order in which alternatives are considered depends on the part of the organization in which the decision is being made and past experience in considering alternatives. [. . .]

Four major relational concepts

In the course of developing the three sub-theories, we have developed a relatively small number of relational concepts. In many respects, they represent the heart of our theory of business decision-making. The four major concepts used in the theory are

1 quasi resolution of conflict

2 uncertainty avoidance

3 problemistic search

4 organizational learning

In this section we review briefly the meaning of each of these concepts. [. . .]

Quasi resolution of conflict

In keeping with virtually all theories of organizations, we assume that the coalition represented in an organization is a coalition of members having different goals. We require some procedure for resolving such conflict. The classic solution is to posit an exchange of money from some members of the coalition to other members as a way of inducing conformity to a single, consistent set of goals – the organizational objective.

We propose an alternate concept of organizational goals and an alternate set of assumptions about how conflict is resolved. Basically we have argued that most organizations most of the time exist and thrive with considerable latent conflict of goals. Except at the level of non-operational objectives, there is no internal consensus. The procedures for 'resolving' such conflict do not reduce all goals to a common dimension or even make them obviously internally consistent.

GOALS AS INDEPENDENT CONSTRAINTS In our framework, organizational goals are a series of independent aspiration-level constraints imposed on the organization by the members of the organizational coalition. These constraints may include non-essential demands (i.e. demands that are already satisfied when other constraints are met), sporadic demands (i.e. demands that are made only occasionally), non-operational demands (i.e. demands for which there are no operational measures), as well as essential, continuous, operative goals. In general, although we recognize the importance of goals that are non-essential (because they might become essential), of goals that are ordinarily sporadic (because they occasionally are enforced), and of goals that are non-operational (because they sometimes can be made operational), we will focus on those constraints that are essential, continuous, and operative.

Specifically, in the case of price and output models of the business firm, we assume a profit goal, a sales goal, a market share goal, an inventory goal, and a production goal. In any particular firm we expect some subset of these objectives to be essential, continuous, and operative. Moreover, we expect that subset to pose problems for the organization in the form of potential conflict. Thus, we require assumptions about procedures for resolving conflict. We assume that conflict is resolved by using local rationality, acceptable-level decision rules, and sequential attention to goals.

LOCAL RATIONALITY We assume that an organization factors its decision problems into subproblems and assigns the sub-problems to sub-units in the organization. From the point of view of organizational conflict, the importance of such local rationality is in the tendency for the individual sub-units to deal with a limited set of problems and a limited set of goals. At the limit, this reduces to solving one problem in terms of only one goal. The sales department is primarily responsible for sales goals and sales strategy; the production department is primarily responsible for production goals and production procedures; the pricing department is primarily responsible for profit goals and price decisions; and so on.

Through delegation and specialization in decisions and goals, the organization reduces a situation involving a complex set of interrelated problems and conflicting goals to a number of simple problems. Whether such a system will in fact 'resolve' the conflict depends, of course, on whether the decisions generated by the system are consistent with each other and with the demands of the external environment. In our theory consistency is facilitated by two characteristics of the decision process: acceptable-level decision rules and sequential attention to goals.

ACCEPTABLE-LEVEL DECISION RULES In the classic arguments for decentralization of decision-making, we require strong assumptions about the effectiveness of the 'invisible hand' in enforcing proper decisions on a system of local rationality. Consistency requires that local optimization by a series of independent decision centers results in overall optimization. On the other hand, we are persuaded that organizations can and do operate with much weaker rules of consistency (i.e. we require that local decisions satisfying local demands made by a series of independent decision centers result in a joint solution that satisfies all demands). Such rules are weaker in two senses:

1 There will ordinarily be a large number of local decisions that are consistent with other local decisions under such a rule. The demand constraints do not uniquely define a solution.

2 Any such system will tend to underexploit the environment and thus leave excess resources to absorb potential inconsistencies in the local decisions.

SEQUENTIAL ATTENTION TO GOALS Ordinarily when we talk of 'consistency' of goals or decisions we refer to some way of assessing their internal logic at a point in time. As a result, in classic theories of organizations we are inclined to insist on some consistency within a cross-section of goals. Such an insistence seems to us inaccurate as a characterization of organizational behavior. Organizations resolve conflict among goals, in part, by attending to different goals at different times. Just as the political organization is likely to resolve conflicting pressures to 'go left' and 'go right' by first doing one and then the other, the business firm is likely to resolve conflicting pressures to 'smooth production' and 'satisfy customers' by first doing one and then the other. The resulting time buffer between goals permits the organization to solve one problem at a time, attending to one goal at a time.

Uncertainty avoidance

To all appearances, at least, uncertainty is a feature of organizational decision-making with which organizations must live. In the case of the business firm, there are uncertainties with respect to the behavior of the market, the deliveries of suppliers, the attitudes of shareholders, the behavior of competitors, the future actions of governmental agencies, and so on. As a result, much of modern decision theory has been concerned with the problems of decision-making under risk and uncertainty. The solutions involved have been largely procedures for finding certainty equivalents (e.g. expected value) or introducing rules for living with the uncertainties (e.g. game theory).

Our studies indicate quite a different strategy on the part of organizations. Organizations avoid uncertainty by, firstly, avoiding the requirement that they correctly anticipate events in the distant future by using decision rules emphasizing short-run reaction to short-run feedback rather than anticipation of long-run uncertain events. They solve pressing problems rather than develop long-run strategies. Secondly, they avoid the requirement that they anticipate future reactions of other parts of their environment by arranging a negotiated environment. They impose plans, standard operating procedures, industry tradition, and uncertainty-absorbing contracts on that environment. In short, they achieve a reasonably manageable decision situation by avoiding planning where plans depend on predictions of uncertain future events and by emphasizing planning where the plans can be made self-confirming through some control device.

FEEDBACK-REACT DECISION PROCEDURES We assume that organizations make decisions by solving a series of problems; each problem is solved as it arises; the organization then waits for another problem to appear. Where decisions within the firm do not naturally fall into such a sequence, they are modified so that they will.

Consider, for example, the production-level decision. In most models of output determination, we introduce expectations with respect to future sales and relate output to such predictions. Our studies indicate, to the contrary, that organizations use only gross expectations about future sales in the output decision. They may, and frequently do, forecast sales and develop some long-run production plans on paper, but the actual production decisions are more frequently dominated by day-to-day and week-to-week feedback data from inventory, recent sales, and salesmen.

This assumption of a 'fire department' organization is one of the most conspicuous features of our models. Under a rather broad class of situations, such behavior is rational for an organization having the goal structure we have postulated. Under an even broader set of situations, it is likely to be the pattern of behavior that is learned by an organization dealing with an uncertain world and quasi-resolved goals. It will be learned because by and large it will permit the organization to meet the demands of the members of the coalition.

NEGOTIATED ENVIRONMENT Classical models of oligopoly ordinarily assume that firms make some predictions about the behavior of their environment, especially those parts of the environment represented by competitors, suppliers, customers, and other parts of the organization. Certainly such considerations are important to any decisions made by the firm. Our studies, however, lead us to the proposition that firms will devise and negotiate an environment so as to eliminate the uncertainty. Rather than treat the environment as exogenous and to be predicted, they seek ways to make it controllable.

In the case of competitors, one of the conspicuous means of control is through the establishment of industry-wide conventional practices. If 'good business practice' is standardized (through trade associations, journals, word of mouth, external consultants, etc.), we can be reasonably confident that all competitors will follow it. We do not mean to imply that firms necessarily enter into collusive agreements in the legal sense; our impression is that ordinarily they do not, but they need not do so to achieve the same objective of stability in competitive practices.

For example, prices are frequently set on the basis of conventional practice. With time, such variables as the rate of mark-up, price lines, and standard costing procedures become customary within an industry. [. . .] The net result of such activity with respect to prices (and comparable activity with regard to suppliers and customers) is that an uncertain environment is made quite highly predictable.

Such negotiation among firms is not obviously collusion for profit maximization. Rather, it is an attempt to avoid uncertainty while obtaining a return that satisfies the profit and other demands of the coalition. The lack of a profit-maximizing rationale is suggested both by the stability of the practices over time and by the occasional instances of success by firms willing to violate the conventional procedures (e.g. discount houses in retailing).

In a similar fashion, the internal planning process (e.g. the budget) provides a negotiated internal environment. A plan within the firm is a series of contracts among the sub-units in the firm. As in the case of industry conventions, internal conventions are hyperstable during the contract period and tend to be relatively stable from one period to the next (e.g. in resource allocation). As a result, they permit each unit to avoid uncertainty about other units in making decisions.

Problemistic search

In the framework proposed [. . .], the theory of choice and the theory of search are closely intertwined. Necessarily, if we argue that organizations use acceptable-level goals and select the first alternative they see that meets those goals, we must provide a theory of organizational search to supplement the concepts of decision-making. In our models we assume that search, like decision-making, is problem-directed. By *problemistic search* we mean search that is stimulated by a problem (usually a rather specific one) and is directed toward finding a solution to that problem. In a general way, problemistic search can be distinguished from both random curiosity and the search for understanding. It is distinguished from the former because it has a goal, from the latter because it is interested in understanding only insofar as such understanding contributes to control. Problemistic search is engineering rather than pure science.

With respect to organizational search, we assume three things:

1 *Search is motivated.* Whether the motivation exists on the buyer or seller side of the alternative market, problemistic search is stimulated by a problem, depressed by a problem solution.

2 *Search is simple-minded.* It proceeds on the basis of a simple model of causality until driven to a more complex one.

3 *Search is biased.* The way in which the environment is viewed and the communications about the environment that are processed through the organization reflect variations in training, experience, and goals of the participants in the organization.

MOTIVATED SEARCH Search within the firm is problem-oriented. A problem is recognized when the organization either fails to satisfy one or more of its goals or when such a failure can be anticipated in the immediate future. So long as the problem is not solved, search will continue. The problem is solved either by discovering an alternative that satisfies the goals or by revising the goals to levels that make an available alternative acceptable. Solutions are also motivated to search for problems. Pet projects (e.g. cost savings in someone else's department, expansion in our own department) look for crises (e.g. failure to achieve the profit goal, innovation by a competitor). In the theory we assume that variations in search activity (and search productivity) reflect primarily the extent to which motivation for search exists. Thus, we assume that regular, planned search is relatively unimportant in inducing changes in existing solutions that are viewed as adequate.

SIMPLE-MINDED SEARCH We assume that rules for search are simple-minded in the sense that they reflect simple concepts of causality. Subject to learning (see below), search is based initially on two simple rules: search in the neighborhood of the problem symptom and search in the neighborhood of the current alternative.

These two rules reflect different dimensions of the basic causal notions that a cause will be found 'near' its effect and that a new solution will be found 'near' an old one.

The neighborhood of symptom rule can be related to the sub-units of the organization and their association with particular goals and with each other. A problem symptom will normally be failure on some goal indicator. Initial reaction, we assume, will be in the department identified with the goal. Thus, if the problem is the failure to attain the sales goal, the search begins in the sales department and with the sales program. Failing there, it might reasonably proceed to the problem of price and product quality and then to production costs.

The neighborhood of existing policy rule inhibits the movement of the organization to radically new alternatives (except under circumstances of considerable search pressure). Such an inhibition may be explained either in terms of some underlying organizational assumptions of continuity in performance functions or in terms of the problems of conceiving the adjustments required by radical shifts.

When search, using the simple causal rules, is not immediately successful, we assume two developments. First, the organization uses increasingly complex ('distant') search; secondly, the organization introduces a third search rule: search in organizationally vulnerable areas.

The motivation to search in vulnerable areas stems from two things. On the one hand, the existence of organizational slack will tend to lead search activity in the direction of slack parts of the organization. On the other hand, certain activities in the organization are more easily attacked than others, simply because of their power position in the system. One general phenomenon is the vulnerability of those activities in the organization for which the connection with major goals is difficult to calculate concretely (e.g. research in many firms). In either case, a solution consists in either absorbing slack or renegotiating the basic coalition agreement to the disadvantage of the weaker members of the coalition.

BIAS IN SEARCH We assume three different kinds of search bias: bias reflecting special training or experience of various parts of the organization; bias reflecting the interaction of hopes and expectations; and communication biases reflecting unresolved conflict within the organization. Bias from prior experience or training is implicit in our assumptions of search learning (below), local specialization in problem solving (above), and sub-unit goal differentiation (above). Those parts of the organization responsible for the search activities will not necessarily see in the environment what those parts of the organization using the information would see if they executed the search themselves. The bias in adjusting expectations to hopes has the consequence of decreasing the amount of problem-solving time required to solve a problem and of stimulating the growth of organizational slack during good times and eliminating it during bad. We assume that communication bias can be substantially ignored in our models except under conditions where the internal biases in the firm are all (or substantially all) in the same direction or where biases in one direction are located in parts of the organization with an extremely favorable balance of power.

Organizational learning

Organizations learn: to assume that organizations go through the same processes of learning as do individual human beings seems unnecessarily naive, but organizations exhibit (as do other social institutions) adaptive behavior over time. Just as adaptations at the individual level depend upon phenomena of the human physiology, organizational adaptation uses individual members of the organization as instruments. However, we believe it is possible to deal with adaptation at the aggregate level of the organization, in the same sense and for the same reasons that it is possible to deal with the concept of organizational decision-making.

We focus on adaptation with respect to three different phases of the decision process: adaptation of goals, adaptation in attention rules, and adaptation in search rules. We assume that organizations change their goals, shift their attention, and revise their procedures for search as a function of their experience.

ADAPTATION OF GOALS The goals which we deal with are in the form of aspiration levels, or – in the more general case – search equivalence classes. In simple terms, this means that on each dimension of organizational goals there are a number of critical values – critical, that is, from the point of view of shifts in search strategy. These values change over time in reaction to experience, either actual or vicarious.

We assume, therefore, that organizational goals in a particular time period are a function of

1 organizational goals of the previous time period

2 organizational experience with respect to that goal in the previous period

3 experience of comparable organizations with respect to the goal dimension in the previous time period. [. . .]

ADAPTATION IN ATTENTION RULE Just as organizations learn what to strive for in their environment, they also learn to attend to some parts of that environment and not to others. One part of such adaptation is in learning search behavior, which we will consider in a moment. Here we wish to note two related, but different, adaptations. First, in evaluating performance by explicit measurable criteria, organizations learn to attend to some criteria and ignore others. For example, suppose an organization sub-unit has responsibility for a specific organizational goal. Since this goal is ordinarily stated in relatively non-operational terms, the sub-unit must develop some observable indices of performance on the goal. Among the indices objectively available to the sub-unit, which will be used? Observation suggests this is a typical case of learning. Sub-units in the short run do not change indices significantly. However, there are long-run shifts toward indices that produce generally satisfactory results (i.e. in this case, usually show the sub-unit to be performing well).

Secondly, organizations learn to pay attention to some parts of their comparative environment and to ignore other parts. We have assumed that one of the parameters in the goal adaptation function is a parameter reflecting the sensitivity of the organization to external comparisons. This parameter is not fixed. We would expect it to change over time as such comparisons do or do not produce results (in the form of goals) that are satisfactory to the important groups in the coalition. [. . .] With which attributes of which organizations should we compare ourselves? Although in a relatively short-run model we might reasonably consider this fixed, we would expect that in the long-run we would require a model in which such attention factors changed.

ADAPTATION IN SEARCH RULES If we assume that search is problem-oriented, we must also assume that search rules change. Most simply, what we require in the models are considerations of the following type: when an organization discovers a solution to a problem by searching in a particular way, it will be more likely to search in that way in future problems of the same type; when an organization fails to find a solution by searching in a particular way, it will be less likely to search in that way in future problems of the same type. Thus, the order in which various alternative solutions to a problem are considered will change as the organization experiences success or failure with alternatives.

In a similar fashion, the code (or language) for communicating information about alternatives and their consequences adapts to experience. Any decision-making system develops codes for communicating information about the environment. Such a code partitions all possible states of the world into a relatively small number of classes of states. Learning consists in changes in the partitioning. In general, we assume the gradual development of an efficient code in terms of the decision rules currently in use. Thus, if a decision rule is designed to choose between two alternatives, the information code will tend to reduce all possible states of the world to two classes. If the decision rules change, we assume a change in the information code, but only after a time lag reflecting the rate of learning. The short-run consequences of incompatibilities between the coding rules and the decision rules form some of the more interesting long-run dynamic features of an organizational decision-making model.

The basic structure of the organizational decision-making process

We have described four basic concepts that seem to us fundamental to an understanding of the decision-making process in a modern, large-scale business organization. The quasi resolution of conflict, uncertainty avoidance, problemistic search, and organizational learning are central phenomena with which our models must deal. In our judgement, the natural theoretical language for describing a process involving these phenomena is the language of a computer program. It is clear that some parts of the theory are susceptible to representation and solution in other forms, but the general structure of the process can be conveniently represented as a flow chart. Such a flow chart is outlined in its most general form in Figure 3.1. [. . .]

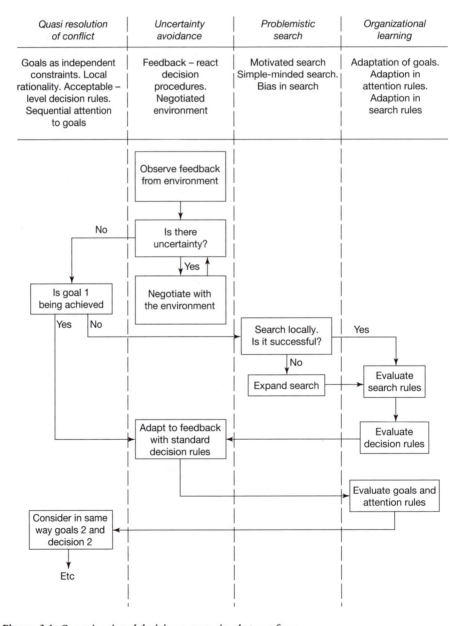

Figure 3.1 *Organizational decision process in abstract form*

Figure 3.1 is intended to illustrate two things. On the one hand, it shows abstractly the step-by-step decision process. For convenience, we have started the process at the point of receiving feedback from past decisions. Since the decision process is continuous, this start is arbitrary. Starting from the feedback, the figure shows the sequence of steps taken by a particular sub-unit in the firm with respect to a specific decision and a specific goal. Other decisions by other sub-units using other goals would occur in parallel with this one. Loose connections among the sub-units and decisions are secured by the environmental feedback and (when indicated) by expanded search.

At the same time, the figure shows (by the vertical columns) the relation between the basic concepts of the theory and the decision process flow chart. At a general level, each of the concepts is represented in a decision process having this structure. Obviously, when a specific decision in a specific content [. . .] is considered, this abstract description of the process must be substantially elaborated with specific content.

Clearly, models based on these concepts will deviate significantly from models based on the approach of classical economics. Such differences are not surprising. We have emphasized the fact that the behavioral theory of the firm is designed to answer a set of questions different from those to which traditional theory of the firm is directed. We think that these concepts will prove useful in dealing with organizational decision-making as it is reflected in business firms. The demonstration of the utility of the concepts, however, depends on defining specific models, based on the concepts, that yield definite, testable predictions.

Decision-making in Organizations

SUSAN J. MILLER, DAVID J. HICKSON AND
DAVID C. WILSON*

The area of organizational decision-making is part of the broader field of organization studies and organization theory. It has therefore followed a similar pattern of evolution, drawing on a variety of paradigms and perspectives and being characterized by a multiplicity of theories, models and methodologies.

This chapter charts its development as a subject of study. The chapter attempts to show how competing views and alternative theoretical frameworks of the way in which decisions are made have shaped both the methods of enquiry and subsequent explanations. The central concepts of rationality and power in decision-making are discussed. Further, the understanding of decision-making as an organizational *process* is explored in detail, as is the relatively neglected area of implementation. Decision-making overlaps other areas, notably strategic management, so the ways in which strategic decisions and strategies may be related are addressed.

Finally, the chapter recognizes that most work on decision-making implicitly assumes culturally bounded Western views of the world and its management processes.

Why decision-making?

Why should decision-making be studied at all? Although its popularity has waxed and waned over time it has continually stayed on the stage of organizational debate, though not always in the spotlight. Why should this be so?

* Sage Publications Ltd. for Miller, S., Hickson, D. and Wilson, D. 'Decision-making in organisations', in S. Clegg et al. (eds), *Handbook of Organisation Studies*. Copyright © Susan J. Millar, David J. Hickson and David C. Wilson 1996.

There are a number of reasons. Certainly the increasing complexity of 'modern organizations' which needed both differentiation and integration (Lawrence and Lorsch, 1967) meant that key decisions about the organization of central operational and transformational processes were required. The overarching paradigm of structural functionalism (which continues to be a dominant perspective) viewed management as being fundamentally concerned with rational decision-making in order to facilitate the smooth running and goal attainment of the modern, complex, structurally and functionally differentiated organization. Rational-legal authority (Weber, 1947) appeared to both empower and compel managers to take rational decisions. This emphasis upon unemotional, impersonal. objective logic has persuasively shaped managerial beliefs and action, and will be discussed further in this chapter.

If the dynamics of organizing created a need for decision-making, studies of managerial work confirmed that this was indeed how managers spent a large proportion of their time. Mintzberg's (1973) early work and Stewart's (1967; 1976; 1983) ongoing studies have both placed decision-making high on the managerial agenda, while Simon (1945) has suggested that 'managing' and 'decision-making' are practically synonymous.

A further reason concerns the intrinsic nature of the decision-making process itself. Decisions can be viewed as being fundamentally concerned with the allocation and exercise of power in organizations. The making of decisions, especially the larger, consequential ones which govern what things are done and shape the future direction of the organization and the lives of people within it, are of vital significance to organizational stakeholders. The issues of who is involved in the making of decisions; who is left out or kept out; who is in a position to exercise influence; who is able to introduce items on to the decision-making agenda or keep them off; are all central to an understanding of the politics of organizational behaviour. The study of decision-making is crucial to the comprehension of how and why organizations come to be what they are and to control whom they do.

To summarize, there are a number of reasons why this topic is of interest to both practitioners and theorists. Modern organizations need decisions to be made in order that they can function effectively; managers spend much of their time in making decisions at both the operational and the strategic level; and decision-making can be seen to focus political activity in organizations and so provide a window on to a less observable but nonetheless influential 'underworld'. There is clearly a contrast here between seeing decision-making as a functional prerequisite of effective organization and seeing it as a maelstrom of political activity and sectional conflict, where power games are played out in an arena which is only partially open to view, and this accounts in part for the differences in approaches to research and discussion.

The variety of contrasting assumptions and preconceptions is compounded because the subject crosses several academic disciplines. Choice behaviour under optimum and sub-optimum conditions is examined using rational choice models from economics and modelling techniques from mathematics and statistics;

the behavioural aspects of making decisions in organizations are discussed by organization theorists, sociologists and social psychologists; while psychologists concentrate on individual cognitive behaviour. This chapter will not and could not address all these perspectives. What it will do is focus on the way in which decisions are made and implemented in an organizational setting. It will therefore draw mainly on material from organization theory which takes the organization with its members as the subject of analysis. Drawing the boundary in this way does not mean that what is inside it is a discrete area of understanding; the influence of the other disciplines mentioned above still permeates the discourse.

The next section will begin our scrutiny in earnest, by looking at the beginnings of decision theory. The approach first taken, with its central notion of rational behaviour, still retains a pivotal position in the field: an orthodox, normative model of decision-making within a paradigm which many other approaches still need to acknowledge before they attempt to dismantle its arguments.

Managerial rationality in decision-making

Neo-classical economic assumptions lie at the heart of rational choice models of decision-making. Predicated on the supposition that individuals normally act as maximizing entrepreneurs, decisions are thought to be arrived at by a step-by-step process which is both logical and linear. Essentially, the decision-makers identify the problem or issue about which a decision has to be made, collect and sort information about alternative potential solutions, compare each solution against predetermined criteria to assess degree of fit, arrange solutions in order of preference and make an optimizing choice. Often such models leave out, or assume, the implementation stage which in principle follows the formal decision itself. Throughout the thrust is to maximize rewards and minimize costs for those involved.

As Zey (1992: 9) has shown, this kind of logic, although by no means new, has increasingly dominated many areas of government and business over the last 20 years, especially in the United States and Western Europe. The implicit assumption is that if individuals behave in accordance with rationality then little or no interference is required by any superordinate bodies.

At the level of the organization, or firm, this view aggregates the behaviour of individuals and groups without compunction. Since individual managers make rational decisions, the decisions made by groups within organizations will be equally rational. At the macro level, a competitive economic environment is both efficient and equitable because of its inherent dynamic logic.

Such a view of organizations and decision-making represents a mainstay of functionalist thinking and has been elaborated by other writers, notably Williamson (1975) with his account of what he terms 'markets and hierarchies', hierarchies here meaning organizations. However, the limitations of the approach have long been recognized by theorists from inside and outside the neo-classical paradigm.

Simon (1945) was one of the earliest authors to provide a comprehensive critique of the limitations of 'rational economic man' or the 'rational actor' model. Simon asserted that, constrained as they were by the complexity of modern organizations and by their own limited cognitive capacities, decision-makers were unable to operate under conditions of perfect rationality. The issue for decision is likely to be unclear or open to varying interpretation; information about alternatives may be unavailable, incomplete or misrepresented; and criteria by which potential solutions are to be evaluated are often uncertain or not agreed. In addition, the time and energy available to decision-makers to pursue a maximizing outcome is both limited and finite. Searching for better choices can simply take too long. The net result of these constraints is that the outcome is likely to be a 'satisficing' rather than an optimizing choice: one which both satisfies and suffices in the circumstances, for the time being. The absolutely rational model is beyond reach. Decision-making does not work that way.

Simon accepts that managers have to operate within a 'bounded rationality'. They intend to be rational, and indeed their behaviour is *reasoned* – it is not *irrational*, which is an important distinction – but it is unrealistic to expect them to meet the stringent requirements of wholly rational behaviour. Human frailties and demands from both within and outside the organization limit the degree of rationality which can be employed.

Even so, Simon makes the important observation that different types of decisions can be processed in different ways. Some decision processes may approximate to rational prescriptions, others may not. Decisions which occur more frequently, which are familiar, almost routine, may be made in a relatively straight-forward fashion. These decisions are comprehensible to managers and usually there exist tried and tested protocols, formulae or procedures for making them. They are 'programmed' (Simon, 1960), in the sense that they can be made by reference to existing rubrics. Programmed decisions are often made lower down in the organizational hierarchy; they are the operational decisions which can be safely left to subordinates. It is likely that they can be made in a way which closely parallels the prescripts of rational choice models. In fact there may be little in the way of formal deciding to be done.

In contrast, 'non-programmed' decisions are those which are unfamiliar: they have not been encountered in quite the same way before, they are to some extent novel, unusual. They therefore present a challenge to managers, for there are no obvious well-trodden paths to follow. To make matters even more challenging, these decisions are usually about the more significant areas of organizational activities. They will have consequential repercussions and will set precedents for other decisions which follow. Since decisions are intended to shape actions for the future and since the future is inherently uncertain, the potential consequences of non-programmed, or *strategic* decisions have worrying implications for managers. Because of their consequentiality, these decisions are usually sanctioned or authorized by the most senior executives in the elite. Since there is less likely to be an existing template to shape the process by which they are made, what happens may differ considerably from what might be fully rational. The topic for decision may be complex, making definition problematic; information may be needed which is difficult both to collect and to categorize; potential solutions may be hard to recognize and may in turn create new problems. It is not easy to follow a step-by-step, smoothly escalating, sequential process under such conditions. 'Problemistic search' may occur, where activity is spurred by the immediate problem, rather than being an orderly collection of information prompted by foresight (Cyert and March, 1963).

This continuum of decisions along a programmed/non-programmed dimension represents an early but significant step in distinguishing the characteristics of decisions and associating them with types of process. It is a field of enquiry that has been explored in greater detail since Simon, and we will return to this later in the chapter.

The issue of rationality in decision-making is therefore a vexed one. Decisions in organizations are subject to constraints endemic to the context in which they are made. The lone decision-maker making choices about his or her own interests might be thought to act rationally (although psychologists may argue the evidence here) but the complexities of managerial decision-making in concert with others have been well documented (for example, see Asch, 1955; Janis, 1972).

So rational choice models have been the target of sustained criticism for over four decades. Although there are those who continue to call for attempts at synthesis and reconciliation of contradictions (Schoemaker, 1993), it has been suggested (Eisenhardt and Zbaracki, 1992) that it is time for theorists concerned with organizational behaviour to drop such models in favour of a more realistic approach to decision-making, particularly one which recognizes how it is imbued with power.

Decision-making as the enactment of power

In Simon's definition of the term, 'bounded rationality' is the result of human and organizational constraints. It can be argued that this view underplays the role of power and political behaviour in setting those constraints. Many writers have pointed out that decision-making may be seen more accurately as a game of power in which competing interest groups vie with each other for the control of scarce resources.

Power is an ever-present feature of organizational life. Legitimate power is allocated to positions of authority in the hierarchy. This 'rational-legal' power (Weber, 1947) is given according to status and regularizes access to the decision-making process. Those with the requisite authority can participate in what occurs. Some can both discuss decisions and authorize them. The contribution of others is relegated to just the providing or cataloguing of data, or the recording of outcomes. Still others do not take part at all, and in the majority of organizations they are the great majority.

However the use of power legitimately is not the only way in which influence is exercised. Power-holders may choose to behave in ways which further their own, or others', interests. They may frame the matter for decision in a way which suits their own ends or blocks the objectives of others. They push for preferred alternatives, whether or not these will lead to decisions which are of organizational benefit. They manipulate information, withhold it, ignore some or all of it. They negotiate for support and suppress opposition. This applies not only to those who are directly engaged in the process, but also to those who, although only indirectly involved, still have the power to influence the process in some way – such as by having access to those who are closely involved, or by providing information for the process. Since all interest groups may be engaging in similar behaviour the process may be characterized by various forms of bargaining, negotiation and compromise that may lead to outcomes which are less than optimum for all parties. So although it might seem rational for each to pursue their own sectional interests in this way, from the perspective of neo-classical theory this can lead to outcomes which for the whole are less than rational. Thus the *means* by which decisions are made may be separably rational while the *ends* may not be. [. . .]

One way of explaining this kind of power play is to see it as the inevitable outcome of the way we organize. The intrinsic nature of organizations as entities which are driven by the imperatives of division of authority and division of labour leads inexorably to fragmentation. Differentiation, which is required to maintain efficiency and cope with turbulent, unpredictable environments, also creates sectional interests, each with their own needs and priorities. A functionalist paradigm has difficulty with the notion of goal dissensus, but the reality of organizations appears to be that once organizational groups are given different tasks they a begin to formulate their own sets of norms and goals. They either reinterpret objectives or construct personal goals which serve their own interests.

This notion of differentiation is at the heart of the resource dependence perspective (Pfeffer and Salancik, 1978). This explores how some parts of the organization gain power as a result of their ability to control access to resources. In this view, an organization, being an 'open system' which interacts with its environment in order to survive, is crucially dependent on obtaining resources from suppliers. Power accrues to those parts of the organization that can control the flow of resources, especially if these are scarce and critical for organizational functioning. [. . .]

This power is conditional upon it being sufficiently central and non-substitutable for the others to be dependent upon it. So, for example, a market department which can iron out fluctuations in demand by shrewd pricing and advertising gains influence. It is this *coping with uncertainty* which confers power. Since organizations are beset by uncertainty arising from suppliers, customer competitors, outside agencies, government and so on, as well as from internal difficulties, the ability to manage uncertainty on behalf of others provides a vital power base.

Hence organizations can be seen as *ensembles des jeux* (Crozier and Friedberg, 1980) where individuals and groups jockey for position in a hierarchy which is mediated by ongoing negotiation and bargaining. There are shifting, multiple coalitions of interests and thus only 'quasi-resolution of conflict' as interests seek to impose their own 'local rationalities' on any given decision (Cyert and March, 1963). The existing structural framework undergoes subtle (or even radical) change as a result of the day-to-day interactions of organizational members. It functions as a 'negotiated order' (Strauss et al., 1982). Particular decisions will enfold particular subsections, drawn into the game by the nature of what is being decided. The topics on hand will attract those who have something to protect: they will want to be involved because they are affected by what is being decided or they see a chance to influence matters in their favour. The matter for decision therefore shapes the interests which become involved and the way the game is played. In this way power positions are formed and transformed depending on what is on the agenda. [. . .]

Pluralist positions are predicated upon the notion of unequal but shifting power relations among elites, under the auspices of a largely neutral set of institutional arrangements. Here Schattsneider's statement begins to have resonance: 'All forms of political organisation have a bias in favour of some kinds of conflict and the suppression of others because organisation is the mobilisation of bias. Some issues are organised into politics while others are organised out' (1960: 71). This suggests that something else is happening 'behind the scenes' of even the pluralists' complex scenario – that the action is not all that it might seem at first glance. This in turn implies that to gain an even deeper understanding of power in organizations we need to look beyond what is readily observable. So attending solely to manifest conflict reveals only the most easily discernible 'face' of power. Ideally, what is going on beneath the surface also needs to be fully understood: the less explicit, more covert, subtle and insidious exercise of power which is used to suppress conflict in the first place. Conflict can be kept quiet; it is not allowed to surface into open debate and so does not become an item for discussion. This means that some decisions do not get onto the agenda. This is the 'second face' of power which Bachrach and Baratz (1962) argue has such import for organizational decision-making. This is the sphere of 'non-decisions'.

What then are non-decisions and do they have a place in the study of decision-making? Bachrach and Baratz maintain that non-decisions are equally if not more important than the decisions which are overtly made. Non-decisions are the covert issues about which a decision has effectively been taken that they will not be decided. They are the controversial topics which go against the interests of powerful stakeholders: they do not engender support, they do not fit with the prevailing culture, they are not considered acceptable for discussion, so they are quietly side-stepped or suppressed or dropped. A knowledge of what these issues are is likely to be as revealing, or more so, as knowledge of what is overtly being discussed. They are what is really going on, not just on the surface but underneath it. The decisions which are being discussed in the board room, in meetings, by executives and management represent the tip of the iceberg, according to this view. [. . .]

Decision-making is far removed from the coolly logical appraisal and selection of alternatives. Rather it is at the centre of political machinations and intrigue, the true nature of which is not always fully recognized, even by those involved.

So although some may see conflict as an endemic, but controllable, part of organizational life, created by the dysfunctions of a functional drive for efficiency, others explain conflict as arising from inherently inequitable power relationships in wider society. In the former view, the context for decision-making is the ongoing power play between interest groups, in which situations of disharmony are an expected but usually reconcilable by-product of organizational structure. In the latter view, decisions are shaped in ways which are not always obvious, by unseen influential power-holders playing within a larger arena. [. . .]

Processes, prescriptions and explanations

Empirical studies of decision-making have added weight to the criticisms of rational choice models as being idealized prescriptions, depicting an unreality.

Lindblom's early work in the American public sector (Lindblom, 1959; Braybrooke and Lindblom, 1963) quickly dispelled the myth that decision-making, in public institutions at least, was a linear, sequential process. Decisions here were made in a halting 'incremental' way with periods of recycling, iteration and reformulation. The process was a non-linear one.

So instead of final choices being arrived at after the full rational process of search and evaluation is completed, small adjustments are made to ongoing strategies. The full range of alternative solutions is not considered, only ones which do not differ markedly from the status quo. Decisions proceed by a series of small steps, rather than attaining and implementing the complete solution in one large step. For Lindblom the advantages of this approach are clear. Because each step, in itself, is not too dissimilar from what is already being done, it does not upset too many stakeholders. They do not feel threatened by radical change so it is possible to gain commitment for what is being done. The repercussions from changes which, initially at least, are relatively minor, are likely to be less serious and more predictable. Most importantly, the decision has more chance of being 'undone' if necessary; it is more reversible. Once each small step has been taken it gives a clearer picture of what has to be done and the future becomes more focused. If the chosen path now seems unlikely to lead to the desired destination, or if changing circumstances make the destination less appropriate, the step can be retraced with less difficulty than a larger one.

Lindblom argues that this is not only a description of what is done in organizations but also what ought to be done, given the inherent unpredictability of the context in which most decision-makers work. The incrementalist model is therefore in the interesting position of being both normative and descriptive as Smith and May (1982) have commented.

Some have suggested that incrementalism, or 'muddling through' as Lindblom has referred to it, is less a recipe for change, more likely a formula for inertia. It has been argued that small decisions which are only marginally different from the status quo are fine – if the current position is acceptable. But if change needs to be immediate and substantial, for example if the organization is in crisis, then incrementalism is not enough. Lindblom has countered that radical change can be equally swift whether it is effected by a series of small frequent steps or one large stride. In fact, smaller steps may be quicker since they may encounter less opposition. [. . .]

Quinn's (1978; 1980) development of the concept into 'logical incrementalism' comes from the very similar processes which can be found in private sector organizations. It appears that all kinds of decision-makers operate in an incremental fashion.

When Mintzberg and his colleagues (1976) studied 25 strategic decisions in a variety of Canadian organizations they found even clearer evidence of cycling and recycling of information and alternatives, again showing that the making of this level of decision is likely to require constant adjustment and reappraisal. Their study distinguished seven kinds of process: simple impasse, political design, basic search, modified search, basic design, blocked design, and dynamic design processes. Most of these experience delays and interruptions, and repeated reconsideration. Nutt's (1984) work analysed 73 decisions in health-related organizations in the USA and noticed some similar patterns occurring in search processes.

On the other hand [. . .], it is claimed that in periods of crisis decisions can be made in a relatively speedy and straightforward way (Dutton, 1986; Rosenthal, 1986). When organizations are in trouble and urgent action is required, those in authority can be given great freedom to act, even by subordinates whose jobs may be affected, particularly if they are perceived to have the necessary grasp of the situation and are likely be able to do something to help.

So whilst it has become a truism that decision-making by the elite takes place in a state of political excitation and is not at all straightforward, this is a view that can be taken too far. All decision-making need not be so. Not all decisions are made the same way. Why is this? Why are decision processes the way that they are? What factors influence process?

The Bradford Studies: Finding explanations for process

The Bradford Studies (Hickson et al., 1986; also Cray et al., 1988; 1991) set out to try and answer these questions. The Bradford team investigated the making of 150 decisions in 30 organizations in England (5 decisions in each), covering manufacturing and service industries in both public and private sectors. [. . .]

Three kinds of processes were found, labelled *sporadic*, *fluid* and *constricted*. The sample of cases divided almost evenly between each cluster, so about a third of all the decisions studied were made in sporadic ways, a third were made in a fluid manner, while a third followed a constricted path.

Sporadic processes are subject to more disrupting delays than either fluid or constricted processes. The information used will be uneven in quality, some good, some bad, and will come from a wide range of sources, and there will be scope for negotiation. This kind of process is 'informally spasmodic and protracted' (Hickson et al., 1986: 118). [. . .]

Fluid processes are almost the opposite of sporadic ones. There is much less informal interaction and the process flows more through formal meetings with fewer impediments and delays. These processes are rather faster and the decision is likely to be made in months, rather than years. In short, a fluid process is 'steadily paced, formally channelled and speedy' (Hickson et al., 1986: 120).

Lastly, constricted processes share some of the characteristics of each of the other two but have features distinctive from both. They are less fluid than the fluids and less sporadic than the sporadics, but constrained in a way that neither of the others is. They tend to revolve around a central figure such as a finance or production director who draws on a wide range of expertise in other departments before arriving at a decision. In short, they are 'narrowly channelled' (1986: 122).

Although public sector organizations and manufacturing firms each show some bias towards sporadic processes, each process is found in every type of organization. The type of organization is not the strongest determinant of process. So what is? The Bradford team found that the primary and 'dual' explanation is the degree of *politicality* and *complexity* inherent in the matter for decision itself.

In other words, it is the political and complex nature of what is being decided which is all-important. With regard to politicality, all decisions draw in a specific 'decision set' of interests: those who have a stake in the outcome. These are drawn from inside and outside the organization: individuals, departments, divisions, owners, suppliers, government agencies and so on. But not all interests are equally influential and not every decision draws in the same number or configuration of them. Some decisions attract less attention: they are less controversial, perhaps, or require work to be done by relatively fewer people. Others are a whirl of interested activity. So every decision is shaped to some degree by the influence of the decision set. Politicality refers to the degree of influence which is brought to bear on a decision and how this influence is distributed within and without the organization.

Complexity refers to the problems which making the decision encompasses. The reasons for complexity are varied. Some decisions are more unusual than others: they may require information to be garnered from more diverse sources, they may have more serious or widespread consequences, or set more fundamental precedents for the future. Since each decision process is made up of various problems – some of which are more complex that others – decisions will vary in terms of how comprehensible they are. Some will be relatively straightforward while others will be more problematic, depending on the nature of the issues involved.

Together, these concepts of politicality and complexity are the primary explanation of why strategic decisions follow the processes they do. [. . .]

There is another body of thought, to which this chapter now turns, that stands distinct from both rational models and politicized views. Both of these are attempts to elucidate causal relationships between events and outcomes. From this other more challenging perspective, both are misunderstandings of the world in general and organizations in particular.

Strategies and garbage-cans: chaos and disorganized order

The most imaginative, coherent and penetrating perspective is that of the evocatively named 'garbage-can' model (Cohen et al., 1972). This is a depiction of decision-making which turns much of what we have previously discussed on its head. Garbage-cans are found predominantly in 'organized anarchies', complex organizations whose internal processes are not really understood, even by people working in them. In these situations the means and ends of decisions become 'uncoupled' (Weick, 1976) so that actions do not lead to expected outcomes, but are hijacked along the way by other decisions and other actions. The main components of decisions – problems, solutions, participants and choice situations – pour into the organizational garbage-can in a seemingly haphazard way, a stream of demands for the fluid attention and energy of decision-makers. If problem, solution, participant and choice situation happen to collide appropriately, then a decision occurs. It may not be foreseen. It may not be one which actually solves the problem to which it has been attached. For not only are the means and ends of decisional processes disconnected, but solutions to problems are in existence before the problems themselves are recognized.

All the while participants move in and out of decision-making processes since 'every entrance is an exit somewhere else' (March and Olsen, 1976), which creates discontinuity. Perversely, actors jostle for the right to get involved and then appear uninterested either in exercising it, or in whether decisions are carried out. The conventionally accepted order of things is transformed put back to front, jumbled beyond recognition. The picture is one of seeming chaos, of disorder. And yet there are some patterns under the confusion and these can be modelled once the parameters are known. The process is not truly random and can be predicted to some extent, although it can feel like chaos to participants. Decisions do get made, although the process is about as far removed from rational choice prescriptions as it is possible to get. [. . .]

Mapping the terrain of decision process research

The range of work on decision-making covered in this chapter may be contrasted along two key dimensions. One is concerned with the nature of the decision process itself over time, the other with the involvement of various interests in the process. They may be termed the dimension of process *action* and the dimension of political *interest*. The principal researchers are 'mapped' on them in Figure 4.1 to present an

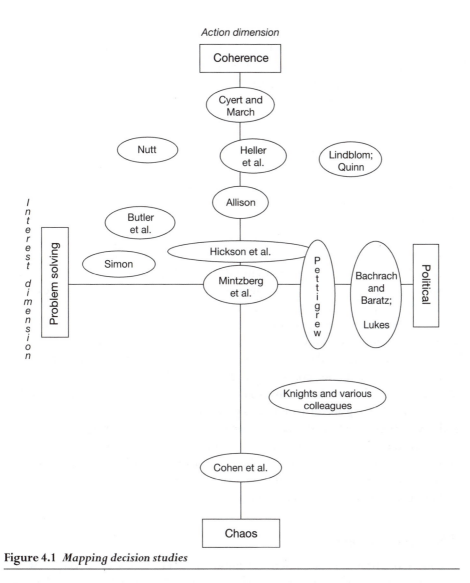

Figure 4.1 *Mapping decision studies*

overview of research and researchers. This is as we see it, of course, and others, especially the researchers and theorists themselves, may have differing views on where particular work should be positioned. Such a diagram is illustrative rather than precise.

The action dimension

On the action dimension, decision-making processes may be viewed as running from the more *coherent* to the more *chaotic*. Authors who take a predominantly coherent view of process subscribe to the notion that decision process trajectories can be relatively sequenced and linear, and reflect attempts by decision-makers to achieve step-by-step progress toward stated goals or objectives. Lindblom's (1959) incrementalism and Quinn's (1980) description of progressive change through step-by-step actions are examples of the coherent approach, as are Heller et al.'s (1988) linear phases. Coherence implies 'intended rationality' (Cyert and March, 1963). Individuals strive to achieve rational decision-making, but are prevented from achieving this through lack of perfect knowledge, through cognitive limits and so on. Nevertheless, the intention is coherence. Butler et al. (1993) show how coherence can be better achieved by attention to specific factors (inspiration, judgement and computation). Hickson et al. (1986) claim to have uncovered a spectrum of process characteristics, so logically they also tend toward the coherent view, since their characterizations presuppose some degree of detectable order in the process.

A diametrically opposite perspective on process is adopted by those who argue that coherence is a myth derived from rational economics. Neat and precise its descriptions may be, but they do not describe the reality of decision processes which are not necessarily linear, sequenced or intendedly rational. At the extreme of this chaotic view of decision process lie the garbage cans of Cohen et al. (1972). Here, solutions are generated prior to processes and are attached to problems in a seemingly random fashion. Cohen et al. (1972) stand alone to define the chaos end of the action dimension. Processes are part of the embeddedness of the organization and are not always under control (e.g. Knights and Morgan, 1991; Knights and Murray, 1992) Chaotic action can also be seen in less extreme form in Mintzberg et al.'s (1976) recycling and discontinuous processes. Here, decisions stop, start again, and revisit their point of origin. They are still processes occurring over time, yet they lack the apparent linear sequential characteristics of their more coherent counterparts. It is very visible that this lower half of Figure 4.1 is least filled (or most empty). The intellectual boldness and empirical ingenuity to follow where Cohen et al. (1972) led does not come easily.

The interest dimension

The more political interest dimension runs from a purely *problem-solving* view to a negotiated order view in which diverse interests give a *political* colour to decision-making.

The problem-solving view is perhaps best typified by Simon's (1960) description of decision-making as a 'new science. It is 'new', because Simon rejected the prevailing orthodoxy of his coeval economists, who believed economic models of individual choice behaviour could be applied directly to organizational decision processes. It is 'scientific', however, since Simon still held centrally the notion of problem-oriented behaviour from those involved. Goals were specified, targets were set and the overall problem was held in view, whilst decision participants sought solutions which were satisfactory and which were sufficient to address the problem. This 'satisficing' behaviour is firmly rooted in the problem-solving perspective. Radical though Simon's ideas may have been to economists at the time, his relative orthodoxy is revealed when reflected against the more political perspectives which gained momentum in the 1970s. At the other extreme are the analyses of Bachrach and Baratz (1962; 1970), who completely eschew problem-solving approaches. All activity is politically driven, they argue, to the extent that certain items are deliberately kept off decision agenda. Whoever defines the agenda or the problem holds the key to decision-making. Bachrach and Baratz are clear about emphasizing politics over problem-solving perspectives, yet reveal far less detail about the action dimension of the decision process. Presumably to them this could be either chaotic or coherent. To them the most important dimension is the extent to which decisions are either made in advance, or kept off the agenda altogether by powerful interests. Pettigrew (1973; 1985; 1987) is less extreme, taking problems as given and overt, but agreeing that the predominant focus is political, as gatekeepers screen information or as interests negotiate in the decision arena. This places Pettigrew's work firmly on the political end of the interest dimension, but there is a similar lack of attention in his work to the relative degrees of coherence and chaos in the process. Hence his location on Figure 4.1 spans only a small range on the action dimension.

Since the explanation of differences in process advanced by Hickson et al. (1986) includes both the nature of the problem and its politics, their work is shown as extending in both directions along the interest dimension.

All the authors in Figure 4.1 have focused on decision-making *per se*. They have started from the decision as the unit of analysis around which other factors might vary. Decisions may vary in content (what they are about) and in process (how the decision moves through the organization) and they may vary in importance (operational or strategic). The common feature, however, is that the concept of decision is the primary unit of analysis. Suppose that the decision itself cannot be taken for granted? Suppose that the very idea of 'a decision' is misleading?

The concept of 'a Decision'

The realism of much of the decision-making research has been called into question by those who feel that the very concept of decision has outlived its usefulness. According to writers such as Mintzberg and Waters (1990) it 'gets in the way' of understanding organizational processes. They argue that there are inherent problems with the concept, one of these being that while decisions imply a commitment to action there are situations where actions are taken without decisions having been made. They argue that to see organizational shifts in terms of the deliberate making of decisions over-concretizes the rather ambiguous, uncertain processes of change and underplays the continual redefinition, reshaping and reformulation which commitments to action constantly undergo. It is possible that the 'quasi-decisions' about foregone conclusions mentioned earlier (Hickson et al., 1986) are an empirical verification of this.

Mintzberg and Waters (1990) claim the notion of decision is particularly unhelpful when thinking about strategies which organizations pursue. This opens up a large area which has not yet received full attention. For although the literature on strategic decisions often discusses corporate strategy (and vice versa) the links between the two are implicit rather than defined. Do strategic decisions implement some overarching strategy, are they made within the context of pre-existing strategies, and what is the interactive effect of decisions and strategies? Are decisions more successful if they are part of a 'global' strategy, or do they exist separately, and does this matter?

Mintzberg and Water's (1982) earlier work on strategy formulation prompted their subsequent musings. In this earlier work they defined strategy as a 'pattern in a stream of decisions'. Yet further ruminations along the lines discussed above refined the description to a 'pattern in a stream of actions' (Mintzberg and Waters, 1985). Thus strategies may *emerge* rather than be deliberately decided in advance. Organizations may find themselves going in a particular strategic direction without anyone explicitly having decided that they should do so [. . .]. They maintain that the usefulness of the concept outweighs its limitations.

Subsuming the analysis of individual decisions into the patterns made by planned or emergent strategies is one example of the different levels of analysis in decision theory. Another in sharp contrast rests on the premise that decision-making is best studied by looking at interactions, interpretations of meaning and the significance of symbols, given by common-sense accounts by individuals of how and why they acted in certain ways. Such accounts produce a richness of data, largely consisting of definitions of the situation and interpretations by individuals (see Silverman, 1970; Clegg, 1973; Goffman, 1982). [. . .]

Although these perspectives draw heavily from earlier works concerned with existentialisn (e.g. Sudnow, 1965), concerns with postmodernity have also prompted decision theory to re-examine its basic assumptions. As Jeffcutt (1994: 241) says, 'the understanding of organization is inseparable from the organization of understanding.' It remains to be seen whether decision theory will look like this in the future, or whether it could even exist, then, as a separate focus of research since decision is a false construct itself through postmodern eyes.

At a macro level, organizations can be seen to be imitative whereby their managements follow leads taken by other organizations in the sector and sometimes outside it (see Grinyer and Spender, 1979; Hinings and Greenwood, 1988; Fombrun and Shanley, 1990). This follow-my-leader approach has some appeal, since competing firms within the same business sector will be likely to adapt and react to each other's strategies and may be seen to be following one another. [. . .] Cyert and March's (1963) characterizations of 'satisficing' or 'sequential attention to goals' could be interpreted as cautious corporate action taken with an eye on the competition in the sector (rather than as managerial limitations). [. . .]

Keat and Abercrombie (1990) go further and imply that the study of individual decisions in an organization is inappropriate since they fit into a pattern determined largely by socio-political factors. They cite the emergence of the 'enterprise culture' in Britain (1979 onwards) whereby particular strategic decisions in firms are framed by interventionist government policies such as privatization (for public sector organizations), reduction of dependencies (on suppliers and government agencies) and an increased emphasis on the customer as a major influence in product and service decisions. They argue that although individual strategic decisions may vary in topic content they will fit into this overall pattern if a wide enough frame of reference is adopted.

Yet even at this level of analysis, Child (1972) argues that managers do have a choice. They are not, he argues, deterministically led by the actions of other organizations. [. . .]

Voluntarist–determinist debates are provoked here. Do managers have the content and process of decision imposed upon them, or do they exercise a degree of strategic choice?

One final challenge to the contentious but stimulating area of research that this chapter has described arises from the differences in socio-economic context around the world. Yet the knowledge base from which virtually all decision theory emanates is socio-culturally North American or western European. [. . .]

The trite conclusion to this chapter therefore can only be that more research is needed. Trite it may be, but specifically it means more research beyond the confines of the (Northern) Western world. Of course, work should continue within that world on patterns of process, their conclusions, implementations, and consequences, and hopefully researchers doing this will become more cognizant than hitherto of the cultures they are working within. But research on decision-making at the managerial apex should extend to organizations in other societies. In this it is lagging behind the rest of organization theory. More has been done in more societies on the use of authority, on bureaucratization, on commitment and loyalties, on the use of time, and so on. Perhaps this is because of the empirical obstacles. Even Western managers accustomed to talking impersonally to all comers in comparatively open societies are cautious enough when asked to reveal to strangers something as sensitive as how a major decision is arrived at. Many managers elsewhere in the world would see no reason for doing anything so peculiar. Researchers in this difficult area will have to find means to break its culture bounds, nonetheless. Unless they can, Western models of decision-making will remain bounded by Western thinking and by Western con- stituted organizations. Although these organizations do make up a large proportion of the world's most developed economies, they are managed by and employ only a small proportion of humankind. Those who research their decision-making have come from an even smaller minority of human societies. Conceptual progress needs the stimulus of both non-Western data and non-Western researchers.

References

Asch, S.E. (1955) 'Studies in independence and conformity: a minority of one against unanimous majority', *Psychological Monographs*, 20 (whole no. 416).

Bachrach, P. and Baratz, M.S. (1962) 'The two faces of power', *American Political Science Review*, 56: 947–52.

Bachrach, P. and Baratz, M.S. (1970) *Power and Poverty: Theory and Practice*. London: Oxford University Press.

Braybrooke, D. and Lindblom, C. E. (1963) *A Strategy of Decision*. New York: Free Press.

Butler, R.J., Davies, L., Pike, R. and Sharp, J. (1993) *Strategic Investment Decisions*. London: Routledge.

Child, J. (1972) 'Organizational structure, environment and performance: the role of strategic choice', *Sociology*, 6: 1–22.

Clegg, S. (1975) *Power, Rule and Domination*. London: Routledge and Kegan Paul.

Cohen, M.D., March, J.G. and Olsen, J.P. (1972) 'The garbage can model of organizational choice', *Administrative Science Quarterly*, 17 (March): 1–25.

Cray, David, Mallory, Geoffrey R., Butler, Richard J., Hickson, David J. and Wilson, David C. (1988) 'Sporadic, fluid and constricted processes: three types of strategic decision-making in organizations', *Journal of Management Studies*, 25(1): 13–39.

Cray, David, Mallory, Geoffrey R., Butler, Richard J., Hickson, David J. and Wilson, David C. (1991) 'Explaining decision processes', *Journal of Management Studies*, 28(3): 227–51.

Crozier, Michel and Friedberg, Erhard (1980) *Actors and Systems*. Chicago: University of Chicago Press (published in French in 1977 by Editions du Seuil).

Cyert, R. and March, J.G. (1963) *A Behavioural Theory of the Firm*. Englewood Cliffs, NJ: Prentice-Hall.

Dutton, Jane E. (1986) 'The processing of crisis and non-crisis strategic issues', *Journal of Management Studies*, 23(5): 501–17.

Eisenhardt, K. and Zbaracki, M.J. (1992) 'Strategic decision making', *Strategic Management Journal*, 13: 17–37.

Fombrun, C. and Shanley, M. (1990) 'What's in a name? Reputation building and corporate strategy', *Academy of Management Journal*, 33(2): 233–58.

Goffman, E. (1982) *The Presentation of Self in Everyday Life*. Harmondsworth: Penguin.

Grinyer, P.H. and Spender, J.C. (1979) 'Recipes, crises and adaptation in mature businesses', *International Studies of Management and Organization*, IX(3): 113–33.

Heller, F., Drenth, P. Koopman, P. and Rus, V. (1988) *Decisions in Organizations – a Three Country Comparative Study*, London: Sage.

Hickson, D.J., Butler, R.J., Cray, D., Mallory, G.R. and Wilson, D.C. (1986) *Top Decisions: Strategic Decision-Making in Organizations*. Oxford: Basil Blackwell. San Francisco: Jossey-Bass.

Hinings, C.R. and Greenwood, R. (1988) 'The normative prescriptions of organizations', in L.G. Zucker (ed.), *Institutional Patterns and Organizations: Culture and Environment*. Cambridge, MA: Ballinger.

Janis, I.L. (1972) *Victims of Groupthink: a Psychological Study of Foreign Policy Decisions and Fiascos*. Boston: Houghton Mifflin.

Jeffcutt, P. (1994) 'From interpretation to representation in organizational analysis: postmodernism, ethnography and symbolism', *Organization Studies*, 15(2): 241–74.

Keat, R. and Abercrombie, N. (eds) (1990) *Enterprise Culture*. London: Routledge.

Knights, D. and Morgan, G. (1991) 'Corporate strategy, organizations and subjectivity', *Organization Studies*, 12(2): 251–73.

Knights, D. and Murray, F. (1992) 'Politics and pain in managing information technology: a case study from insurance', *Organization Studies*, 13(2): 211–28.

Lawrence, P.R. and Lorsch, J.W. (1967) *Organization and Environment*. Cambridge, MA: Harvard Graduate School of Business Administration.

Lindblom, C.E. (1959) 'The science of "muddling through"', *Public Administrative Review*, 19(2): 79–88.

March, J.G. and Olsen, J.P. (1976) *Ambiguity and Choice in Organizations*. Bergen, Oslo, and Tromsø: Universitetsforlaget.

Mintzberg, H. (1973) *The Nature of Managerial Work*. New York: Harper & Row.

Mintzberg, H., Raisinghani, D. and Theoret, A. (1976) 'The structure of "unstructured" decision processes', *Administrative Science Quarterly*, 21: 246–75.

Mintzberg, H. and Waters, J.A. (1982) 'Tracking strategy in an entrepreneurial firm', *Academy of Management Journal*, 25(3): 465–99.

Mintzberg, H. and Waters, J.A. (1985) 'Of strategies, deliberate and emergent', *Strategic Management Journal*, 6: 257–72.

Mintzberg, H. and Waters, J.A. (1990) 'Studying deciding: an exchange of views between Mintzberg and Waters, Pettigrew, and Butler', *Organization Studies*, 11(1): 2–16.

Nutt, Paul C. (1984) 'Types of organizational decision processes', *Administrative Science Quarterly*, 29(3): 414–50.

Pettigrew, A.M. (1973) *The Politics of Organizational Decision-Making*. London: Tavistock.

Pettigrew, A.M. (1985) 'Examining change in the long term context of culture and politics', in J.M. Pennings (ed.), *Organizational Strategy and Change*. San Francisco: Jossey-Bass.

Pettigrew, A.M. (1987) 'Context and action in the transformation of the firm', *Journal of Management Studies*, 24(6): 649–99.

Pfeffer, J. and Salancik, G.R. (1978) *The External Control of Organizations: a Resource Dependence Perspective*. London: Harper & Row.

Quinn, James B. (1978) 'Strategic change: logical incrementalism', *Sloan Management Review*, Fall: 7–21.

Quinn, James B. (1980) *Strategies for Change: Logical Incrementalism*. Homewood, IL: Irwin.

Rosenthal, U. (1986) 'Crisis decision-making in the Netherlands', *The Netherlands Journal of Sociology*, 22(2): 103–29.

Schattsneider, E. (1960) *Semi-Sovereign People: a Realist's View of Democracy in America*. Austin, Texas: Holt, Rinehart and Winston. (Quoted in Anthony G. McGrew and M.J. Wilson (eds) (1982), *Decision-Making: Approaches and Analysis*. Manchester University Press.)

Schoemaker, Paul J.H. (1993) 'Strategic decisions in organizations: rational and behavioural views', *Journal of Management Studies*, 30(1): 107–29.

Silverman, David (1970) *The Theory of Organizations*. London: Heinemann.

Simon, Herbert A. (1945) *Administrative Behaviour*, 2nd edn. New York: Free Press.

Simon, Herbert A. (1960) *The New Science of Management Decision*. New York: Harper & Row.

Smith, G. and May, D. (1982) 'The artificial debate between rationalist and incrementalist models of decision-making', in Anthony G. McGrew and M.J. Wilson (eds), *Decision Making: Approaches and Analysis*. Manchester University Press.

Stewart, R. (1967) *Managers and their Jobs*. Maidenhead: McGraw-Hill.

Stewart, R. (1976) *The Reality of Management*. London: Pan.

Stewart, R. (1983) 'Managerial behaviour: how research has changed the traditional picture', in M. Earl (ed.), *Perspectives on Management: a Multidisciplinary Analysis*. Oxford: Oxford University Press. pp. 82–98.

Strauss, A., Schatzman, L., Ehrlich, D., Bucher, R. and Sabshin, M. (1982) 'The hospital and its negotiated order', in *People and Organisations*. Essex, UK: Longman.

Sudnow, D. (1965) 'Normal crimes: sociological features of the penal code in a public defender office'. *Social Problems*, 12(3): 255–76.

Weber, Max (1947) *The Theory of Social and Economic Organization*, translated by A. Henderson and T. Parsons. Glencoe, IL: Free Press.

Weick, Karl E. (1976) 'Educational organizations as loosely coupled systems', *Administrative Science Quarterly*, 21(1): 1–19.

Williamson, O.E. (1975) *Markets and Hierarchies*. New York: Free Press.

Zey, Mary (1992) *Decision Making: Alternatives to Rational Choice Models*. London: Sage.

Understanding Decision-making: Understanding Organizations

Herbert Simon, one of the forefathers of our concern with decision-making in organizations made the point which this section addresses. In a challenge to the rational approach to, and description of, organizations he argued that it:

> suffers currently from superficiality, oversimplification, lack of realism. It has confined itself too closely to the mechanism of authority, and has failed to bring within its orbit the other, equally important modes of influence on organizational behaviour. It has refused to undertake the tiresome task of studying the actual allocations of decision-making functions. It has been satisfied to speak of 'authority', 'centralisation', 'spans of control', 'function', without seeking operational definitions of these terms. (Simon, 1952: 53)

This 'tiresome task' is what this section is about: Its role is to develop an analysis and understanding of two key approaches to decision-making. The rational choice approach to decision-making assumes a rational form of organization. Critiques of, or alternatives to, this approach, if they attempt to do more than simply note the normal limitations of the model assert an alternative model of how decisions are made.

The approaches to the analysis of decision-making discussed in this section regard the sorts of decision-making that classical or rationalistic theorists would regard as aberrant and odd decision-making as normal within their approach to organizational functioning. They define the rational model of decision-making as heavily idealized – as prescribing what *should* take place rather than describing what *actually* takes place.

Theories of organizational decision-making described in this section offer two ways of understanding decision-making. The chapters by Cyert and March, and by Miller et al. in the previous section identify a number of types of explanation (or theory) of decision-making. They suggest that theories of decision-making are concerned with politics and processes. An example of politics is Cyert and March's comment that ' . . . an organization is a coalition of members having different goals . . . ' An example of process being important is these authors' concept of 'problemistic search' where activity is initiated by an immediate problem rather than by an orderly and systematic process of search and analysis. These approaches differ radically from views of decision-making which see organizations as deliberately constructed machines whose structures and systems operate rationally and efficiently to achieve clear and shared organizational goals. This view of organizations stresses the deliberate or purposeful aspect of organizations. But Section 2 of this book presents approaches to organization and decision-making which stress the processual, negotiated, emergent aspect of organizations. It sees them not as machines designed for, and achieving, their purposes, but as made up of different groups with different views, priorities, power, negotiating decisions and outcomes; it stresses how notions of rationality, or even of facts and information, are not simple or given, but vary. It shows that rules and procedures do not always achieve what their designers intended but are adapted by employees in their everyday life.

The co-existence of both political and process factors is illustrated in Chapter 8. When clarifying and distinguishing his approach the author says:

> The study reported here . . . is not concerned with *how adequately the formal programme of the organization and the structural arrangements whereby it is implemented provide for 'rational' goal accomplishment* . . . Nor is it directed to the specification of the conditions under which *personnel comply with or depart from their prescribed duties as set forth in the formal programme, or come to be more or less partisan to organizational objectives.* Its primary concern is to investigate the *variety of practices and mundane considerations involved in determinations of the operational meaning and situational relevance of policies and procedures for ongoing, everyday organizational activities.*
> (Zimmerman, this volume: italics added)

The first italicized passage describes the rational perspective; the second summarizes the political perspective, and the third the focus on processes of organizational understanding and cognition. These latter two approaches constitute the concern of this section.

The political perspective is clearly identified by Cyert and March and Miller et al. Chapter 5 by Andrew Pettigrew sets out a view of organizations – and decision-making – as a political arenas in which organizational units with differentiated or opposed interests, loyalties, and mindsets struggle for advantage, with obvious implications for the nature and outcome of decision-making. As Pettigrew notes in this reading, political behaviour follows the unequal distribution of organizational resources and the creation of specialized loyalties and perspectives through organizational differentiation. Pettigrew – and the perspective he describes in this reading – sees political activity as central to organizational structures and processes: divisions of interest follow from the hierarchical nature of power.

References

Simon, H.A. (1952) 'Some further requirements of bureaucratic theory', in R.K. Merton, A.P. Grey, B. Hockey and H.C. Selvin (eds), *Reader in Bureaucracy*. New York: Free Press, pp. 51–9.

Zimmerman, D. (1971) 'The practicalities of rule use', in J. Douglas (ed.), *Understanding Everyday Life*. London: Routledge and Kegan Paul. pp. 221–38.

Decision-making as a Political Process

ANDREW M. PETTIGREW*

The idea of analysing organizations as political systems is not yet a popular one. In 1962 Norton Long noted: 'People will readily admit that governments are organizations. The converse – that organizations are governments – is equally true but rarely considered (1962: 110). Long gives two main reasons for this neglect: first, a lack of concern with the 'political' structure of the organization and a consequent over-attention to the formal structure of power and legitimacy: secondly, a heavy reliance on a psychological orientation with a lack of emphasis on sociological analysis. Burns (1961) has also made a plea for the study of the 'political' in organizations. He raises the issue of the difficulty of studying such behaviour: 'The problem is no one regards himself as a politician, or as acting politically, except of course on occasions when he is led into accounts of successful intrigue and manoeuvering when he bolsters his self-esteem and reputation by projecting the whole affair into the safe social context of a game or joke' (1961: 260). There is, in addition, the problem that those who are politically involved usually claim that they are acting in the interests of the company as a whole. This is how they legitimate their behaviour.

Nevertheless, a few empirical studies of political behaviour in organizations have appeared. Dimock (1952) provides a rather extreme example. He sees the executive as a tactician and philosopher who 'must live by his wits, his competitive instincts, his understanding of social forces, and his ability as a leader' (1952: 290). The bureaux that Dimock talks of are engaged in conflict as a result of overlapping jurisdictions, competing loyalties, and incompatible objectives. Strauss (1962) in a study of lateral organizational relationships deals with what he calls 'office politics' and 'bureaucratic gamesmanship'. He describes the various tactics used by purchasing agents to control the inputs to their role and thereby increase their

---

* Tavistock for Pettigrew, A. 'Decision-making as a political process', in A. Pettigrew, *The Politics of Organisational Decision-Making*. Copyright © Andrew Pettigrew 1973

status. [. . .] Crozier (1964), dealing with the triadic relationship, demonstrates how a person with formally the lowest power and prestige is able, in part at least, to control the initiation of action by others. His main explanatory variables are uncertainty, immobility and commitment. The technical engineer, because of his control over the major source of uncertainty in the routine of factory life, his relative immobility and his high commitment to his job, is able to exert some power over his superiors. [. . .]

In the present study the organization is considered an open political system. The division of work in an organization creates sub-units. These sub-units develop interests based on specialized functions and responsibilities. Although such sub-units have specialized tasks, they may also be interdependent. This interdependence may be played out within a joint decision-making process. Within such decision- making processes, interest-based demands are made. Given heterogeneity in the demand-generating process and the absence of a clearly set system of priorities between those demands, conflict is likely to ensue. Sub-units with differential interests make claims on scarce organizational resources. The extent of the claims is likely to be a reflection of the unit's perception of how critical the resources up for negotiation are to its survival and development. The success any claimant has in furthering his interests will be a consequence of his ability to generate support for his demand.

It is the involvement of sub-units in such demand- and support-generating processes within the decision-making processes of the organization that constitutes the political dimension. Political behaviour is defined as behaviour by individuals, or, in collective terms, by sub-units, within an organization that makes a claim against the resource-sharing system of the organization. [. . .]

As long as organizations continue as resource-sharing systems where there is an inevitable scarcity of those resources, political behaviour will occur: 'The specialization of function not only proceduralizes and so restrains power, it also creates functionaires with a function to defend and a constituency to represent and draw strength from' (Long, 1962: 114). If the dominant occupational ideology defines success as career mobility and if people continue to be rewarded for that mobility, they will attempt to influence the procedures for mobility established in any occupation.

One of the major hypotheses of this study is that such political behaviour is likely to be a special feature of large-scale innovative decisions. These decisions are likely to threaten existing patterns of resource-sharing. New resources may be created and appear to fall within the jurisdiction of a department or individual who has not previously been a claimant in a particular area. This department, or its principal representative, may see this as an opportunity to increase its, or his, status and rewards in the organization. Those who see their interests threatened by the change may invoke resistance in the joint decision process. In all these ways new political action is released and ultimately the existing distribution of power is endangered.

The impact of a large-scale computer installation, it is suggested, will have substantially similar consequences for the organization concerned. In the joint decision process involving the Old Guard and the New Guard (Kahn et al., 1964: 128), the issues that are likely to arise will have to do with the relative contribution that either side can claim for its knowledge or skill contributed as resources, and the right thereby to the greater or lesser share of command over total resources. In the present case, the control problem involving the inclusive leadership system and its innovating subsystem is complicated by the control problem within the innovating subsystem itself. In the 15 or so years in which computers have been used commercially, there have been dramatic changes in computer technology. These changes have not only kept user task environments in a considerable state of flux and uncertainty, but also brought changes in the occupational structure of the industry. The relative statuses of the various occupational groups have changed: programmers no longer occupy the high status they once did. Status systems, however, are slow to adjust, and recognition frequently lags behind capabilities. Newer specialties are often more expansionist than older ones, since they have not been accepted and are still trying to prove themselves. To use Thompson's (1961) phrase, power conflicts thus arise over perceptions of 'the reality of interdependence'. In a changing technological environment the right to review or to be consulted may be distributed in a manner inconsistent with the distribution of ability. This may lead to jurisdictional struggles until a further balance in the state of interdependence is achieved.

[. . .] The theoretically most developed analyses of organizational decision-making, those of March and Simon (1958) and Cyert and March (1963), are lacking in certain respects. [. . .]

First, the above theories are virtually untestable on an aggregate basis because they are presented in a universal and non-structural form. Theories, even in a universal form, should be specified in a societal context and related to societal structures and organizations. Secondly, decisions are not made by individuals or by role occupants, but via processes which are affected by properties of the unit or units in which the decision is to be made. Information failures that characterize 'bounded rationality' are rooted in structural problems of hierarchy, specialization and centralization, and do not just reflect the malfunctioning of thought processes. Conflict in a joint decision-making process may arise not only as a result of differences in goals and perceptions but with regard to the transference of authority over a particular area from one sub-unit to another. While 'satisficing man' may be a considerable advance in realism over the economist's maximizing man, the former is never operationally defined. In consequence, the role that powerful interests might play in the search and choice processes tends to be played down. Finally, although Cyert and March (1963) discuss conflict they are never specific about its determinants. They offer only vague discussions of sub-goal identification. Their model of coalition formation, while smacking of realism, lacks depth of presentation. There is no mention of the organizational structure of the firm, nor therefore of the membership of the bargaining sub-groups in the coalition. Little attention is given to how and why coalitions are formed and changed, or to the generation of support and how the structure of the organization might limit such a process.

While our analysis has gone much further than Cyert and March in discussing the determinants of the political behaviour they describe, if it is going to add to existing work, an attempt must be made to explain processually the relationship between the strategies pursued by the various interested parties and the final decisional outcome. Such an analysis involves tracing out the generation of demands and the mobilization of support for those demands. Finally, for the sake of analytical precision the concept of politics requires differentiation into the elements of power and authority.

Power and organizational decision-making

In 1964, Kahn wrote: 'The descent from theory to data is often painful. With respect to power, there are a few extra twinges involved in that downward journey because the research results so far available are few and modest' (1964: 52). He then went on to describe three studies of superior–subordinate relationships and a study of control in a trade union, all carried out at Michigan. By 1968, Silverman was arguing [. . .] for 'an analysis of the balance of power within an organization and of the factors that govern it' (1968: 234). Mouzelis (1967) talked of feats already achieved as far as intra-organizational power relations were concerned: 'What is most needed . . . is to combine in a more systematic way this new awareness of the internal power structure of an organization with the wider problems of power in modern societies' (1967: 162). [. . .]

As far as organizational studies of power are concerned, one of the main problems is gaining access to do research. In many cases, sociologists rely upon the co-operation and financial support of those who control the organizations they seek to study. As Mouzelis (1967: 163) has stated, the practical issue then becomes whether 'groups would systematically oppose and hinder the sociologists' attempts to bring into the open the power structure and political struggles taking place in the organization'. [. . .]

Aside from the practical problem of limited research access, the concept of power has received scant empirical attention because of controversy over its conceptual elaboration and operational definition. [. . .]

There are as many different definitions of the concepts of authority and power as there are of the concept of role. This is not the place to effect yet another survey of them. However, a number of important theoretical distinctions must be made if our analysis is to move off on a sound footing. For Talcott Parsons, authority refers to the legitimate position of an individual or group: 'Authority is essentially the institutional code within which the use of power as medium is organized and legitimized' (1967: 319). Authority is then, for Parsons, a basis of power, in fact the only basis of power, rather than a kind of power. The use of power is restricted entirely to the achievement of collective goals: 'Power rests on the consensual solidarity of a system . . . in this sense it is the capacity of a unit in the social system, collective or individual, to establish or activate commitments to performance that contributes to, or is in the interest of, attainment of the goals of a collectivity' (1967: 504). Giddens (1968) holds that Parson's collectivistic orientation to power shares some of the basic difficulties and deficiencies of his general theory: 'By treating power as necessarily (by definition) legitimate, and thus starting from the assumption of consensus of some kind between power-holders and those subordinate to them, Parsons virtually ignores . . . the necessarily hierarchical character of power, and the divisions of interest which are frequently consequent upon it' (1968: 264). Clearly, positions of power offer to their incumbents definite material and psychological rewards, and thereby stimulate conflicts between those who want power and those who have it. This brings into play a multiplicity of possible strategies of coercion, deceit, and manipulation which can be used either to acquire or to hold on to power: 'Any sociological theory which treats such phenomena as "incidental", or as 'secondary and derived", and not as structurally intrinsic to power differentials, is blatantly inadequate' (Giddens. 1968: 264). [. . .]

The formal structure of power and legitimacy is regarded as problematic. This issue has been expressed in the literature in a number of ways. Barnard (1938) talks of the authority of position and the authority of leadership, while Bass (1960) distinguishes between power of position and personal power. More recently, Peabody (1964) has discussed the differences between formal and functional authority. All these authors imply that authority requires to be fortified in interaction. A position may give a leader authority, but the exercise of authority requires interaction. It is at this point that the leader's problems begin. Blau (1955) has posited that a superior's ability to exercise authority depends on the willingness of his subordinates to obey him. The superior not only controls but is controlled. Crozier (1964: 150) similarly considers subordinates as 'free agents who can discuss their own problems and bargain about them, who not only submit to a power structure but also participate in that structure'.

[. . .] If certain groups within a social system compare their share of power, wealth and status with that of other groups and question the legitimacy of this distribution, discontent and overt conflict are likely to ensue. The critical consideration is, then, what factors lead groups and individuals to question at a certain point the legitimacy of the system of distribution of authority and rewards? A further source of discontent in certain poorly institutionalized social systems is the possibility that individuals may not know what either their superiors or their subordinates regard as legitimate behaviour.

The present, question is, however. how superiors attain and sustain legitimacy. The key issue is the norms and values adhered to by both superior and subordinate. According to Blau (1964: 199): 'Compliance is a cost that is judged on the basis of social norms of fairness. Excessive demands lead to disapproval.' As a group representative the superior will be expected to some extent to symbolize the values and standards of the group. And yet the contact the superior has with the norms of the external environment, coupled with his need for some acceptance by that environment if he is to be an effective group representative. may place on him pressures to conform to norms contrary to his group's. Michels (1949: 311), quoting the example of the 'deproletarianization' of socialist leaders, suggests that this is a special problem for minority group leaders. Other empirical examples of this same phenomenon have been provided by Gluckman (1949) in discussing the village headman's role, and more recently by Kaplan (1959) and Evan (1965) in examining the research administrator's role. Data will be presented shortly to demonstrate that the head of a Management Services department is faced with a similar problem.

Evidence from experimental psychology has established that 'competence in helping the group achieve its goals, and early conformity to its normative expectations for members, provide the potential for acting as a leader and being perceived as such' (Hollander and Julian, 1969). [. . .] Julian and Hollander (1966) found that, aside from the significance of task competence, a leader's 'interest in group members' and 'interest in group activity' were significantly related to group members' willingness to have him continue in that position. While it is doubtful that in a non-laboratory situation subordinates could exert sufficient pressure to remove their superior, the above findings certainly support the conclusion that the leader's source of authority is perceived and reacted to as a relevant element in the leadership process.

In contrast to prestige and authority structures, power structures rest primarily not on a social consensus concerning expectations about privileges or rights between superiors and subordinates, but on the distribution of the resources by means of which compliance with demands can be enforced. Following Dahl (1957: 203), power involves 'A having power over B to the extent that he can get B to do something that B would not otherwise do'. Power is, then, a property of social relationships, not an attribute of the actor. An essential aspect of this theory of power is the notion of dependency. [. . .]

An examination of the determinants of dependency should uncover the power base of an actor in respect of his role set: 'The base of an actor's power consists of all the resources, opportunities, acts, objects that he can exploit in order to affect the behavior of another (Dahl, 1957: 203). Dependency is, then, a product of an imbalance of exchange between individuals and the ability of one actor to control others through his possession of resources. Such resources must not only be possessed by the power aspirant, but also be controlled by him. Bannester (1969: 386) makes this point succinctly: 'It is immaterial who owns the gun and is licensed to carry it; the question is who has his finger on the trigger.'

Mechanic (1962: 352) has shown that within organizations dependency can be generated by controlling access to the resources of 'information, persons and instrumentalities'. To the extent that these resources can be controlled, 'lower participants make higher-ranking participants dependent upon them. Thus, dependence together with the manipulation of the dependency relationship is the key to the power of lower participants' (1962: 256). Unfortunately there are few empirical examples describing such a process. Scheff (1961) analyses the failure of a state mental hospital to bring about intended reform because of the opposition of the hospital attendants. The power of the ward attendants largely derived from the dependence on them of the physicians. This dependence resulted from the physicians' short tenure, their lack of interest in administration, and the large amount of administrative responsibility they had to assume. An agreement developed between the physicians and the attendants whereby the attendants would take on some of the responsibilities and obligations of the physicians in exchange for increased power in decision-making processes concerning patients. If a physician failed to honour his part of the agreement, the attendants would disrupt his contact with patients by withholding information and being disobedient and generally un-co-operative. Sykes (1961) quotes a similar example, this time describing the dependence of prison guards on inmates. Although guards could report prisoners for disobedience, too many reports from a particular guard would give his superiors the impression that he was ineffective. The result was a trading agreement whereby the guards allowed violation of certain rules in return for cooperative behaviour.

Control over information is a critical resource for mobilizing power in a decision-taking situation. McCleery (1960) has provided interesting data on power relations in a prison. His main point is that the formal system of authority relations could be considerably modified by the location and control of communication channels. Because all reports had to pass through the custodial hierarchy, this group was able to subvert the industrial and reform goals represented by the Prison Professional Services and Industry Programs. The head of the custodial hierarchy, the prison captain, was for the same reason able to exert considerable control over decisions made by his immediate superior, the warden. McCleery concludes that while 'the institutional autocrat is not responsible to his subordinates, he is no less responsible than any other executive to those who define the premises of his discretion' (1960: 51).

The pertinent research question [. . .] is: Under what conditions is a superior likely to be most dependent on his subordinates? Walter (1966), in a study of decision-making in two cities, confirmed his hypothesis that 'the influence of subordinates over superiors on non-programmed choices is greater than the influence of superiors over subordinates' (1966: 206). His reasons for this were somewhat inconclusive: 'This outcome is apparently a function of the subordinate's greater knowledge, or, perhaps, the shared presumption by superiors that subordinates know more than they do.'

Given our interest in innovative decision-making jointly involving executives and computer experts, what power the experts have over their immediate superior and the executives is likely to be consequent upon the amount of dependency in the relationship. The expert can maintain a power position over high-ranking persons in the organization as long as they are dependent upon him for special skills and access to certain kinds of information. It is expected that innovative decisions will be characterized by uncertainty. Such uncertainty can be used as a major power resource by the expert. Crozier (1964: 131) cites the example of the technical engineer who is able to control the actions of his director by setting technical limits on what it is and what it is not possible to do. Others also have referred to the role of uncertainty in power relations. [. . .] Zald (1962) found that the degree of uncertainty in the relation of administrative means to organizational ends was a contributory factor to both the power balance and the level of conflict in five correctional institutions. Gordon and Becker (1964) draw attention to the instability of expert power. They attribute shifts in power within hospitals from physicians to administrators to the impact of modern medical techniques. These enable administrators to specify the procedures and resources to be used in treatment. Specified procedures improve administrative co-ordination, but mounting conflict may be anticipated as physicians defend their discretionary prerogatives against the encroaching rules.

In a joint decision process the expert is unlikely to be omnipotent even with the most technically uncertain problem. There is the factor of political access. The position the expert occupies in the structure of relationships in the organization will affect his ability to control and direct the actions of others, as will his position in the communication structure of the organization. Furthermore, executives generally have ultimate power to hire and fire experts. This is likely to exert a major control over the power strategies of the experts. Also, a superior may attempt to reduce his dependence on any group of experts by arranging to pick up the specialist information they possess from other sources. In doing so, however, he will create an exchange imbalance in his relationship with them. He may, of course, attempt to coerce his experts into giving him advice or, alternatively, resign himself to doing without it. Dahl (1967: 238) has noted that a further strategy used by leaders 'is to co-opt rivals into the central leadership group. Another is to buy them off, or to undercut their support by making concessions to their followers.' Georg Simmel (1950), in his discussion of coalition formation in triads, describes the strategy of divide and rule used by a leader faced with a coalition of subordinates. All these strategies may be used by an executive seeking to reduce his dependence on an expert group.

The expert, however, need not simply rely upon the presumed dependency of others that his expertise can give him. He can seek support for the demands he is making. Again, the amount of support a person achieves in a situation will be conditional on the structure and nature of his organizational relationships. Respect might be an important factor here, as will be general personal acceptability and particular feelings of indebtedness felt by relevant others. [. . .]

Crozier (1964) has analysed the evolution of power relationships in systems. He underlines the self-defeating nature of expert power:

> The invasion of all domains by rationality, of course, gives power to the expert who is an agent of this progress. But the expert's success is constantly self-defeating. The rationalization process gives him power, but the end results of rationalization curtail this power. As soon as a field is well covered, as soon as the first intuitions and innovations can be translated into rules and programs, the expert's power disappears (1964: 165).

Crozier also hypothesizes that, 'in the long run, power will tend to be closely related to the kind of uncertainty upon which depends the life of the organization'

(1964: 164). It has already been hypothesized that innovative decisions will be characterized by uncertainty. Expert power might be expected to be maximal when the expert is involved in an innovative decision in that area of the business upon which the life of the organization depends.

Theoretical bearings

The analyses of organizational decision-taking proposed by March and Simon (1958) and Cyert and March (1963), while noteworthy for their political realism, have been found wanting. The present analysis seeks to complement existing work by exploring the nature of the 'political' in the context of an innovative decision process. For reasons already given, such political behaviour is likely to be especially pronounced in the uncertain task environment surrounding an innovative decision. The political dimension will be analysed with reference to authority and power relations in the decision process.

Particular emphasis will be given to the part played by individuals in the structuring of social action over time. By their ability to exert power over others, individuals can change or maintain structures as well as the norms and expectations upon which these structures rest. An individual's behaviour is therefore governed not only by the structure of the situation in which he participates but also by his ability to shape and mould that structure to suit his own interests. He can do this only if he has sufficient power to impose his will on others despite their opposition. The weapons of such contests are the resources that individuals possess, control, and can manipulate, and the ties of dependency that they can form with relevant others.

Within decision-taking processes, power *strategies* are employed by the various interested parties through their *demands*. Strategies are the links between the intentions and perceptions of officials and the political system that imposes restraints and created opportunities for them (Wildavsky, 1964: 63). A demand 'is an expression of opinion that an authoritative allocation with regard to a particular subject matter should or should not be made by those responsible for doing so' (Easton, 1965: 38). The more complex, heterogeneous, and differentiated a political structure is, the more likely are disparate demands to be made. Such disparities are a product of organizational position, professional training, and adherence to sub-group values and reference groups. A joint decision process involving an inclusive leadership system and an innovative subsystem will be characterized by disparate demands. Not all demands can be met. A competitive struggle will develop in which the innovating subsystem (which may be differentiated itself) will attempt to utilize its various resources to generate support for its demands. Where a demand is voiced, who articulates it, who hears it, and how widely it is diffused are all matters of signal importance for the future stages of its career. The processing of demands and the generation of support are the principal components of the general political structure through which power may be wielded. The final decisional outcome will evolve out of the processes of power mobilization attempted by each party in support of its demand.

References

Bannester, D. M (1969) 'Socio-dynamics: an integrating theorem of power, authority, interinfluence and love', *American Sociological Review*, 24: 374–93.

Barnard, C. I. (1938) *The Functions of the Executive*, Cambridge, MA: Harvard University Press.

Bass, B. A. (1960) *Leadership, Psychology, and Organizational Behavior*, New York: Harper.

Blau, P. M. (1955) *The Dynamics of Bureaucracy*. Chicago: University of Chicago Press.

Blau, P. M. (1964) *Exchange and Power in Social Life*. New York: Wiley.

Burns, T. (1961) 'Micropolitics: mechanisms of institutional change', *Administrative Science Quarterly*, 6(3): 257–81.

Crozier, M. (1964) *The Bureaucratic Phenomenon*. Chicago: University of Chicago Press; London: Tavistock.

Cyert, R. M. and March, J. G. (1963) *A Behavioral Theory of the Firm*. Englewood Cliffs, NJ: Prentice-Hall.

Dahl, R. A. (1957) 'The Concept of power', *Behavioral Science*, 2: 201–18.

Dahl, R. A. (1967) 'The politics of planning', in *Decisions and Decision Makers in the Modern State*. Paris: UNESCO.

Dimock, M. (1952) 'Expanding jurisdiction: a case study in bureaucratic conflict', in R. K. Merton et al. (eds), *Reader in Bureaucracy*. Glencoe, ILL: Free Press. pp. 282–90.

Easton, D. A. (1965) *A Systems Analysis of Political Life*. New York: Wiley.

Evan, W. M. (1965) 'Superior–subordinate conflict in research organizations', *Administrative Science Quarterly*, 10: 53–64.

Giddens, A. (1968) '"Power" in the recent writings of Talcott Parsons', *Sociology*, 2(3): 257–72.

Gluckman, M. (1949) 'The village headman in British Central Africa', *Africa*, 19(2): 89–106.

Gordon, G. and Becker, S. (1964) 'Changes in medical practice bring shifts in the patterns of power', *The Modern Hospital*, 102(2).

Hollander, E. P. and Julian, J. W. (1969) 'Contemporary trends in the analysis of leadership processes', *Psychological Bulletin*, 71(5): 387–97.

Julian, J. W. and Hollander, E. P. (1966) 'A study of some role dimensions of leader–follower relations', *Technical Report No. 3*. State University of New York at Buffalo.

Kahn, R. L. (1964) 'Field studies of power in organizations', in R. L. Kahn and E. Boulding (eds), *Power and Conflict in Organizations*. New York: Basic Books; London: Tavistock.

Kahn, R. L., Wolfe, D. M., Snoek, R. P., Diedrick, J. and Rosenthal, R. A. (1964) *Organizational Stress*. New York: Wiley.

Kaplan, N. (1959) 'The role of research administrator', *Administrative Science Quarterly*, 4: 20–42.

Long, N. E. (1962) 'The administrative organization as a political system', in S. Mailick and E. H. Van Ness (eds), *Concepts and Issues in Administrative Behavior*. Englewood Cliffs, NJ: Prentice-Hall.

McCleery, R. (1960) 'Communication patterns as basis of systems of authority and power', in *Theoretical Studies in Social Organization of the Prison*. New York: Social Science Research Council, Pamphlet 15.

March, J. G. and Simon, H.A. (1958) *Organizations*. New York: Wiley.

Mechanic, D. (1962) 'Sources of power of lower participants in complex organizations', *Administrative Science Quarterly*, 7: 349–64.

Michels, R. (1949) *Political Parties*. Glencoe, ILL: Free Press.

Mouzelis, N. P. (1967) *Organization and Bureaucracy*. London: Routledge and Kegan Paul. (Chicago: Aldine, 1968.)

Parsons, T. (1967) *Sociological Theory and Modern Society*. New York: Free Press.

Peabody, R. L. (1964) *Organizational Authority*. New York: Atherton Press.

Scheff, T. J. (1961) 'Control over policy by attendants in a mental hospital', *Journal of Health and Human Behavior*, 93–105.

Silverman, D. (1968) 'Formal organizations or industrial sociology: towards a social action analysis of organizations', *Sociology*, 2(2): 221–38.

Simmel, G. (1950) *The Sociology of Georg Simmel*. Translated and edited by K. H. Wolff. Glencoe, ILL: Free Press.

Strauss, G. (1962) 'Tactics of lateral relationships: the purchasing agent', *Administrative Science Quarterly*, 7: 161–86.

Sykes, G. M. (1961) 'The corruption of authority and rehabilitation', in A. Etzioni (ed.), *Complex Organizations*. New York: Holt, Rinehart and Winston.

Thompson, V. A. (1961) 'Hierarchy, specialization, and organizational conflict', *Administrative Science Quarterly*, 5(4): 485–521.

Walter, B. (1966) 'Internal Control Relations in Administrative Hierarchies', *Administrative Science Quarterly*, 11(2): 179–206.

Wildavsky, A. (1964) *The Politics of the Budgetary Process*. Boston: Little, Brown.

Zald, M. N. (1962) 'Power balance and staff conflict in correctional institutions', *Administrative Science Quarterly*, 7: 22–49.

The Irrationality of Action and Action Rationality: Decisions, Ideologies and Organizational Actions

NILS BRUNSSON*

[...]

The decision-making perspective and irrationality

A characteristic of social science is the multitude of perspectives used by different researchers. The significant differences between research fields lie less often in what is described than in how it is described. One important way of developing a social science is to apply new perspectives to a part of reality, thereby highlighting new features of the reality. Perspectives determine what data are seen, what theories are developed and what kinds of results turn up.

One of the most influential perspectives has been the decision-making perspective which conceives of human behaviour as resulting from decisions made by individuals, groups or organizations. A decision is normally described as a conscious choice between at least two alternative actions. Researchers have studied the choosing among alternatives, the generating of alternatives and the forming of criteria for choice (goals, objectives).

The attractiveness of the decision-making perspective has several explanations. One explanation is that diverse social theories can be stated in

* Blackwell Publishers for an extract from Brunsson, N. 'The irrationality of action and action rationality: decisions, ideologies and organizational actions', *Journal of Management Studies*, 19(1) (1982). Copyright © Blackwell Publishers 1982.

decision-making terms. This is true for parts of microeconomics and of political science. Another explanation is that the perspective lends itself to experimentation; psychological researchers can create experimental decision situations by giving people objectives and information, and then they study the resulting choices. In addition, social development has spawned situations where the decision-making perspective seems relevant from a commonsense point of view. The establishment and growth of large organizations have added hierarchy to society and, consequently, many actions are determined by forces outside the actors themselves [. . .]. This separates cognition from action and makes it natural to say some individuals decide and others carry out the decisions. The decision-making perspective seems almost imperative in democratic conventions. According to the existing law for industrial democracy in Sweden, for example, the employees' influence should be guaranteed by their participation in decisions.[. . .]

Still, the decision-making perspective has derived from studies of individual behaviour rather than organizational. An individual has less difficulty going from decision to action than does an organization. This emphasis on individual behaviour might explain why the choosing of actions has received much more attention than the carrying out of actions. Organizational decision processes are described in essentially the same terms as individual decision processes, and research has often characterized organizations as being led by single powerful entrepreneurs (as in microeconomic theory) or by coalitions [. . .].

The decision-making perspective has been most elaborated in normative research which prescribes how decisions should be made. This kind of research sets the criteria for a 'rational' decision. Strong efforts have been devoted to prescribing how a best choice should be made, given a specific problem, specific alternatives and specific information. Typically, a problem is described as one where there is either too little information or too much. Little attention has been paid to other phases of decision-making processes or to implementing the decisions made.

Normative research has engendered an increasing consensus among researchers as to what kinds of decision-making should be called rational. At the same time, empirical research has found ample evidence of decision-making processes that appear irrational by the normative standards [. . .]. What is more, the apparent irrationalities are not limited to insignificant decisions: people behave similarly when making major decisions on strategic issues. It can even be argued that the apparent irrationalities are largest in major decisions. Janis (1972) demonstrated how decisions with serious actual or potential effects – such as the decision by the Kennedy administration to start the invasion in the Bay of Pigs – were made without normative rationality. Disturbing information was suppressed, and false illusions of unanimity were built up among the decision-makers, who took immense and unjustified risks.

There are three common ways of explaining the irrationality found in practice. One chauvinist explanation is that the people studied are not clever enough to behave rationally. For instance, difficulties of implementing models from operations research have been explained by managers' emotional reactions or by their cognitive styles [. . .]. If decision-makers only had the brain capacities and knowledge of scientists, they would behave as the rational decision models prescribe. Thus, decision-makers ought to be selected better and trained better.

A second explanation derives from recent psychological research, which indicates that certain types of irrationality are inherent characteristics of human beings, and these characteristics are difficult to change by training [. . .]. Consequently, not even experts can be fully rational, and full rationality can only be reached by mathematical formulae or computer programs.

A third way of explaining apparently irrational behaviour is to point out practical restrictions. In realistic decision situations, values, alternatives and predictions interact; so decision-makers have incomplete information, or they have more information than human beings can grasp. This view implies that normative research should design systems for gathering and processing data. Not many years ago, some people expected computer-based information systems to solve numerous management problems [. . .]. Also, recognizing that objectives may be difficult to compare with each other, normative research has produced cost-benefit analysis and multiple-criteria methods [. . .].

These traditional explanations are made within the decision-making perspective. They refer to diverse phenomena that disturb decision processes. Like the decision processes themselves, the disturbances are described as being cognitive; they arise from deficiencies in perceived information or deficiencies in decision-makers' mental abilities.

These ways of explaining irrationality cannot be said to be inherently wrong, but there is much evidence that these explanations do not suffice. Computer-based information systems have not been used in the prescribed ways; recommendations given by operations-research models have not been followed; cost-benefit analyses have not been done or have been neglected even by competent and successful managers and politicians [. . .].

If actual behaviour is to be understood, other explanations are needed. As long as actual behaviour is not fully understood, the recommendations of normative research may be irrelevant, confusing or even harmful.

The main purpose of this article is to argue that an action perspective will be more fruitful for understanding large areas of organizational behaviour. The action perspective explains behaviour within attempts to change and differences in abilities to achieve changes. Because organizational actions do not lend themselves to laboratory experiments, the article is based on studies of major organizational changes or stabilities in seven organizations. The organizations include industrial companies, governmental agencies and local governments. Processes of change were observed, and people's ways of describing both the changes and the general situations were measured.

The decision-making perspective fails to recognize that practitioners do more than make decisions. Making a decision is only a step towards action. A decision is not an end product. Practitioners get things done, act and induce others to act.

An action perspective makes it easier and important to observe that there exist both decisions without actions and actions without decisions. Some actions are not preceded by weighing of objectives, evaluating of alternatives or choosing; and decision processes and decisions do not always influence actions, particularly not when the actions precede the decisions. On the other hand, decision processes often comprise some of the processes associated with actions. Because managers and representatives in political bodies describe part of their work as decision-making, decisions and decision-making should remain important topics for study.

In fact, the very relationship between decision-making and action helps explain why decisions deviate from normative rationality. Since decision processes aim at action, they should not be designed solely according to such decision-internal criteria as the norms of rationality; they should be adapted to external criteria of action. Rational decisions are not always good bases for appropriate and successful actions.

How can decisions lay foundations for actions? [. . .]

Decisions as initiators of actions

Making decisions is just one way among several of initiating actions in organizations. However, it is a familiar one. Actions are often preceded by group activities which the participants describe as decision-making steps. Certain issues are posed in forms that allow them to be handled by decision processes: several alternative actions are proposed, their probable effects are forecasted, and finally actions are chosen. Sometimes the decision-makers even formulate goals or other explicit criteria by which the alternatives can be evaluated. The final results are called decisions.

For decisions to initiate actions, they must incorporate cognitive, motivational and committal aspects. One cognitive aspect of a decision is expectation: the decision expresses the expectation that certain actions will take place. A decision also demonstrates motivation to take action, and it expresses the decision-makers' commitments to specific actions. By making a decision, decision-makers accept responsibility both for getting the actions carried out and for the appropriateness of the actions.

To go from decision to action is particularly complicated and difficult when there are several decision-makers and several actors and when decision-makers and actors are different persons. These conditions are typical of organizations. Thus, organizations should provide motivational and social links from decisions to actions. Strong motivations, sometimes even enthusiasm, are needed to overcome big intellectual or physical obstacles. Co-operating actors should be able to rely on certain kinds of behaviours and attitudes from their collaborators, so they should construct mutual commitments: the actors should signal to one another that they endorse proposed actions, for example, by presenting arguments in favour of them or by expressing confidence in success. Actors should also elicit commitments from those who will evaluate their actions afterwards, because committed evaluators are more likely to judge actions as successful (Brunsson, 1976).

Thinking, motivation and commitment are aspects of all actions. However, the importance of each aspect might differ in various situations, depending on such variables as the actors' time horizons, the degrees of change that the actions involve, and the power relationships within the organization. Cognitive activities probably become more important where the actors expect more information to be beneficial. Motivations would be more important where actors lack information needed for predicting the consequences of acting, where the negative consequences could be great, or where great efforts are essential; motivations would be less important where the actions are highly complex and the actors must collaborate extensively (Zander, 1971). Commitments would be more important where many people are involved in actions, agreements from many people are necessary, efforts must be tightly co-ordinated, or results depend upon the actions or evaluations of collaborators who are accessible through communication. Since motivations and commitments represent internal pressures for action, they are particularly influential where external pressures are weak. This is true of wait-and-see situations where people think that it may be possible to take no action: the actors can reject one proposed action without having to accept another at the same time.

The stronger the expectation, motivation and commitment expressed in a decision, the more power that decision exerts as a basis for action. Insofar as the constituents of decisions are determined by decision processes, the likelihoods of actions can be influenced by designing the decision processes. However, effective decision processes break nearly all the rules for rational decision-making: few alternatives should be analysed, only positive consequences of the chosen actions should be considered, and objectives should not be formulated in advance.

The following subsections explain how irrationalities can build good bases for organizational actions.

Searching for alternatives

According to the rational model, all possible alternatives should be evaluated. This is impossible, so the injunction is often reformulated as evaluating as many alternatives as possible.

In reality, it seems easier to find decision processes which consider few alternatives (typically two) than ones which consider many alternatives. It is even easy to find decision processes which consider only one alternative. This parsimony makes sense from an action point of view, because considering multiple alternatives evokes uncertainty, and uncertainty reduces motivation and commitment. If actors are uncertain whether a proposed action is good, they are less willing to undertake it and to commit themselves to making it succeed. For example, in order to facilitate product-development projects, uncertainty should not be analysed but avoided (Brunsson, 1980). If people do not know which action will actually be carried out, they have to build up motivations for several alternatives at the same time, and this diffuses the motivations supporting any single alternative. For the same reasons, commitments may be dispersed or destroyed by the consideration of several alternatives. Therefore, very early in decision processes, if possible before the processes even start, decision-makers should get rid of alternatives that have weak to moderate chances of being chosen.

On the other hand, alternatives with no chance to being chosen do not have these negative effects: they may even reinforce motivation and commitment. One strategy is to propose alternatives which are clearly unacceptable but which highlight by comparison the virtues of an acceptable alternative. This defines the situation as not being of the wait-and-see type: rejecting one alternative means accepting another. Another and more important effect is that commitments become double-sided: commitments arise not only through endorsements of acceptable alternatives but also through criticisms of unacceptable alternatives. Thus, considering two alternatives can lay a stronger foundation for action than considering only one alternative if one of the two alternatives is clearly unacceptable.

One example is the decision process following the merger of Sweden's three largest steel companies. The merger was supposed to make production more efficient by concentrating each kind of production in one steelworks. A six-month-long decision process considered several alternative ways of redistributing production. Besides the alternative that was actually chosen, however, only one alternative was investigated thoroughly. This was the alternative to make no change at all. Because this alternative would have made the merger meaningless, no one considered it a practical action.

Estimating consequences

Decision-makers who want to make rational decisions are supposed to consider all relevant consequences that alternatives might have; positive and negative consequences should get equal attention. But such a procedure evokes much uncertainty, for inconsistent information produces bewilderment and doubt, and stimulates conflicts among decision-makers (Hoffman, 1968). Also, it is difficult to weigh positive and negative consequences together (Slovic, 1966).

One way of avoiding uncertainty is to search for consequences in only one direction – to seek support for the initial opinion about an alternative. People tend to anchor their judgements in the first cues they perceive (Slovic, 1972; Tversky and Kahneman, 1974). Searching for positive consequences of an acceptable alternative has high priority, while negative consequences are suppressed. The purpose is not only to avoid uncertainty: active search for arguments in favour of an alternative also helps to create enthusiasm and to increase commitments. If negative consequences do pop up, adding more positive consequences can at least help to maintain commitment and motivation.

For example, in a company with high propensity to undertake innovative product-development projects, personnel spent most of their discussions collecting arguments in favour specific projects. This helped them to build up enthusiasm for project – an enthusiasm that they deemed necessary to overcome difficulties (Brunsson, 1976).

Evaluating alternatives

The rational model prescribes that alternatives and their consequences should be evaluated according to predetermined criteria, preferably in the form of objectives. Decision-makers are told to start with objectives and then to find out what effects the alternatives would have on them. This is a dangerous strategy from the action point of view because there is a high risk that decision-makers will formulate inconsistent objectives and will have difficulties assessing alternatives. Data are needed that are difficult or impossible to find, and different pieces of information may point in conflicting directions.

For producing action, a better strategy is to start from the consequences and to invent the objectives afterwards (Lindblom, 1959). Predicted consequences are judged to be good because they can be reformulated as desirable objectives. The relations between alternatives and objectives are not investigated in detail, only enough to demonstrate some positive links. The objectives are arguments, not criteria for choice; they are instruments for motivation and commitment, not for investigation. The argumentative role of objectives becomes evident in situations where objectives are abandoned after data indicate that they will not be promoted by preferred actions.

For instance, the calculations in the merged steel company actually demonstrated that the no-change alternative would be at least as profitable as the alternative that was chosen. The decision makers then shifted their criterion from profitability as defined in the calculations to criteria such as access to a harbour and the age of a steelworks – criteria which favoured the alternative to be chosen.

Choosing

Within the decision-making perspective, a decision is normally described as a choice which follows automatically from preceding analysis. But when decision-making initiates action, a choice is not merely a statement of preference for one alternative but an expression of commitment to carrying out an action. A choice can be formulated in diverse ways which express different degrees of commitment and enthusiasm. Which people participate in choosing influences which people participate in acting.

A local government with an unstable majority postponed for eight years a decision about where to build new houses. Yet, at every time, there existed a majority favouring one location. Majority support was not thought to be a sufficient basis for the complicated and time-consuming planning work to follow (Brunsson, 1981; Jönsson, 1982).

Making rational use of irrationality

The purpose of action calls for irrationality. Some irrationalities are consistent with the prescriptions of Lindblom (1959) who argued that thorough rational analyses are irrelevant for the incremental steps in American national policy. But irrationality is even more valuable for actions involving radical changes, because motivation and commitment are crucial.

Much of the decision irrationality observed in decision processes can be explained as action rationality. The hypothesis that such may be the case is worth considering at least in situations where motivation and commitment are highly beneficial. For example, this kind of explanation can be applied to some of the strategic decisions described by Janis (1972). Much of the irrationality Janis observed in the decision of the Kennedy administration to invade Cuba can be explained by the fact that such risky and normally illegitimate actions needed extreme motivation and commitment to be adopted. Strong motivations and commitments seem actually to have arisen, and they led to very strong efforts to complete the action in spite of great difficulties and uncertainties.

According to Janis, better alternatives would have been found if the decision process had been more rational, giving room for more criticism, alternative perspectives and doubts. Perhaps so. But deciding more rationally in order to avoid big failures is difficult advice to follow. If the decisions should initiate actions, the irrationality is functional and should not be replaced by more rational decision procedures. Rational analyses are more appropriate where motivation and commitment offer weak benefits. This is true for actions which are less significant, less complicated and short-term. Lundberg (1961) observed that investment calculations are made for small, marginal investments but not for large, strategic ones. If one believes that rational decision processes lead to better choices, this observation should be disquieting. Moreover, important actions tend to be carried out with strong motivations and commitments, which make it difficult to stop or change directions if the actions prove to be mistakes.

There is also the opposite risk – that decision rationality impedes difficult but necessary actions. For actions involving major organizational changes, the magnitudes of the issues and the uncertainties involved may frighten people into making analyses as carefully as possible. At the same time, the uncertainty potentials and the involvements of many people heighten the risks that rational decision-making will obstruct action.

One extreme and pathological case of decision-making giving no basis for action is decision orientation. This occurs when people regard decision-making as their only activities, not caring about the actions and not even presuming that there will be actions. In full accordance with the decision-making perspective, these people look upon decisions as end points. In one political organization, for instance, the politicians facilitated their decision-making substantially by concentrating on making decisions and ignoring subsequent actions. Since the decisions were not to be carried out, the politicians did not have to worry about negative effects, and they could easily reach agreements. On the other hand, the lack of actions threatened the survival of the organization.

To sum up, rational decision-making procedures fulfill the function of choice – they lead to the selection of action alternatives. But organizations face two problems: to choose the right thing to do and to get it done. There are two kinds of rationality, corresponding to these two problems: decision rationality and action rationality. The one is not better than the other, but they serve different purposes and imply different norms. The two kinds of rationality are difficult to pursue simultaneously because rational decision-making procedures are irrational from an action perspective; they should be avoided if actions are to be facilitated. [. . .]

References

Brunsson, N. (1976) *Propensity to Change*. Göteborg, Sweden: BAS.

Brunsson, N. (1980) 'The functions of project evaluation', *R & D Management*, 10: 61–5.

Brunsson, N. (1981) *Politik och administration*. Stockholm: Liber.

Hoffman, P. J. (1968) 'Cue-consistency and configurality in human judgement', in B. Kleinmetz (ed.), *Formal Representation of Human Judgement*. New York: Wiley.

Janis, I. L. (1972) *Victims of Groupthink*. Boston, MA: Houghton Muffin.

Jönsson, S. A. (1982) 'Cognitive turning in municipal-problem solving', *Journal of Management Studies*, 19: 63–73.

Lindblom, C. E. (1959) 'The science of "muddling through"', *Public Administration Review*, 19: 79–88.

Lundberg, E. (1961) *Produktivitet och räntabilitet*. Stockholm: SNS.

Slovic, P. (1966) 'Cue consistency and cue utilization in judgement', *American Journal of Psychology*, 79: 427–34.

Slovic, P. (1972) *From Shakespeare to Simon*. Portland, OR: Oregon Research Institute.

Tversky, A. and Kahneman, D. (1974) 'Judgement under uncertainty: heuristics and biases', *Science*, 185: 1124–31.

Zander, A. (1971) *Motives and Goals in Groups*. New York: Academic Press.

CHAPTER 7

The Hospital and its Negotiated Order

A. STRAUSS, L. SCHATZMAN, D. EHRLICH,
R. BUCHER AND M. SABSHIN*

In the pages to follow, a model for studying hospitals will be sketched, along with some suggested virtues of the model. It grew out of the authors' research, which was done on the premises of two psychiatric hospitals. [. . .]

Our model bears upon that most central of sociological problems, namely, how a measure of order is maintained in the face of inevitable changes (derivable from sources both external and internal to the organization). Students of formal organization tend to underplay the processes of internal change as well as overestimate the more stable features of organizations – including its rules and its hierarchical statuses. We ourselves take our cue from Mead (1936), who some years ago, when arguing for orderly and directed social change, remarked that the task turns about relationships between change and order:

> How can you bring those changes about in an orderly fashion and yet preserve order? To bring about change is seemingly to destroy the given order, and yet society does and must change. That is the problem, to incorporate the method of change into the order of society itself.

Without Mead's melioristic concerns, one can yet assume that order is something at which members of any society, any organization must work. For the shared agreements, the binding contracts – which constitute the grounds for an expectable, non-surprising, taken-for-granted even ruled orderliness – are not binding and shared for all time. Contracts, understandings, agreements, rules – all have appended to them a temporal clause. That clause may or may not be explicitly discussed by the contracting parties, and the terminal date of the agreement may or may not be made specific, but none can be binding forever – even if the parties

* Macmillan (New York) for Strauss, A. et al. 'The hospital and its negotiated order', in E. Friedson et al. (eds), *The Hospital in Modern Society*. Copyright © Macmillan NY 1963.

believe it so, unforeseen consequences of acting on the agreements would force eventual confrontation. Review is called for, whether the outcome of review be rejection or renewal or revision, or what not. In short, the bases of concerted action (social order) must be reconstituted continually; or, as remarked above, 'worked at'.

Such considerations have led us to emphasize the importance of negotiation – the processes of give-and-take, of diplomacy, of bargaining – which characterizes organizational life. In the pages to follow, we shall note first the relationship of rules to negotiation, then discuss the grounds for negotiation. Then, since both the clients and much of the personnel of hospitals are laymen, we wish also to underscore the participation of those laymen in the hospital's negotiative processes. Thereafter we shall note certain patterned and temporal features of negotiation; then we shall draw together some implications for viewing social order. A general summary of the argument and its implications will round out the chapter.

[. . .]

A professionalized locale

A hospital can be visualized as a professionalized locale – a geographical site where persons drawn from different professions come together to carry out their respective purposes. At our specific hospital, the professionals consisted of numerous practising psychiatrists and psychiatric residents, nurses and nursing students, psychologists, occupational therapists, and one lone social worker. Each professional echelon has received noticeably different kinds of training and, speaking conventionally, each occupies some differential hierarchical position at the hospital while playing a different part in its total division of labour.

But that last sentence requires elaboration and emendation. The persons within each professional group may be, and probably are, at different stages in their respective careers. Furthermore, the career lines of some may be quite different from those of their colleagues: thus some of our psychiatrists were just entering upon psychoanalytic training, but some had entered the medical speciality by way of neurology, and had dual neurological-psychiatric practices. Implicit in the preceding statement is that those who belong to the same profession also may differ quite measurably in the training they have received, as well as in the theoretical (or ideological) positions they take toward important issues like aetiology and treatment. Finally, the hospital itself may possess differential significance for colleagues: for instance, some psychiatrists were engaged in hospital practice only until such time as their office practices had been sufficiently well established; while other, usually older, psychiatrists were committed wholeheartedly to working with hospitalized patients.

Looking next at the division of labour shared by the professionals: never do all persons of each echelon work closely with all others from other echelons. At our hospital it was notable that considerable variability characterized who worked closely with whom – and how – depending upon such matters as ideological and hierarchical position. Thus the services of the social worker were used not at all by some psychiatrists, while each man who utilized her services did so somewhat differently. Similarly some men utilized 'psychologicals' more than did others. Similarly, some psychiatrists were successful in housing their patients almost exclusively in certain wards, which meant that, wittingly or not, they worked only with certain nurses. As in other institutions, the various echelons possessed differential status and power, but again there were marked internal differences concerning status and power, as well as knowledgeability about 'getting things done'. Nor must it be overlooked that not only did the different professions hold measurably different views – derived both from professional and status positions – about the proper division of labour; but different views also obtained within each echelon. (The views were most discrepant among the psychiatrists.) All in all, the division of labour is a complex concept, and at hospitals must be seen in relation to the professionalized milieu.

Ruled and unruled behaviour

The rules that govern the actions of various professionals, as they perform their tasks, are far from extensive, or clearly stated or clearly binding. This fact leads to necessary and continual negotiation. It will be worth deferring discussions of negotiation *per se* until we have explored some relationships between rules and negotiation, at least as found in our hospital; for the topic of rules is a complicated one.

In Michael Reese Hospital, as unquestionably in most sizeable establishments, hardly anyone knows all the extant rules, much less exactly what situations they apply to, for whom, and with what sanctions. If this would not otherwise be so in our hospital, it would be true anyway because of the considerable turnover of nursing staff. Also noticeable – to us as observers – was that some rules once promulgated would fall into disuse, or would periodically receive administrative reiteration after the staff had either ignored those rules or forgotten them. As one head nurse said, 'I wish they would write them all down sometimes' – but said so smilingly. The plain fact is that staff kept forgetting not only the rules received from above but also some rules that they themselves had agreed upon 'for this ward'. Hence we would observe that periodically the same informal ward rules would be agreed upon, enforced for a short time, and then be forgotten until another ward crisis would elicit their innovation all over again.

As in other establishments, personnel called upon certain rules to obtain what they themselves wished. Thus the nurses frequently acted as virtual guardians of the hospital against some demands of certain attending physicians, calling upon the resources of 'the rules of the hospital' in countering the physicians' demands. As in other hospital settings, the physicians were only too aware of this game, and accused the nurses from time to time of more interest in their own welfare than in that of the patients. (The only difference, we suspect, between the accusatory language of psychiatrists and that of internists or surgeons is that the psychiatrists have a trained capacity to utilize specialized terms like 'rigid' and 'overcompulsive'.) In so dredging up the rules at convenient moments, the staff of course are acting identically with personnel in other kinds of institutions.

As elsewhere, too, all categories of personnel are adept at breaking the rules when it suits convenience or when warrantable exigencies arise. Stretching the rules is only a further variant of this tactic, which itself is less attributable to human nature than to an honest desire to get things accomplished as they ought, properly, to get done. Of course, respective parties must strike bargains for these actions to occur.

In addition, at the very top of the administrative structure, a tolerant stance is taken both toward extensiveness of rules and laxity of rules. The point can be illustrated by a conversation with the administrative head, who recounted with amusement how some members of his original house staff wished to have all rules set down in a house rule book, but he had staved off this codification. As will be noted more fully later, the administrative attitude is affected also by a profound belief that care of patients calls for a minimum of hard and fast rules and a maximum of innovation and improvization. In addition, in this hospital, as certainly in most others, the multiplicity of medical purpose and theory, as well as of personal investment, are openly recognized: too rigid a set of rules would only cause turmoil and affect the hospital's overall efficiency.

Finally, it is notable that the hospital must confront the realities of the attending negotiations with patients and their families – negotiations carried out beyond the physical confines of the hospital itself. Too many or too rigid rules would restrict the medical entrepreneurs' negotiation. To some degree any hospital with attending men has to give this kind of leeway (indeed, the precise degree is a source of tension in these kinds of hospitals).

Hence, the area of action covered directly by clearly enunciated rules is really very small. As observers, we began to become aware of this when, within a few days, we discovered that only a few very general rules obtained for the placement of new patients within the hospital. Those rules, which are clearly enunciated and generally followed, can, for our purposes, be regarded as long-standing shared understandings among the personnel. Except for a few legal rules, which stem from state and professional prescription, and for some rulings pertaining to all of Michael Reese Hospital, almost all these house rules are much less like commands, and much more like general understandings: not even their punishments are spelled out; and mostly they can be stretched, negotiated, argued, as well as ignored or applied at convenient moments. Hospital rules seem to us frequently less explicit than tacit, probably as much breached and stretched as honoured, and administrative effort is made to keep their number small. In addition, rules here as elsewhere fail to be universal prescriptions: they always require judgement concerning their applicability to the specific case. Does it apply here? To whom? In what degree? For how long? With what sanctions? The personnel cannot give universal answers; they can only point to past analogous instances when confronted with situations or give 'for instance' answers, when queried about a rule's future application.

The grounds for negotiation

Negotiation and the division of labour are rendered all the more complex because personnel in our hospital – we assume that the generalisaton, with some modification, holds elsewhere share – only a single, vaguely ambiguous goal. The goal is to return patients to the outside world in better shape. This goal is the symbolic cement that, metaphorically speaking, holds the organization together: the symbol to which all personnel can comfortably and frequently point – with the assurance that *at least* about this matter everyone can agree! Although this symbol, as will be seen later, masks a considerable measure of disagreement and discrepant purpose, it represents a generalized mandate under which the hospital can be run – the public flag under which all may work in concert. Let us term it the institution's constitutional grounds or basic compact. These grounds, this compact, are never openly challenged; nor are any other goals given explicit verbal precedence. (This is so when a hospital, such as ours, also is a training institution.) In addition, these constitutional grounds can be used by any and all personnel as a justificatory rationale for actions that are under attack. In short, although personnel may disagree to the point of apoplexy about how to implement patients' getting better, they do share the common institutional value.

The problem, of course, is that when the personnel confront a specific patient and attempt to make him recover, then the disagreements flare up – the generalized mandate helps not at all to handle the specific issues – and a complicated process of negotiation, of bargaining, of give-and-take necessarily begins. The disagreements that necessitate negotiation do not occur by chance, but are patterned. Here are several illustrations of the grounds that lead to negotiation. Thus, the personnel may disagree over what is the proper placement within the hospital for some patient; believing that, at any given time, he is more likely to improve when placed in one ward rather than in another. This issue is the source of considerable tension between physicians and ward personnel. Again, what is meant by 'getting better' is itself open to differential judgement when applied to the progress – retrogression – of a particular patient. This judgement is influenced not only by professional experience and acquaintance with the patient but is also influenced by the very concept of getting better as held by the different echelons. Thus the aides – who are laymen – have quite different notions about these matters than do the physicians, and on the whole those notions are not quite equivalent to those held by nurses. But both the nurses and the aides see patients getting better according to signs visible from the patient's daily behaviour, while the psychiatrist tends to relate these signs, if apprehended at all, to deeper layers of personality; with the consequence that frequently the staff thinks one way about the patient's 'movement' while the physician thinks quite otherwise, and must argue his case, set them right, or even keep his peace.

To turn now to another set of conditions for negotiation: the very mode of treatment selected by the physician is profoundly related to his own psychiatric ideology. For instance, it makes a difference whether the physician is neurologically trained, thus somatically oriented, or whether he is psychotherapeutically trained and oriented. The former type of physician will prescribe more drugs, engage in far more electric shock therapy, and spend much less time with each patient. On occasion the diagnosis and treatment of a given patient runs against the judgement of the nurses and aides, who may not go along with the physician's directives, who may or may not disagree openly. They may subvert his therapeutic programme by one of their own. They may choose to argue the matter. They may go over his head to an administrative officer. Indeed, they have many choices of action – each requiring negotiative behaviour. In truth, while physicians are able to command considerable obedience to their directives at this particular hospital, frequently they must work hard at obtaining co-operation in their programming. The task is rendered all the more difficult because they, as professionals, see matters in certain lights, while the aides, as laymen, may judge matters quite differently – on moral rather than on strictly psychiatric grounds, for instance.

If negotiation is called for because a generalized mandate requires implementation, it is also called for because of the multiplicity of purpose found in the hospital. It is incontestable that each professional group has a different set of reasons for working at this hospital (to begin with, most nurses are women, most physicians are men); and of course colleagues inevitably differ among themselves on certain of their purposes for working there. In addition, each professional develops there his own specific and temporarily limited ends that he wishes to attain. All this diversity of purpose affects the institution's division of labour, including not only what tasks each person is expected to accomplish but also how he manoeuvres to get them accomplished. Since very little of this can possibly be prefigured by the administrative rule-makers, the attainment of one's purposes requires inevitably the co-operation of fellow workers. This point, once made, scarcely needs illustration.

However, yet another ground of negotiation needs emphasizing: namely, that in this hospital, as doubtless elsewhere, the patient as an 'individual case' is taken as a virtual article of faith. By this we mean that the element of medical uncertainty is so great, and each patient is taken as – in some sense – so unique, that action round and about him must be tailor-made, must be suited to his precise therapeutic requirements. This kind of assumption abets what would occur anyhow: that only a minimum of rules can be laid down for running a hospital, since a huge area of contingency necessarily lies outside those rules. The rules can provide guidance and command for only a small amount of the total concerted action that must go on around the patient. It follows, as already noted that where action is not ruled it must be agreed upon.

One important further condition for negotiation should be mentioned. Changes are forced upon the hospital and its staff not only by forces external to the hospital but also by unforeseen consequences of internal policies and negotiations carried on within the hospital. In short, negotiations breed further negotiations.

[. . .]

The patients and negotiated order

The patients are also engaged in bargaining, in negotiative processes. (As some public-administration theorists have put it, clients are also part of the organizational structure.) Again, a significant aspect of hospital organization is missing unless the clients' negotiation is included. They negotiate, of course, as laymen, unless they themselves are nurses or physicians. Most visibly they can be seen bargaining, with the nurses and with their psychiatrists, for more extensive privileges (such as more freedom to roam the grounds); but they may also seek to affect the course and kind of treatment – including placement on given wards, amounts of drugs, and even choice of psychiatrist, along with the length of stay in the hospital itself. Intermittently, but fairly continually, they are concerned with their ward's orderliness, and make demands upon the personnel – as well as upon other patients – to keep the volume of noise down, to keep potential violence at a minimum, to rid the ward of a trouble-making patient. Sometimes the patients are as much guardians of ward order as are the nurses, who are notorious for this concern in our hospital. (Conversely, the nursing personnel must also seek to reach understandings and agreements with specific patients; but sometimes these are even collective, as when patients pitch in to help with a needy patient, or as when an adolescent clique has to be dealt with 'as a bunch'.)

An unexpected dividend awaits anyone who focuses upon the patients' negotiations. An enriched understanding of their individual sick careers – to the hospital, inside it, and out of it – occurs. In the absence of a focus upon negotiation, ordinarily these careers tend to appear overly regularized (as in Parsons and Fox, 1952) or destructive (as in Goffman, 1959). When patients are closely observed 'operating around' the hospital, they will be seen negotiating not only for privileges but also for precious information relevant to their own understandings of their illness. We need only add that necessarily their negotiations will differ at various stages of their sick careers.

What Caudill et al. (1952) and Goffman (1957) have written of as patient culture is roughly equivalent to the demands and expectations of the patients; but their accounts require much supplementation by a conception of patients entering, like everyone else, into the overall negotiative process. How demands and claims will be made and met, by whom, and in what manner – as well as who will make given demands and claims upon them, how, and in what manner – are of utmost importance for understanding the hospital's structure. When patients are long-term or chronic, then their impact upon structure is more obvious to everyone concerned; but even in establishments with speedy turnover, patients are relevant to the social order.

Patterned and temporal features of negotiation

To do justice to the complexity of negotiative processes would require far more space than can be allowed here. For present purposes, it should be sufficient to note only a few aspects. In our hospital, as elsewhere, the various physicians institute programmes of treatment and care for their patients. Programming involves a mobilization and organization of action around the patient (and usually involves the patient's co-operation, even in the psychiatric milieu). Some physicians in our hospital had reached long-standing understandings with certain head nurses, so that only a small amount of communication was necessary to effectuate their treatment programmes. Thus a somatically oriented psychiatrist typically would attempt to get his patients to those two wards where most electric-shock treatment was carried out; and the nurse administrators there understood quite well what was expected in handling 'their type of patients'. It was as if the physician were to say 'do the usual things' (they sometimes did) – little additional instruction being needed. We ourselves coined the term 'house special' (as opposed to '*à la carte*') treatment, to indicate that a patient could be assigned to these wards and handled by the ward staff without the physician either giving special instructions or asking for special favours. However, an original period of coaching the nurses and of reaching understandings was necessary. Consequently when personnel leave, for vacations or permanently, then arrangements must be instituted anew. Even with house special treatment, some discussion will be required, since not every step of the patient's treatment can be imagined ahead of time. The nurses are adept (as in non-psychiatric hospitals) at eliciting information from the physician about his patient; they are also adept both in forcing and fostering agreements about action vis-à-vis his patient. We have watched many a scene where the nurse negotiates for such understandings, as well as many staff meetings that the nurses and aides consciously convert into agencies for bringing recalcitrant physicians to terms. When physicians choose, they can be equally concerned with reaching firm agreements and understandings.

It is important that one realizes that these agreements do not occur by chance, nor are they established between random parties. They are, in the literal sense of the word, patterned. Thus, the somatically oriented physicians have long-standing arrangements with a secretary who is attached to the two wards upon which their patients tend to be housed; this secretary does a variety of jobs necessitated by these physicians' rather medical orientation. The more psycho-therapeutically minded physicians scarcely utilize her services. Similarly, the head nurses and the administrative residents attached to each ward reach certain kinds of understandings and agreements, which neither tends to establish with any other type of personnel. These latter agreements are less in evidence when the resident is new; then the nurse in some helplessness turns to the next highest administrative officer, making yet other contracts. Again, when an attending physician is especially physician is especially recalcitrant, both resident and nurse's aide seek to draw higher administrators into the act, negotiating for support and increased power. This kind of negotiation occurs with great predictability: for instance, certain physicians because of their particular philosophies of treatment use the hospital in certain ways; consequently, their programmes are frequently troublesome for the house staff, who must then seek to spin a network of negotiation around the troublesome situation. When the ward is in high furore, then negotiative activity of course is at its most visible!

In sum: there is a patterned variability of negotiation in the hospital pertaining to who contracts with whom, about what, as well as when these agreements are made. Influencing this variability are hierarchical position and ideological commitments, as well as periodicities in the structure of ward relationships (for instance, because of a rotational system that moves personnel periodically on and off given wards).

It is especially worth emphasizing that negotiation – whether characterised as 'agreement', 'understanding', 'contract', 'compact', 'pact' or by some other term – has a temporal aspect, whether that aspect is stated specifically or no by the contracting parties. As one listens to agreements being made in the hospital, or watches understandings being established, he becomes aware that a specific termination period, or date line, is often written into the agreement. Thus a physician after being accosted by the head nurse – who may in turn also be responding to her own personnel – may agree to move his patient to another ward after this specific ward has agreed 'to try for two more days'. What he is doing is issuing to its personnel a promissory note that if things don't work out satisfactorily, he will move his patient. Sometimes the staff breaks the contract, if the patient is especially obstreperous or if tempers are running especially high, and transfers the patient to another ward behind the back of the physician. However, if the patient does sufficiently better, the ward's demands may subside. Or, interestingly, it often happens that later both sides will negotiate further, seeking some compromise: the staff, for instance, wishing to restrict the patient's privileges or to give him stronger drug prescriptions, and the physician giving in on these issues to gain some ends of his own. On less tender and less specific grounds, the physician and the head nurse may reach nodding agreement that a new patient should be handled in certain ways 'until we see how he responds'. Thus there exists a continuum running from specific to quite non-specific termination dates. But even those explicit and long-term permissions that physicians give to nurses in all hospitals – such as to administer certain drugs at night without bothering to call upon the physicians – are subject to review and withdrawal along with later qualified assent.

It should be added that the very terms 'agreements' and 'understandings' and 'arrangements' – all used by hospital personnel – point out that some negotiations may be made with full explicitness, while others may be established by parties who have scarcely talked. The more implicit or tacit kinds of contracts tend to be called 'understandings'. The difference can be highlighted by the following contrasting situations: when a resident suggests to a nurse that an established house rule temporarily be ignored, for the good of a given patient, it may be left implicit in their arrangement that he must bear the punishment if administration discovers their common infraction. But the nurse may make this clause more explicit by demanding that he bear the possible public guilt, otherwise she will not agree to the matter. It follows that some agreements can be both explicit and specific as to termination, while others are explicit but non-specific as to termination, and so on. What might be referred to as 'tacit understandings' are likely to be those that are neither very specific nor very explicitly discussed. When a physician is not trusted, the staff is likely to push him for explicit directives with specific termination clauses.

Negotiation, appraisal and organizational change

We come now to the full import of the above discussion, for it raises knotty problems about the relationships that exist between the current negotiated order and genuine organizational change. Since agreements are patterned and temporal, today's sum total of agreements can be visualized as different from tomorrow's – and surely as quite different from next week's. The hospital can be visualized as a place where numerous agreements are continually being terminated or forgotten, but also as continually being established, renewed, reviewed, revoked, revised. Hence at any moment those that are in effect are considerably different from those that were or will be.

Now a sceptic, thinking in terms of relatively permanent or slowly changing structure might remark that from week to week the hospital remains the same – that only the working arrangements change. This contention only raises the further question of what relationship exists between today's working agreements and the more stable structure (of rules, statuses and so on).

With an eye on practicality, one might maintain that no one knows what the hospital 'is' on any given day unless he has a comprehensive grasp of what combination of rules and policies, along with agreements, understandings, pacts, contracts, and other working arrangements, currently obtains. In any pragmatic sense, this is the hospital at the moment: this is its social order. Any changes that impinge upon this order – whether something ordinary like a new staff member, a disrupting event, a betrayed contract; or whether unusual, like the introduction of a new technology or a new theory – will call for renegotiation or reappraisal, with consequent change in the organizational order. [. . .]

Summary and implications

The model presented has pictured the hospital as a locale where personnel, mostly but not exclusively professionals, are enmeshed in a complex negotiative process in order both to accomplish their individual purposes and to work – in an established division of labour – toward clearly as well as vague phrased institutional objectives. We have sought to show how differential professional training, ideology, career and hierarchical position all affect the negotiation. [. . .] We have outlined important relationships between daily working arrangement and the more permanent structure.

[. . .]

But what of other organizations, especially if sizeable or complex – is this kind of interactional model also relevant to them? The answer, we suggest, is strongly in the affirmative. Current preoccupation with formal organization tends to underplay – or leave implicit – the interactional features underscored in the foregoing pages. Yet one would expect interactional features to jump into visibility once looked for systematically. We urge that whenever an organization possesses one or more of the following characteristics, such a search be instituted: if the organization, first of all utilizes personnel trained in several different occupations, or secondly, if each contains an occupational group including individuals trained in different traditions, then they are likely to possess somewhat different occupational philosophies, emphasizing somewhat different values; then also if at least some personnel are professionals, the latter are likely to be pursuing careers that render them mobile – that is, carrying them into and out of the organization. The reader should readily appreciate why those particular characteristics have been singled out. They are, of course, attributes of universities, corporations, and government agencies, as well as of hospitals. If an organization is marked by one or more of those characteristics, then the concept of 'negotiated order' should be an appropriate way to view it.

References

Caudill, W. et al. (1952) 'Social structure and interaction processes on a psychiatric ward', *American Journal of Orthopsychiatry*, 22: 314–34.

Goffman, E. (1957) 'On the characteristics of total institutions', *Proceedings of the Symposium on Preventive and Social Psychiatry*, Walter Reed Army Institute of Research.

Goffman, E. (1959) 'The moral career of the mental patient', *Psychiatry*, 22: 123–42.

Mead, G. H. (1936) 'The problem of society – how we become selves', in *Movements of Thought in the Nineteenth Century*. Chicago: University of Chicago Press.

Parsons, T. and Fox, R. (1952) 'Illness, therapy, and the modern urban American family', *Journal of Social Issues*, 7: 31–44.

The Practicalities of Rule Use

DON ZIMMERMAN*

[. . .]

This chapter examines certain aspects of the work activities of [. . .] bureaucratic actors in a public assistance organization. Drawing on observational materials collected in the setting, it describes in detail the work of reception personnel in inducting applicants for public assistance into the organizational routine. The analysis is concerned particularly with the judgemental work of receptionists in employing a procedure for assigning applicants to intake case-workers.

This study reported here, [. . .] is to investigate the variety of practices and mundane considerations involved in determinations of the operational meaning and situational relevance of policies and procedures for ongoing, everyday organizational activities. The ways in which this concern contrasts with the traditional viewpoint may be clarified by reference to the considerations below.

Numerous studies of formal organizations have found that some significant portion of the observed practices of bureaucrats are not easily reconciled with the investigator's understanding of what the formally instituted rules and policies dictate. Bureaucrats, in conducting their ordinary everyday affairs in organizations, have been seen in study after study to honour a range of formally, extraneous considerations in making decisions and concerting actions. The asserted contrasts between theory and practice reported by organizational studies are so commonplace that documentation seems hardly necessary.

[. . .]

It is typically the case that the issue of what [. . .] rules mean to, and how they are used by, personnel on *actual occasions* of bureaucratic work is ignored as an empirical issue. For the investigator to make decisions about rules without clarifying the basis of such decisions – particularly without reference to how

* Routledge & Keegan and Paul and Aldine Press for Zimmerman, D. (1971) 'The practicalities of rule use', in J. Douglas (ed.), *Understanding Everyday Life*.

personnel make such decisions – invites the treatment of rules as idealizations, possessing stable operational meanings invariant to the exigencies of actual situations of use, and distinct from the practical interests, perspective and interpretative practices of the rule user. [. . .]

It is sometimes argued by students of organization that rules and policies are to some degree abstract and general, and hence by their very nature incapable of completely encompassing the perversely contingent features of manifold and changing organizational situations. This conception would seem to speak to the concerns of this chapter.

However, this 'defect' of rules is typically dealt with by proposing that informal rules and policies develop in response to this lacuna that warrant modification, redefinition or circumvention of the formal rules by personnel in light of operating conditions. Invoking one set of rules to account for the interpretation of another set dodges the issue.

In addition, this line of reasoning would propose that whatsoever patterned conduct is observed, it is formulable as conduct in accord with *some* rule. This view slights the question of *what it takes* to warrant the application of any rule – formal or informal – in concrete situations, thus failing to address as a crucial problem the judgemental processes that members must use to employ rules on relevant occasions.

A related issue of interest here is the way in which 'departures' from the formal organizational plan are dealt with. It has been consistently found that bureaucrats [. . .] are keenly attuned to a number of practical matters at hand as these are grasped as constraints or facilities, justifications or contra-indications, resources or troubles in the course of pursuing bureaucratic work. Indeed, these practical matters often seem to be critical elements informing the bureaucrats' use of the rules, resources and formal arrangements of the organization.

Investigators typically invoke such features of the bureaucrats' circumstances, and their situationally enforced interests in coming to terms with them, in order to account for the asserted discrepancy between the formally ordained and observed 'actual' state of organization affairs. These circumstances are often conceived to be obstacles – or problems to be solved – on the way to rational goal accomplishment. [. . .]

The problem that concerns this chapter is how the formal plan of an organization (or some aspect of it) is used by the organization's members to deal with everyday work activities. What are the features [. . .] that members use to recognize, to interpret, and to instruct others about the operational intent and behavioural implications of such a plan? Thus conceived, the problem dictates, first of all, that the relationship of the formal plan to actual conduct be investigated with specific reference to how members of the organization reconcile the two on a day-to-day basis. This approach [. . .] consists in entertaining the possibility that these circumstances may in fact be consulted by bureaucrats in order to decide what the formal plan might reasonably be taken to mean and 'what it would take' to implement it in the first instance.

This argument is not to be taken to mean that rule violations do not occur, or that bureaucrats might not respect alternative informal rules in doing their work [. . .] . The point is that the issue of what rules, policies and goals mean for the bureaucratic actor upon the concrete occasion of their use (for example, to guide, to account for or to justify action) must be treated as problematic. In accordance with this view, the major assumption guiding the present endeavour is that the relationship of such idealizations to conduct may be found only by investigating the features of the circumstances in which they are deemed relevant and used by members.

Following a brief discussion of the setting of the study, receptionists' use of an intake assignment procedure will be described in detail. This procedure is examined within its organizational context, with close attention paid to the features of actual occasions of its use and the contingencies encountered upon these occasions. Analysis will suggest that the operational import of formal rules and organizational policy (of which the assignment procedure is an instance) is decided by personnel on a case-by-case basis and warranted on 'reasonable grounds'.

It will be argued that the 'reasonableness' of such decisions, from the point of view of personnel, relies upon a taken-for-granted grasp of, and implicit reference to, the situated practical features of task activity (actual task structure). [. . .]

The setting

The study was conducted in one district office of the Metropolitan County Bureau of Public Assistance, located in a large western state. In broad terms, the Bureau – like other public assistance organizations in the country – administers several programmes of federal-state financed assistance (Aid to Families with Dependent Children or AFDC, etc.) as well as a county financed 'residual' programme (GA, or General Assistance), which provides for those persons not meeting the eligibility criteria of the categoric aids.

Administration of these programmes requires an investigation of the applicant's circumstances in order to provide a 'factual' basis for determining need and entitlement to assistance under the provisions of the several categories. In the Metropolitan County Bureau this responsibility is discharged by the intake division.

Once certified as eligible, the applicant comes under the supervision of the 'approved' division. The routine administration of the case, including periodic reinvestigation of the applicant's eligibility for assistance, is the responsibility of this division.

Within the 'Lakeside Office' of the Bureau (one of several district offices in the county) the inquiry was focused upon the day-to-day operation of the intake function. Concentration on the work activities of intake personnel led as a matter of course to observation of the work done by reception. Just as the approved worker's caseload is assembled by virtue of the work of the intake worker in certifying eligibility, so the intake worker's investigation is preceded by the work of reception-ists in pre-processing new applications for assistance. A discussion of the reception function follows.

The reception function

A major responsibility of reception (and a prominent concern of receptionists) is to provide for the orderly and appropriately paced pre-processing of applicants for public assistance and their assignment to an intake case-worker, who investigates their claim and decides its merit. As accomplished work, pre-processing and assignment appear to be contingent upon receptionists' performance of a series of related tasks that may be referred to as the 'steps' in the reception process.

These steps involve, but are not exhausted by, screening persons entering the office (determining the business bringing the person 'in'), categorizing those persons discovered to be new applicants for public assistance as one or another type of application (as AFDC or GA, etc.), collecting preliminary information relevant to the subsequent processing of the application (name, age, residence data, etc.), generating and updating records (providing for the initiation of or search for a previous dossier on the applicant) and, at the terminus of these activities, assigning the applicant to an intake worker, accomplished by use of a procedure operationalizing the maxim, 'first come, first served'.

Assignment by this procedure is effected by the use of an intake book, a looseleaf binder the pages of which are ruled to form a matrix. One axis of the matrix represents the order in which the panel of intake workers on duty on a given day are to receive assignments; the other axis represents the order of assignments for a given worker (typically six in total). By use of the rule, top to bottom, left to right, in that order (that is, the 'next available cell'), applicants are assigned to the cells in the order in which their processing was initiated. The execution of the procedure as described above, invariant to any situational exigencies may be termed a literal [. . .]

From the vantage point of an observer not involved in the work process of reception, the execution of these steps has the appearance of a busy but nonetheless orderly round of activities. Applicants (and others) coming into the office appear to be integrated into the reception process in a matter-of-course way.

The routine character of the process will be seen to be one of its most salient features, one to which receptionists orient and, by their management of work activities, seek to preserve. That is, receptionists (and other personnel as well) orient to the management of the day's work so as to provide for the defensible claim that it was accomplished in sufficient-for-all-practical-purposes accord with rule and policy. 'Sufficient for all practical purposes' may be taken to mean the judgement by competent and entitled persons in the setting that the work was acceptably done, forgiving what may be forgiven, ignoring what may be ignored, allowing for what may be allowed based on both tacit and explicit understandings of such matters *in light of* 'what anyone knows' about the practical circumstances of work in general and on particular occasions.

The practical circumstances of work may be encountered in such things as the receptionists' fond hope that applicants *will* conduct themselves properly, their sure knowledge that *some* will not, and the often demanding task of dealing with the 'oddballs' and 'troublemakers' in the context of an ongoing work routine.

That the process is to be kept ongoing is itself a practical feature of the work. To keep things moving requires continual attention to such matters as scheduling and co-ordinating the activities of applicants, receptionists and caseworkers. The receptionist must avoid, insofar as possible, marked disruptions or 'hitches' in the flow of work and at the same time be able to defend if necessary the sanctionable relationship of her practices on achieving the above to the rules and policies of the organization to which these practices are accountable.

In order to examine how the receptionist, as an everyday accomplishment, achieves the reasonable reconciliation of the formal programme of the organization with the practical features of doing work *in* the organization, it is necessary to examine in more detail what will be called the 'actual task structure' of reception. This term refers to the variety of problematic features generated by the attempt to put into practice a programmatically specified task such as that of receptionists outlined above.

Actual task structure in reception

TEMPORAL FEATURES The temporal-co-ordinative contingencies of the reception process are inadequately depicted by speaking of the task as a series of steps, or a 'first this and then that' matter. From the perspective of a given applicant, the process may perhaps have this appearance (first, the initial contact, then the collection of preliminary information, and so on). For the receptionists, however, these steps are discontinuous with respect to each applicant. That is, step one of the process may take place for one applicant at a given time, step two somewhat later, and so on, with the various steps in the processing of other applicants intervening.

The steps in the process for receptionists are thus interspersed over an aggregate of applicants. Reception activities consist in multiple dealings with a set of applicants, imbedded in a sequence of varying maturity, in constant motion, fitted together according to present circumstances and future prospects, and paced with respect to the ebb and flow of applicants in and out of the doors.

Viewed in this light, the appearance of the activities (to an observer or to organization personnel themselves) as a timely and orderly steplike execution of the various phases of the preprocessing and assignment routines is provided for by the work of receptionists in attending to and managing such problems as matching the pace of work to the current demand (the number of applicants – and others – requesting service at a given time) in terms of their practical interests in moving applicants through the process with reasonable speed and a minimum of difficulty.

TROUBLES AND CONSEQUENCES Receptionists' practical interests in the trouble-free development of the workday reflect their knowledge that things sometimes go awry and that they are accountable to others in the setting for their efforts to manage the course of work, to minimize disruptions and control departures from routines. As indicated above, close attention to timing and scheduling are critical features of the receptionists' task of making the workday 'come out right'.

Receptionists were seen to monitor the flow of work with the explicit concern that it be done by a certain time. Accomplishment of the latter required management of such matters as the timely 'closing' of intake, that is, cutting off the processing of new applications so that no excess of applicants awaiting interviews over case-workers available to interviews occurs at the end of the day.

A consideration adding urgency to concerns about timing and co-ordination is the proper utilization of the case-worker as a resource. It is the case-worker's expeditious completion of the intake interview that moves the applicant out of the office completing the process. On the part of the receptionists, 'proper' utilization requires prompt preparation of each applicant for assignment, the promptness gaining its particular temporal specification by reference to the pressing of demands and available resources at the time. The dispatch with which case-workers complete assigned interviews is a factor over which receptionists apparently have little direct control. The occurrence of an inordinately lengthy interview may be potentially troublesome for receptionists, as will be seen in the following section.

Actual task structure and competent rule use

The intake assignment procedure

The 'literal' application of the intake assignment procedure was defined above as the employment of the 'next available cell' rule invariant to any exigencies of the actual situation of use. However, as might be expected, this literal usage was not maintained in every instance of an assignment of an application to an intake worker. If the literal-use model is posited as the 'proper' use of the rule, other alternatives would have to be designated as deviations. As was indicated in the introduction, use of such a model would put out of account any exercise of judgement by the rule user, and leave as unproblematic the empirical issue of what the rule intends and how its operational sense is discovered by attempts to employ it in actual situations.

The task taken here will be to examine such 'deviations' (detectable by reference to the literal-use model) as possibly competent 'uses' of the rule by personnel employing judgements based upon their understanding of the features of the actual situation of use and the practicalities of action in the setting. Two instances of 'deviation' will be analysed.

CASE I A third intake was about to be assigned to worker Jones. At this time, Jones was engaged in conducting an interview with her *first* assigned applicant. From the point of view of receptionists, this interview was presumed to have posed unusual problems since it had not been completed at the time a third assignment was contemplated.

A receptionist commented, in connection with the present case:

> The biggest problem is keeping these people moving. Jones had her first assignment, well, shortly after 8:00 a.m. [It was 10:30 a.m. at this time.] She hasn't picked up her second and here is a third.

At 11:20 a.m., almost an hour after its assignment, the third intake had yet to be picked up. A receptionist called Jones's unit clerk and informed her that 'there's a woman out here who has been waiting a long time'. She was told that Jones was conducting an interview (the assignment). This call had been occasioned by the third applicant's expressed anxiety that she was going to miss a 12:30 doctor's appointment. The receptionist who made the call remarked, 'If she has a doctor's appointment at 12:30 she's not going to make it at the rate Jones is going.'

The senior receptionist then decided that the third applicant would be switched to another worker. The switch entailed a discussion among receptionists concerning which worker to assign her to, as well as taking the next assignment of the worker receiving Jones's case and assigning it to her. The change also required alternation in the intake book and changes in certain other records. The potential third intake of Jones in fact assigned to another worker, thereby 'suspending' the rule. That the suspension was observable as such may be seen in a receptionist's comment at that time that the 'skipped turn' was not 'fair'.

It is proposed here that this suspension be understood in terms of the actual task structure of the reception function. Reception, as depicted above, is a temporally complex system of activities. The prevailing emphasis is placed upon the rapid accomplishment of the pre-processing given case. The concern, aptly expressed by a receptionist, is to 'keep people moving'.

The case reported here posed a dilemma, since it represented a 'snag' upon which several cases were caught. The snag was in part structured into the situation by the intake assignment rule itself, which provided of that each case was taken in order under a literal application. The smoothness with which this literal application effects the movement of applicants out of the office is contingent on the dispatch with which intake workers could accomplish the initial interview. Hence, the rule's capacity (literally applied) to achieve the objective of orderly and rapid processing is contingent upon the intake worker's system of relevances in conducting an interview, which are not necessarily congruent with that of reception, hence, disjuncture is guaranteed for *some* portion of the cases, which may lead to situations of the sort documented above.

One solution to such situations of course, is to maintain the priority of the next available cell rule. Apparently, from the point of view of the receptionist who made the decision, the rule could be suspended and the suspension deemed a 'reasonable' solution to the minor dilemma the situation presented.

The critical consideration here is the fact that the literal application of the assignment rule is apparently deemed adequate most of the time to deal with the typical applicant. Processing, from the point of view of receptionists, proceeds in a routine fashion most of the time. This *sense* of routineness provides receptionists a way to recognize the exceptional character of a given event and, thereby, the good grounds for suspending or otherwise modifying the rule as normally applied. That the use of the rule 'typically' effects the expected outcome, that, 'typically', applicants do not 'stack up' in this fashion, and that for most situations only the most commonplace and regular considerations need be entertained, constitutes the receptionists' sense of an organizationally normal state of affairs.

By suspending the rule in light of the exceptional character of the situation, the intent of the rule might be said to be honoured – its intent being formulable on a particular occasion by situational relevant reference to the 'usual' course of affairs its routine or precedented use typically reproduces. Through the situated judgemental modification of the routine application of the rule, the 'same' business as usual course of affairs may be – for all intents and purposes – reliably reproduced.

In other words, what the rule is intended to provide for is discovered in the course of employing it over a series of actual situations. The use of a procedure, in the way that it is used, generates the state of affairs that, when things go wrong, may be referred to as the end in view 'all along'. For example, the attempt to use a procedure in a given situation may produce an array of troubles that motivate alterations in the manner in which the rules are put into practice, in turn affecting the state of affairs generated. The modification established, the resultant outcomes (if less troublesome) might then be invoked or assumed to argue what the rule intended 'all along' if an issue subsequently arose around what the rule 'really' calls for by way of action.

It may then be argued that the above *kinds* of considerations provide for the receptionist a   reasonable solution for the dilemma confronted. The present argument, however, is not intended to argue the receptionist's case for her, thereby 'justifying' her decisions. The point is rather that receptionists appear to employ such considerations as justifications for the reasonableness of the action. By deciding to suspend the rule in *this* instance of its potential application, the intent of the rule was apparently not seen to be violated. Furthermore, in finding such modifications to be 'reasonable', receptionists appear to provide for ways to ensure that the continuing accomplishment of the normal pacing and minor flow of work may be reconciled with their view of these task activities *as governed by rules*, in this instance, the intake assignment procedure.

If this is generally the case, then it would seem that the notion of action-in-accord-with-a-rule is a matter not of compliance or non-compliance *per se* but of the various ways in which persons *satisfy* themselves and others concerning what is or is not 'reasonable' compliance in particular situations. Reference to rules might then be seen as a commonsense method of accounting for or making available for talk the orderly features of everyday activities, thereby *making out* these activities as orderly in some fashion. Receptionists, in accomplishing a for all practical purposes ordering of their task activities by undertaking the 'reasonable' reconciliation of particular actions with 'governing rules' may thus sustain their sense of 'doing good work' and warrant their further actions on such grounds.

CASE 2 The following incident appears anomalous in terms of the preceding discussion. Here, contrary to the implications of the analysis thus far, a suspension of the rule of assignment was apparently allowed for reasons of 'personal preference' rather than for practical work considerations.

A GA case was prepared by 10:10 a.m. of the same day as the incident reported above. It was assigned to worker Hall at 10:16 a.m. At the same time an OAA case was assigned to worker Kuhn. Several minutes after this, the investigator noted that Hall had taken the OAA case and Kuhn the GA assignment. What had transpired was the intervention of the OAA applicant who specifically requested that Hall process her case.

Here again the rule was suspended. The same senior receptionist had permitted the previous suspension on the grounds of exigent circumstances connected with the routine processing of cases allowed the 'switch' even though, strictly speaking, a disruption of the normal pacing of work was not immediately at issue. She was considerably more circumspect in permitting the suspension, commenting 'We don't do this very often. They're not supposed to get a case just because they want it.'

It may first be noted that this suspension has an illegitimate character to it. By this is meant that it was so treated by the receptionist, even though allowed. If this is the case, why did the receptionist not stand by the rule?

In answer to this problem, it is proposed here that single instances of illegitimate suspension *may* be allowed simply in order to avoid confrontation of the issue of procedural correctness, particularly when 'making an issue of it' might involve a dispute between the receptionists, the worker *and* the applicant. Note that in allowing the impropriety it was cast in terms of a 'one time only' exception. Further, the switch was occasioned by an applicant's specific request: to deny it 'might' have required confrontation of both the applicant and the worker. What is more, the switch was arranged between the two workers, with consent given by both to the change. It is suggested that what is entailed in a circumstance of this sort is a permissiveness in the interest of avoiding difficulties and getting on with the work.

The burden of the preceding argument has been that receptionists orient to a normal course of affairs and seek by their action to guarantee its continuing reproduction. Such an orientation requires judgemental work on the part of receptionists in the use of procedures to effect such results, since contingent circumstance may sometimes render the literal use of such rules inappropriate, that is, the actions that could ordinarily be reconciled with the literal use would lead to 'trouble' – potential or actual. One such circumstance is 'occasional deviance'. By this is meant those instances wherein something recognized as illegitimate in the situations is proposed or encountered, and where such deviance may be permitted to stand by virtue of the explicit provision for its non-precedential character – simply to sidestep possible resistance (and the troubles it might bring) to enforcement of the 'proper' procedure.

It is a moot point whether or not the receptionist's insistence on adherence to the procedure would have generated a serious dispute. The fact remains that she did not so insist, even though she gave clear indication of disapproval. At least two alternative accounts are available. The first would be to assign the instance to a defect in the motivation of the receptionist to enforce the 'legitimate' ordering of events. The second is to refer the permissiveness to the receptionists' interests in preserving the routine flow of work in the setting. Allowance for occasional deviance would appear to be consistent with this latter interest. . . . From the point of view of receptionists, the steps of the reception process, including the use of intake assignment procedure typically achieve the desired outcomes. That is, for all practical purposes, and for most of the time, receptionists are able to co-ordinate applicants (who typically co-operate) and bring off the day's work with respect to even the constraints of timing, pacing and scheduling represented by the described 'actual task structure'. For receptionists, these outcomes are typically effected in an acceptable fashion by actions that are describable by them as in accordance with rules. This provides for the receptionists' sense of, and way of accounting for, normal everyday routine affairs in the setting. Further, these routine affairs are looked to by receptionists to decide what the rule or procedure is 'up to' after all.

On a more general level, it appears that the 'competent use' of a given rule or a set of rules is founded upon members' practical grasp of what particular actions are necessary on a given occasion to provide for the regular reproduction of a 'normal' state of affairs. A feature of the member's grasp of his everyday affairs is his knowledge, gained by that experience, of the typical but unpredictable occurrence of situational exigencies that threaten the production of desired outcomes. Often, troubles develop over which little control is possible, save to restore the situation as well as possible. Certain exigencies may be dealt with on an ad hoc basis and others may be provided for systematically.

The use of formally prescribed procedures viewed from the perspective of the notion of their 'competent use' thus becomes a matter not of compliance or deviance but of judgemental work providing for the reasonableness of viewing particular actions as *essentially* satisfying the provisions of the rule, even though the action may contrast with invocable precedent, with members' idealized versions of what kinds of acts are called for by the rule, or with the sociologists' ideas concerning the behavioural acts prescribed or proscribed by the rule.

Thinking in Organizations

S ection 3 moves our analysis to a different and more detailed level. There are three basic types or levels of explanation for the nature of decision-making *within* organizations. Two – politics and processes – were discussed in the previous section. A third type of explanation relates decision-making criteria, objectives and rationalities to shared ways of thinking within the organization. This is the subject matter of Section 3.

In the conclusion to Chapter 2 Valentin writes that some of the explanation of the 'fatal business strategy' is that '. . . past successes and ideological rigidities can foster dysfunctional inertia and mindsets.' He continues: 'The study centred on a strategy rooted largely in speculative and (predominantly false) analogies and conjectures that became so vivid and available during the planning process that their verity was eventually taken for granted without the benefit of serious objective inquiry' (see p. 58). And Cyert and March have noted that: '. . . when an organization discovers a solution to a problem by searching in a particular way, it will be more likely to search in that way in future problems of the same type . . .' (see p. 71).

These authors – and many others whose work has been presented earlier – are pointing to the issue that is discussed in this section: the ways in which structures of shared meanings within organizations impact on managers' decision-making. Organizations consist of structures of shared meaning. These influence how managers think; they offer common ways for defining and thinking about issues. Shared ways of thinking and shared moralities, prevalent within organizations describe how things are and how they should be and why they are (or why they are not as they should be). They play a major role in decision-making.

Simon has pointed out that people organize new data in terms of pre-existing schema and worldviews. The psychological limitations of individuals' capability for dealing with complexity and non-routine data and stimuli have been thoroughly plotted. Interest in organizations as sources of shared cognitive schema show how these schema influence perceptions, values and beliefs. Much recent research (much of it summarized in this section) has described the ways in which managers' shared cognitive constructs of the external world (markets, competition, industrial structure, etc.) are influenced by entrenched schemas. Managers learn to focus and minimize data processing time in order to achieve efficiencies but these routines may become counter-productive under new circumstances. Systems of organizational learning may lead to the application of shared cognitive routines and assumptions which are historically based but irrelevant for future success. 'As a result, the older, larger, and more successful organizations become, the more likely they are to have a large repertoire of structures and systems which discourage innovation while encouraging tinkering' (Van de Ven, 1986: 596). These are serious and daunting possibilities. That is the purpose of this section.

Reference

Van de Ven, A. (1986) 'Central problems in management of innovation', *Management Science*, 32(5): 590–607.

CHAPTER 9

Strategic Management in an Enacted World

LINDA SMIRCICH AND CHARLES STUBBART*

A major debate within organization theory and strategic management concerns whether environments are objective or perceptual phenomena. This chapter develops a third view – that environments are enacted through the social construction and interaction processes of organized actors. Although this view has been mentioned in some strategic management literature (Miles and Snow, 1978; Pfeffer and Salancik, 1978), its implications have not been explored adequately. This paper demonstrates that enactment implies distinctive strategic management models, new research questions, and different prescriptions for practitioners.

According to most strategic management literature, an organization is an open system that exists within an independently given environment (Thompson, 1967). The objective environment may be accurately or inaccurately perceived, but in either case the task of strategic managers is to maintain congruence between environmental constraints and organizational needs (Lawrence and Dyer, 1983). According to another perspective, derived from interpretive sociology, organizations are socially constructed systems of shared meaning (Burrell and Morgan, 1979; Pfeffer, 1981; Weick, 1979). Organization members actively form (enact) their environments through their social interaction. A pattern of enactment establishes the foundation of organizational reality, and in turn has effects in shaping future enactments. *The task of strategic management in this view is organization making – to create and maintain systems of shared meaning that facilitate organized action.*

The purpose here is not to argue the veracity of these differing perspectives on the organization–environment relationship and on strategic management.

* The Academy of Management for Smircich, L. and Stubbart, C. 'Strategic Management in an Enacted World', *Academy of Management Review*, 10(4). Copyright © 1985 by the Academy of Management. Reproduced with the permission of the Academy of Management in the format textbook via Copyright Clearance Center.

Instead, it is to show how an interpretive approach, with its different emphasis on what is important, can enrich and expand the theory, research, and practice of strategic management.

The potential contributions of an interpretive perspective are well-timed: many of the problems in strategic management – for example, failures in implementation (Kiechel, 1982) – seem to originate primarily in the field's inattention to the fundamentally *social* nature of the strategy formation and organizing processes.

Three models for knowing the environment

For any single 'organization,' the 'environmental' field contains an infinite number of situations and events, each of which could provide some material for environmental scanning. [. . .] Obviously, to consider every situation, event, condition, and so on, and furthermore, to evaluate the vast combinations of environmental relationships is far beyond the capacity of any imaginable method of environmental analysis. Yet, this is what seems to be required for effective strategic management. Somehow, the tidal wave of environmental data must be funneled down to a small pipeline of information. It is like analysing the world's oceans using a glass of water. How can strategic managers accomplish this feat? Three different models that represent ideal types for explaining how organized participants know their environments are offered here.

An objective environment

The words 'organization' and 'environment' create a dichotomy that profoundly shapes thinking about strategic management. This dichotomy clearly underlies the objective environment model which assumes that an 'organization' is embedded within an 'environment' that has an external and independent existence. 'Environments' constitute some thing or some set of forces to be adapted to, coaligned with, controlled, or controlled by. Terms that seem to capture this sense of 'environment' include concrete, objective, independent, given, imminent, out there.

The open system analogy provides a common way of thinking about the relationship between an 'organization' and its objective 'environment' (Miller, 1978; von Bertalanffy, 1968). The open system idea was originally derived from, and applied to, plant and animal communities, but the image of an organization-as-organism is now strongly entrenched in organizational studies (Keeley, 1980; Morgan, 1980). Much of the biologist's theory and language has been borrowed by organization theorists and strategic management theorists (e.g. adaptation, population ecology, the life cycle approach).

Nearly all strategic management research and writing incorporates the assumption that 'organization' and 'environment' are real, material, and separate – just as they appear to be in the biological world. Strategists search for opportunities or threats *in* the 'environment.' Strategists search for strengths and weaknesses *inside* an 'organization.' In the figures theorists draw, an 'organization' and its 'environment' occupy opposite ends of the arrows. This view emphasizes *recognition* of what already exists. Environmental analysis thus entails *discovery*, or finding things that are *already somewhere* waiting to be found. Strategy, naturally, is defined as the fit between an 'organization' and its 'environment.' Given this set of concepts, research proceeds directly to find the successful combinations of organization–strategy–environment.

Within the strategic management literature there is some disagreement about the nature of the relationship between 'organizations' and their 'environments.' Child (1972) emphasizes the importance of strategic choice – the powerful-organization theory. Child argues that organizations can select their environmental domains, that environmental forces are not so confining that they cannot be outflanked or sometimes even safely ignored. On the contrary, Aldrich (1979) maintains that most organizations flounder helplessly in the grip of environmental forces – the weak-organization theory. Aldrich believes that 'environments' are relentlessly efficient in weeding out any organization that does not closely align itself with environmental demands. He doubts that many organizations self-consciously change themselves very much or very often, or that the conscious initiatives by organizations are likely to succeed. Most researchers seem to place themselves somewhere between these polar views. *Despite the heated discussion, however, neither the strategic choicers, nor the environmental determinists, nor those in between, question the pivotal notion of environments as independent, external, and tangible entities.*

Therefore, a strategist must look out into the world to see what is there. Strategists function (in theory) like perfect information processors – able to access, organize, and evaluate data without mistakes. Strategists overcome the problem of deciding what information is worth bothering about by using frameworks or lists (Glueck, 1980; Hofer and Schendel, 1978; Porter, 1980). Within an objective 'environment,' a strategist faces an intellectual challenge to delineate a strategy that will meet the *real* demands and *real* constraints that exist 'out there.'

The perceived environment

The difference between objective 'environments' and perceived 'environments' is *not* attributable to a change in the conception of environment (which remains real, material, and external). Instead, the difference between objective and perceived environments involves a distinction about strategists. Strategists are permanently trapped by bounded rationality (Simon, 1957) and by their incomplete and imperfect perceptions of the 'environment.'

The idea of a perceived environment raises new problems. For now, research has to encompass the *real* external 'environment' *and* the partly mistaken beliefs of organizational strategists [. . .]. Acrimonious debates have cropped up around questions about how accurate perceivers are (or can be) and whether organization behavior is more responsive to the environmental perceptions of strategists or to the real, material, environment [. . .].

From a practical standpoint, the challenge for strategists, who must labor within the confines of flawed perceptions, is minimizing the gap between these flawed perceptions and the reality of their 'environment.'

The enacted environment

Recently, [. . .] another perspective vies for attention. Supporting the work of Mason and Mitroff (1981), Davis (1982), Huff (1982), and Peters (1978) is an assumption that organization and environment are created together (enacted) through the social interaction processes of key organizational participants. From an interpretive worldview, *separate objective* 'environments' simply do not exist (Burrell and Morgan, 1979). Instead, organizations and environments are convenient labels for patterns of activity. What people refer to as their environment is generated by human actions and accompanying intellectual efforts to make sense out of these actions. The character of this produced environment depends on the particular theories and frameworks, patterns of attention, and affective dispositions supplied by the actor–observers.

In an enacted environment model the world is essentially an ambiguous field of experience. There are no threats or opportunities out there in an environment, just material and symbolic records of action. But a strategist – determined to find meaning – makes relationships by bringing connections and patterns to the action.

The timeless practice of scanning the heavens in search of constellations provides an analogy. There is really no Big Dipper in the sky, although people find it useful to imagine that there is. People see the Big Dipper when they furnish imaginary lines to cluster and make sense of the stars. In finding constellations astronomers organize material reality (the stars) using their own imaginations to produce a symbolic reality (Orion, the Lion, etc.). The same is true for strategists. Physical phenomena (like stars) in a strategist's world are real and have an independent existence. The automobiles that roll off the production line in a day, the oil well that was either dry or a gusher, the number of missiles stockpiled by the enemy – these are surely material elements in the material world. By themselves, however, automobiles, oil wells, and missiles are meaningless, and they appear as random as the stars appear to an untrained eye. Strategists create imaginary lines between events, objects, and situations so that events, objects, and situations become meaningful for the members of an organizational world. The majority of many excellent top managers' time and effort goes into this interpretive process – drawing some imaginary lines so that the world of IBM, Hewlett-Packard, or 3M, for example, makes sense to employees and clientele (Peters and Waterman, 1982).

Enactment implies a combination of *attention and action* on the part of organizational members. Processes of action and attention differentiate the organization from not-the-organization (the environment). The action component often is poorly appreciated by theorists who discuss sensemaking processes. An enactment model implies that an environment of which strategists can make sense has been put there by strategists' patterns of action – not by a process of *perceiving* the environment, but by a process of *making* the environment. Consequently, the analogy of finding the constellations is partly an inadequate one for capturing the full scope of enactment. The analogy does not allow an emphasis on how the material records of action (e.g. automobile production, oil wells, missiles) have actually been put there by activities of organizational participants who *subsequently* interpret them. In other words, managers and other organization members create not only their organization, but also their environment.

In summary, theories involving objective or perceived 'environments' envision concrete, material 'organizations' that are within, but separate from, real material 'environments.' The relationships between the two are expressed in terms of cause and effect. On the other hand, enactment theory abandons the idea of concrete, material 'organizations/environments' in favor of a largely socially created symbolic world (Winch, 1958).

Organization and environment from an interpretive perspective

If one accepts the notion that people understand the world through bracketing and chunking experience into meaningful units (Schutz, 1967; Weick, 1979), it then follows that 'organizations' and 'environments' provide convenient, but also arbitrary, labels for some portions of experience. But no inherent rationale compels researchers to employ the everyday language and commonsense understanding of these terms in their analyses (Bittner, 1965). In fact, doing so misdirects one's attention. Misdirection occurs because analysts investigate concepts such as strategy, organization structure, standardization, and technology as if the concepts correspond to freestanding material entities. Researchers often ignore the metaphoric and symbolic bases of organized life that create and sustain these organizational ideas. An interpretive perspective places these processes and symbolic entities at the center of analysis.

To illustrate the differences in approach, consider an interpretive definition of organization. Organization is defined as the degree to which a set of people share many beliefs, values, and assumptions that encourage them to make mutually reinforcing interpretations of their own acts and the acts of others. Organization exists in this pattern of ongoing action–reaction ('interacts,' Weick, 1979) among social actors. For instance, the organization of the music industry rests in particular patterns of beliefs, values, and assumptions that support the ongoing creation, distribution, and enjoyment of the various forms of music. Thus, from an interpretive perspective, such organization is different from the everyday conceptualization of legally constituted 'organization,' and refers instead to a quality of interaction. Organization can extend across 'organizations.' Some 'organizations' are disorganized. From an interpretive perspective the interesting questions concern *how patterns of organization are achieved, sustained, and changed.*

Similarly, environment takes on a different meaning, and different questions are important. From an interpretive view the term environment refers only to a specific set of events and relationships noticed and made meaningful by a specific set of strategists. An interpretive perspective does not treat environment as separate objective forces that impinge on an organization. Instead, environment refers to the ecological context of thought and action, which is not independent of the observer–actor's theories, experiences, and tastes. Multiple groups of people enact the ecological context; neither historical necessity nor the operation of inexorable social laws imposes it on them. From the standpoint of strategic management, strategists' social knowledge constitutes their environment. An interpretive perspective on strategic management and the environment asks questions about *the processes of knowing* – those social processes that produce the rules by which an 'organization' is managed and judged.

Implications of an interpretive perspective

'Organization' and 'environment' are key concepts in the vocabulary of strategic management. The reconceptualization of these building block concepts that flows from an interpretive approach changes perspectives as well as words. The language through which people understand actions powerfully shapes future actions as well as the questions they are likely to ask about those actions. The logic of the interpretive perspective on organization and environment leads to three major implications for strategic management. It also has implications for the way we write research accounts. The editorial policies of journals work against interpretive modes of expression. A strong tradition in scientific writing has been the insistence on the third person and the passive voice. These depersonalize the arguments and lend an aura of 'objectivity' and 'consistency' to the research account. But the interpretive perspective highlights personal involvement with knowledge; it emphasizes that knowledge is standpoint dependent. An interpretive perspective aims to put the author back into the text, as one who *authorizes* the account. Our manuscript has been systematically edited; this has the effect of removing actors from the action and removing the sense of responsibility that comes from being included in the text – exactly what an interpretive perspective seeks to avoid.

ABANDONING THE PRESCRIPTION THAT ORGANIZATIONS SHOULD ADAPT TO THEIR ENVIRONMENTS The conventional wisdom of strategic management urges organizations to adapt to their environments. This taken-for-granted maxim is more problematic than it appears. It obscures a good deal of the complexity, ambiguity, and abstractness in the strategic management process.

When one theorizes from the present into the past as strategic analysts often do, one finds what seems to be a powerful argument about adaptation to an objective 'environment.' But the power of this explanation ends in the present. Although the argument about environmental adaptation may initially seem appealing, it does not provide much help for strategists in the here and now. The advice from much strategic management literature that stresses fit, congruence, and alignment is not sufficient for dealing with issues in day-to-day management. The executives in an industry cannot simply stand outside the action and adjust themselves to trends; their actions make the trends. Thus, if every firm rushes to take advantage of an opportunity. the opportunity vanishes. Trends are complex functions of multilateral behavior, making future outcomes problematic. The nature of what constitutes adaptation can be stated only *retrospectively*, never prospectively. Accordingly, the admonition to adapt to trends and forces is not very helpful.

[. . .]

Analysis of a firm's environment cannot aspire to the status of a science, because there are no independent, authoritative observers. Instead, the choice of frameworks and interpretations becomes a creative and political art. Strategists need to concentrate on their *choices* vis-à-vis frameworks and interpretations. Novel and interesting frameworks may stimulate novel and interesting environments that could in turn preface novel and interesting strategic initiatives.

RETHINKING CONSTRAINTS, THREATS, OPPORTUNITIES Managers face a tidal wave of situations, events, pressures, and uncertainties, and they naturally resort to collective discussion (in the broadest sense) to negotiate an acceptable set of relationships that provide satisfactory explanations of their social worlds. The scope and meaning of events are funneled down to manageable dimensions by formal and informal processes leading to industry wisdom. Huff (1982) points out that industry groups and other industry forums provide organized sensemaking mechanisms.

A corresponding problem occurs, however, when strategic managers, by holding untested assumptions, unwittingly collude to restrict their knowledge. They may suffer from 'collective ignorance' (Weick, 1979).

Evidence of the fragile nature of industry wisdom often draws attention (Cooper and Schendel, 1983). What everyone knows about an industry translates into an opportunity for those who do not know. Many, if not most, really novel and exciting new strategies that invade an industry, are perpetrated by outsiders who do not know the rules. [. . .]

These observations about the way social reality is formed in organizational settings suggest a powerful prescription for strategic managers. They must look first to themselves and their actions and inactions, and not to 'the environment' for explanations of their situations. Indeed, recent research on organizational crises (Nystrom and Starbuck, 1984; Starbuck, 1983) reveals that in many cases top managers' thinking patterns, not external environments, cause crises. As Karl Weick advises:

> If people want to change their environment, they need to change themselves and their actions – not someone else. . . . Problems that never get solved, never get solved because managers keep tinkering with everything but what they do. (Weick, 1979: 152)

Because of the temptation to assign convenient blame, the contributions of strategic management research should help managers reflect on the ways in which managers' actions create and sustain their particular organizational realities. With the development of a greater capacity for self-reflection, corporate officials, governmental policy-makers, and all organization members can examine and critique their own enactment processes. By maintaining a dual focus of attention – an ability to transcend the momentary situation in which they are entangled and to see and understand their actions within a system of meanings that is continually open to reflection and reassessment – strategic managers can challenge the apparent limits and test the possibilities for organizational existence.

THINKING DIFFERENTLY ABOUT THE ROLE OF STRATEGIC MANAGERS The enactment model places strategy makers in an entirely different role from that envisaged by the objective or perceived models. Environmental scanning in those models sends managers 'out' to collect facts and to amass an inventory of information (King and Cleland, 1978). A strategic manager is portrayed as a decision-formulator, an implementer of structure, and a controller of events who *derives* ideas from information.

The interpretive perspective, on the other hand, defines a strategist's task as an imaginative one, a creative one, an art. In the chaotic world, a continuous stream of ecological changes and discontinuities must be sifted through and interpreted. Relevant and irrelevant categories of experience must be defined. People make sense of their situation by engaging in an interpretive process that forms the basis for their *organized* behavior. This interpretive process spans both intellectual and emotional realms. Managers can strategically influence this process. They can provide a vision to account for the streams of events and actions that occur – a universe within which organizational events and experiences take on meaning. The best work of strategic managers inspires splendid meanings (Davis, 1982; Peters, 1978; Pfeffer, 1981; Pondy, 1976; Smircich and Morgan, 1982).

The juxtaposition of events and context, figure and ground, is one mechanism for the management of meaning. Through this process, strategists work in the background to construct the basis on which other people will interpret their own specific experiences. The interpretive background makes a difference because people use it to decide what is happening and to judge whether they are engaged in worthwhile activities or nonsense.

How can strategic managers generate the context for meaning in organizational life? A growing body of literature explains how the management-of-meaning can be accomplished through values and their symbolic expression, dramas, and language (Deal and Kennedy, 1982; Pfeffer, 1981; Pondy et al., 1983). Although researchers are aware of the powerful effects of some value/symbol systems (e.g. advertising), research has only just begun to explore how these processes occur in organizations, how symbolic realities change, and how symbolic realities may be manageable (Broms and Gahmberg, 1983; Peters, 1978). Nevertheless, many strategic managers probably can sharpen their strategic impact by gaining awareness of the less than obvious values/symbols that pervade their organizations.

[. . .]

Powerful language and metaphors set a tone, provide direction, and gain commitment. [. . .] Wise strategic managers take advantage of language, metaphors, and stories to convey their messages. They also pay attention to language, metaphors, and stories that originate elsewhere. [. . .]

Values, dramas, and language comprise the symbolic foundations that support the everyday prosaic realities of management information systems, hierarchy, incentive systems, and so on – the surface architecture of organizations. Until now, strategic managers have been taught to consider organizational design problems exclusively in terms of surface architecture. These conventional approaches to designing organized activity have been further restricted by focusing nearly all attention on intellectual (rather than emotional) issues and on massive, unremittant control (rather than imagination).

An interpretive approach, probing the subjective process of reality-building, redirects the strategic manager's attention toward deep images of organizational life. Strategic managers can improve their efforts – make them *more* strategic – by recognizing the powerful nature of those deep images and by consciously approaching this deeper level. The challenge to management research is to understand that world and to make such knowledge useful.

Following this advice would lead to a major reorientation of some strategic managers' thinking and behavior. Rather than concentrating on issues of product-market strategies, for example, a strategic manager would concentrate on process issues. Rather than concentrating on decisions or design of decision-making structures, a strategic manager would concentrate on the values, symbols, language, and dramas that form the backdrop for decision-making structures. Rather than confining themselves to the technical/intellectual aspects of organizational structures, many strategic managers would learn to express and to elaborate on the social/emotional basis for organizational life.

Managing in an enacted world

Given a world increasingly characterized by organized, rather than individual action, what guidelines can be derived from an interpretive perspective to aid those responsible for managing human affairs?

Managerial analysis

The idea of enactment underscores a view that one's own actions and the actions of others make an 'organization' and its 'environment.' Because of this sequence, environmental analysis is much less critical than managerial analysis. Managerial analysis means challenging the assumptions on which managers act and improving managers' capacity for self-reflection – seeing themselves as enactors of their world (Litterer and Young, 1981; Mason and Mitroff, 1981). This dual (active–reflective) posture toward action is difficult for managers to maintain. In fact, consultants often are called in to help organization members get a different perspective on what members are doing. Consultants state the obvious, ask foolish questions, and doubt – all of which helps organization members get outside of themselves. Management groups can institutionalize the role of 'wise fool' (Kegan, 1981) in order to provoke the capacity for critical self-examination.

Creation of context

The answers to such questions as 'Who are we? What is important to us? What do we do? and What don't we do? set the stage for strategy formulation. These questions elicit the values framework within which activity becomes meaningful. Current literature (Peters and Waterman, 1982) suggests that excellent companies have top management groups who can articulate clear value positions. [. . .]

Encouraging multiple realities

An interpretive perspective urges the consideration of multiple interpretations. But, in strategic management, multiple interpretations often are viewed as communication problems to be overcome by more information, rather than as a natural state of affairs.

Successful strategists have often contemplated the same facts that everyone knew, and they have invented startling insights (e.g. Ray Kroc and the hamburger restaurant chain, or Gene Amdahl's insight into the strategic inflexibility of IBM's pricing). Interesting enactments blossom when strategists draw out novel interpretations from prosaic facts. Quite often, novel interpretations occur when companies enter an industry for which they have no specific experience. They try out novel strategies that run counter to conventional assumptions [. . .].

Testing and experimenting

Every industry is saddled with a long list of do's and don'ts. These stipulated limits should be tested periodically. Enactment means action as well as thinking. [. . .] Assumptions about what is related to what, what works (or doesn't), what we can do (or can't), should be tested periodically by acting as if counter assumptions are viable (Weick, 1979). Strategists should learn to act ambivalently about what they know, so that they do not become straitjacketed by what they know. Learning compels forgetting. In fact, organizational wisdom may require continuous unlearning (Nystrom and Starbuck, 1984).

Managerial analysis, creation of context, encouraging multiple realities, and testing and experimenting are managerial principles derived from an interpretive worldview, recognizing that people enact their symbolic world. These principles of variety are largely ignored by approaches to strategic management that stress scanning of an objective/perceived environment, setting objectives, and manipulating managerial controls.

Can any reality be enacted?

This argument may seem to imply that people can enact any symbolic reality that they choose. In a limited sense the present authors are saying precisely that. Individual people occupy personal, subjective space – space in which intentions, meaning, and sensibility often are quite idiosyncratic – what the world means to *them*. And even those isolated lifeworlds can sometimes be transformed into social worlds [. . .]. But in this paper the special concern is with enactments in which numerous people collectively participate, in which people experience limits to what they can enact.

First, organized people often struggle within the confines of their own prior enactments. Patterns of enactment rooted in prior personal, organizational, and cultural experiences powerfully shape ongoing organizational and cultural options. Starbuck (1983) calls these patterns 'behavior programs' and emphasizes how past thinking gets concretized into standard operating procedures, job specifications, buildings contracts, and so on that take on the aura of objective necessity. Behavior programs – institutionalized as unwritten rules and taken for granted assumptions – seem to dictate how things are and must be done (Zucker, 1977). Changing these patterns requires people to intentionally forget some of what they know and to disbelieve some of what they believe. Depending on the weight of prior commitments, changing may seem risky, foolish, or taxing.

Secondly, enactment means thinking *and acting*. Enactments test one's physical, informational, imaginative, and emotional resources. Without sufficient resources (or without the ability to think imaginatively about what might constitute resources), one simply cannot support many conceivable enactments.

Finally, enactments may compete with each other. In an election, for example, the candidates struggle mightily to discredit an opposition candidacy. In a corporate context, various strategic initiatives compete in a similar fashion. For sizable organizational enactments to succeed, a critical mass of belief and acceptance must be reached. But reaching the critical mass depends on persuasion rather than objective factors.

For these reasons – prior enactments, problems with resources, and competing enactments – organizational enactment processes can be distinguished from fond hopes and castles in the air. [. . .]

Conclusion

Several writers in the field of organizational analysis and strategic management have raised questions about how strategists come to know their environments. Yet the implications of one legitimate answer to these questions – enactment – have not been fully examined. The implications of the enactment perspective for strategic managers given here are extensive and provocative:

1 The eclipse of the 'organization/environment' dichotomy

2 A different mode of strategic analysis

3 An entirely different role for the strategist from the role presently envisaged by most analysts

4 A different research focus

This message to researchers contends that more resources should be devoted to the study of the enactment processes of strategic managers, because these enactment processes form the invisible foundations supporting strategic choice. The role of an analyst is to show the practitioner how the practitioner's patterns for enacting environments can fundamentally alter the range of available choices. By displaying assumptions, beliefs, and norms, consultants/researchers can uncover practices trapping people in cycles of behavior that prohibit scrutiny of enactment processes. Researchers/consultants can facilitate examination of the reality-construction process and evoke possibilities for change.

What prevents one from doing interpretive analysis more frequently? Again, a general acceptance of a deceptively persuasive 'organization–environment' metaphor blinds one to the largely symbolic, social nature of organized life. That metaphor leads theorists to adapt the frame of reference of a focal organization or industry, rather than a perspective of an undisciplined environment enacted by multiple interest groups. Another contributing factor may be the tendency of strategic management researchers to identify closely with those whom they choose to study, so that researchers unquestioningly accept management's commonsense understanding of the environment as something that is 'out there.' An acceptance of 'organization–environment' fundamentally establishes a frame of reference guiding analyses along only certain paths.

This appeal to strategic managers asks that they begin to think of themselves as playwrights more than as heroes, as creators rather than as aligners. They could begin to think more about how they get to know what they know and think less about what they know. In addition, strategic managers may find that their most enduring strategic contributions rest with their unique roles as background-generators and context-composers, not on their direct roles as decision-makers and commanders.

It has been strongly argued here that a strategic analyst should guide the strategic practitioner toward critical self-examination. Similarly, the contribution of this chapter to the field of strategic management guides the field toward a critical examination of one of its major assumptions – the nature of the 'organizatian–environment' relationship. In either case, success should be measured only in terms of raising issues – not in terms of settling them.

References

Aldrich, H. E. (1979) *Organizations and Environments*, Englewood Cliffs, NJ: Prentice-Hall.

Bittner, E. (1965) 'The concept of organization', *Social Research*, 32: 239–55.

Broms, H. and Gahmberg, H. (1983) 'Communication to self in organization cultures', *Administrative Science Quarterly*, 28: 482–95.

Burrell, G. and Morgan, G. (1979) *Sociological Paradigms and Organizational Analysis*. London: Heinemann.

Child, J. (1972) 'Organizational structure, environment and performance: the role of strategic choice', *Sociology*, 6: 1–22.

Cooper, A. C. and Schendel, D. (1983) 'Strategic responses to technological threats', in D. J. McCarthy (ed.), *Business policy and strategy: Concepts and Readings*. Homewood, IL: Irwin. pp. 207–219.

Davis, S. M. (1982) 'Transforming organizations: the key to strategy is context', *Organizational Dynamics*, 3 (10): 64–80.

Deal, T. E. and Kennedy, A. A. (1982) *Corporate Cultures*. Reading, MA: Addison-Wesley.

Glueck, W. F. (1980) *Business Policy and Strategic Management*. New York: McGraw-Hill.

Hofer, C. and Schendel, D. E. (1978) *Strategy Formulation: Analytical Concepts*. St. Paul, MN: West.

Huff, A. S. (1982) 'Industry influences on strategy reformulation', *Strategic Management Journal*, 3: 119–31.

Keeley, M. (1980) 'Organizational analogy: a comparison of organismic and social contract models', *Administrative Science Quarterly*, 25: 337–62.

Kegan, D. L. (1981) 'Contradictions in the design and practice of an alternative organization: the case of Hampshire College,' *Journal of Applied Behavioral Science*, 17(1): 79–97.

Kiechel, W., III. (1982) 'Corporate strategists under fire', *Fortune*, 27 December: 35–9.

King, W. R. and Cleland, D. I. (1978) *Strategic Planning and Policy*. New York: Van Nostrand Reinhold.

Lawrence, P. and Dyer, D. (1983) *Renewing American Industry*. New York: Free Press.

Litterer, J. A. and Young, S. (1981) 'The development of managerial reflective skills. *Proceedings of Northeast American Institute for Decision Sciences*, Boston, MA. pp. 71–4.

Mason, R. O. and Mitroff, I. I. (1981) *Challenging Strategic Planning Assumptions: Theory Cases and Techniques*. New York: Wiley Inter-Science.

Miller, J. G. (1978) *Living Systems*. New York: McGraw-Hill.

Miles, R. E. and Snow, C. C. (1978) *Organizational Strategy, Structure and Process*. New York: McGraw-Hill.

Morgan, G. (1980) 'Paradigms, metaphors, and puzzle solving in organization theory', *Administrative Science Quarterly*, 25: 605–22.

Nystrom, P. C. and Starbuck, W. H. (1984) 'To avoid organizational crises, unlearn', *Organizational Dynamics*, 4(12): 53–65.

Peters, T. J. (1978) 'Symbols, patterns and settings: an optimistic case for getting things done', *Organizational Dynamics*, 2(7): 3–23.

Peters, T. J. and Waterman, R. (1982) *In Search of Excellence*. New York: Harper & Row.

Pfeffer, J. (1981) 'Management as symbolic action: the creation and maintenance of organizational paradigms', in L. L. Cummings and Barry M. Staw (eds), *Research in Organizational Behavior*, Vol. 3. Greenwich, CT: JAI Press. pp. 1–52.

Pfeffer, J. and Salancik, G. R. (1978) *The External Control of Organizations: A Resource Dependence Perspective*. New York: Harper & Row.

Pondy, L. R. (1976) 'Leadership is a language game', in M. McCall and M. Lombardo (eds), *Leadership: Where else can we go?* Durham, NC: Duke University Press. pp. 87–98.

Pondy, L. R., Frost, P., Morgan G. and Dandridge, T. (1983) *Organizational Symbolism*. Greenwich, CT: JAI Press.

Porter, M. E. (1980) *Competitive Strategy*. New York: Free Press.

Schutz, A. (1967) *The Phenomenology of the Social World* (trans., G. Walsh and F. Lehnevet). Evanston, IL: Northwestern University Press.

Simon, H. A. (1957) *Administrative behavior* (2nd edn) New York: Macmillan.

Smircich, L. and Morgan, G. (1982) 'Leadership: The management of meaning', *Journal of Applied Behavioral Science*, 18(3): 257–73.

Starbuck, W. H. (1983) 'Organizations as action generators', *American Sociological Review*, 48: 91–102.

Thompson, J. D. (1967) *Organization in Action*. New York: McGraw-Hill.

von Bertalanffy, L. (1968) *General Systems Theory*. New York: Braziller.

Weick, K. E. (1979) *The Social Psychology of Organizing*. Reading, MA: Addison-Wesley.

Winch, P. (1958) *The Idea of a Social Science and its Relation to Philosophy*. London: Routledge and Kegan Paul.

Zucker, L. G. (1977) 'The role of institutionalization in cultural persistence,' *American Sociological Review*, 42: 726–43.

The Role of Managerial Learning and Interpretation in Strategic Persistence and Reorientation: An Empirical Exploration

THERESA K. LANT, FRANCES J. MILLIKEN AND BIPIN BATRA*

Managers have the difficult task of navigating their organizations through an uncertain and changing environment. One of the most basic strategic decisions top-level managers make is whether to persist with their current strategic orientation or to alter an organization's strategic course. Although persistence frequently improves an organization's efficiency, it can also lead to failure when there are major shifts in an organization's environmental context. Achieving long-term success requires the ability to emphasize efficiency at certain times while maintaining the flexibility to change strategic direction (Thompson, 1967).

However, deciding when to persist and when to change is difficult because there is often uncertainty about the future state of the environment and about the relationships between managers' actions and organizational outcomes [. . .]. Further complicating managers' strategic decision-making efforts is the fact that there are often structural [. . .] political [. . .] and psychological [. . .] pressures to persist with past strategies.

Major changes in an organization's strategic direction often are attributed to visionary, transformational leadership [. . .] or to managers' rational analysis of environmental threats and opportunities [. . .]. Although many researchers acknowledge that executives' perceptions and interpretations play an important

* John Wiley and Sons for Lant, T. K. et al. (1992) 'The role of managerial learning and interpretation in strategic persistence and reorientation', *Strategic Management Journal*, 13(8). Copyright © *Strategic Management Journal* 1992. Reprinted with permission of John Wiley and Sons Limited.

role in these choices [. . .], the precise mechanisms by which these interpretations influence decisions to persist or change have not been fully specified or examined.

The purpose of our research is to examine how past performance, managerial interpretations of their experience, and top management characteristics influence the likelihood of strategic reorientation in different environmental contexts. [. . .] In this paper, we apply a managerial learning framework to build and test a model of the decision-making process that drives strategic transformation.

Organizational learning models typically have several common characteristics. First, managers are assumed to set concrete performance goals to which they compare performance outcomes. It is hypothesized that these goals are a function of past performance (Lant, 1992) and competitor performance [. . .]. Secondly, the discrepancy between goals and performance provides a signal of success or failure to which managers attend in an attempt to simplify the task of interpreting their experience [. . .] and to guide future behavior (Lant, 1992). Thirdly, performance relative to goals and managerial interpretations of their experiences influence the likelihood of organizational change [. . .].

The managerial learning framework we develop and test in this paper examines the roles of past performance and managerial interpretations in influencing the likelihood of strategic reorientations. In addition, since managers typically do not make major strategic decisions in isolation, but rather as part of a top management team (Hambrick and Mason, 1984), we examine the role of top management characteristics in the managerial learning process. Finally, we examine whether industry context influences how past performance, managerial interpretations, and top management team characteristics affect the likelihood of strategic reorientations.

Patterns of strategic reorientation

Punctuated equilibrium models of strategic change (Miller and Friesen, 1980; Tushman and Romanelli, 1985) assert that organizations experience long periods of strategic persistence punctuated by short periods in which major changes occur in strategic direction and supporting structures and systems. [. . .] Reorientations are characterized by 'simultaneous and discontinuous shifts in strategy, the distribution of power, the firm's core structure, and the nature and permissiveness of control systems' (Tushman and Romanelli, 1985: 179).

A key contribution of this literature is the recognition that because of the need to maintain a fit between an organization's strategy and other key elements of its design (e.g. structure, power systems, control systems), major changes in strategy are likely to be accompanied by changes in other key elements of an organization's design. [. . .]

One reason why organizations may go through long periods of convergence punctuated by short bursts of change is that organizations experience tremendous persistence forces that make both the recognition of a need for change and its implementation difficult:

> As webs of interdependent relationships with buyers, suppliers, and financial backers strengthen and as commitments to internal participants and external constituencies are elaborated into institutionalized patterns of culture, norms, and ideologies, the organization develops inertia, a resistance to all but incremental change. (Tushman and Romanelli, 1985: 177)

[. . .] This chapter [. . .] explores how elements of managerial experience affect the likelihood of organizational reorientation. The set of variables we examine is derived from an organizational learning perspective.

The influence of managerial learning on the likelihood of strategic persistence and reorientation

Managerial learning involves managers' attempts to develop an understanding of the connections between their actions and an organization's outcomes, as well as the role that an organization's environmental context plays in influencing these action-outcome linkages. Historically, the organizational learning literature had emphasized the process of trial-and-error learning, where actions associated with positive outcomes are repeated, and actions associated with negative outcomes are not repeated [. . .].

We argue that managerial learning is a more complex process than that implied by simple trial-and-error learning. There are many factors in an organizational setting that make accurate learning difficult. Environmental change and uncertainty may make it difficult for managers to accurately interpret their past performance outcomes and to predict the effects of environmental changes on an organization (Levitt and March, 1988; March and Olsen, 1976). For example, persistence with a previously successful strategy can yield poor performance outcomes when there are major changes in an organization's environment. Similarly, changing strategies can yield poor performance outcomes if the environmental changes to which an organization is reacting are short-lived or misinterpreted. In addition, managers have a limited capacity to process information (Kiesler and Sproull, 1982; March and Simon, 1958) and they operate in organizational contexts that are often characterized by organizational and psychological pressures to persist with prior strategies (Milliken and Lant, 1991). For example, managers who are the architects of past strategies may be reluctant to acknowledge the validity of information that signals the failure of their strategies (Kiesler and Sproull, 1982). They may also tend to be systematically biased in how they attribute causes of an organization's performance outcomes. The tendency to attribute failures to external and temporary phenomena (Ford, 1985; Ford and Baucus, 1987) may short-circuit organizational learning and, thereby, lead to a high likelihood of persistence even in the face of evidence that a strategy has not yielded good performance outcomes in the past. The cumulative effect of these various persistence forces is to make convergence extremely likely and strategic reorientation extremely unlikely.

The application of a learning perspective to an examination of patterns of strategic persistence and change recognizes that managers act on interpretations of their experience and that these interpretations are likely to be systematically influenced by pressures inside an organization towards persistence with past strategies. However, certain organizational and environmental factors may enhance an organization's capacity for learning, and thus, counteract these persistence forces. For example, the characteristics of a top management team are likely to influence both managerial interpretations and the likelihood of strategic change. Nystrom and Starbuck (1984) argue that turnover of top-level managers facilitates the unlearning of old routines, thereby increasing the probability of strategic change. Empirical evidence suggests that top management change may be associated with an increased probability of strategic reorientation (Virany et al., 1992). In addition, there is evidence that the heterogeneity of the top management team is associated with higher levels of strategic change (Bantel and Jackson, 1989; Wiersema and Bantel, 1992); Milliken and Lant (1991) have suggested that more heterogeneous teams are less vulnerable to psychological pressures to persist with past strategies. Further, the context within which managers learn may affect the likelihood of strategic change by influencing what and how they learn and the interpretations they make. An organization's context may also influence the relative importance of other variables, such as past performance, on managers' decisions to persist or change.

Research model

Figure 10.1 summarizes the model we will test in this study. We will begin by discussing our expectations regarding overall rates of reorientation and convergence, and how these are affected by the environmental context. We will then examine how past performance, characteristics of a top management team, and managerial interpretations of their environmental context and their past performance outcomes affect the relative frequency of reorientation. Finally, we will complete our discussion of the model by exploring the effects of past performance on managerial interpretations and top management team characteristics.

We begin with the premise that, in general, organizations are more likely to converge than reorient. This prediction is based on the argument that organizations experience strong persistence forces [. . .].

Hypothesis 1: Organizations are more likely to converge or persist with their strategic direction than to undergo strategic reorientations.

The effect of environmental context on rates of reorientation

Many theorists argue that organizations survive by 'fitting' their strategies and structures to the nature of the industry context they face (Burns and Stalker, 1961;

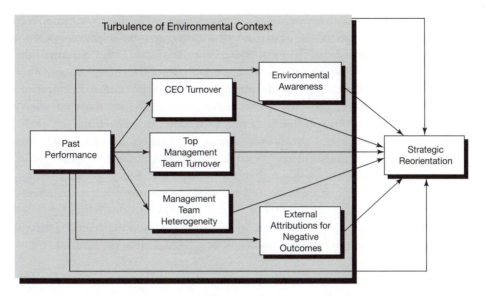

Figure 10.1 *A managerial learning model of strategic reorientation*

Lawrence and Lorsch, 1969; Porter, 1981; Terreberry, 1968). Thus, one would expect that the likelihood of strategic reorientation to vary across industry contexts, with such change being more common in turbulent environments than in stable ones. [. . .] The application of organizational routines (March, 1981) in a rapidly changing and uncertain environment can produce experiences that are not easy to explain within the current interpretive scheme of the organization (Lant and Mezias, 1992). [. . .] Managers whose past experience has been in an environment with constant change are more likely to expect change, to remain vigilant for changes, and to devote resources to environmental scanning; consequently, they might be less likely to underestimate the significance of environmental changes. [. . .]

Hypothesis 2: Organizations in volatile or turbulent environments are more likely to exhibit strategic reorientation than organizations in stable environments.

The managerial learning process and the likelihood of reorientation

This section develops hypotheses about how past performance, top management team characteristics, and managerial interpretations of their environment and their past performance outcomes affect the relative frequency of reorientation.

THE ROLE OF AN ORGANIZATION'S PAST PERFORMANCE OUTCOMES Past performance is a major explanatory variable in most models of organization learning [. . .]. An organization's past performance provides feedback about the relative effectiveness of an organization's chosen strategy. The discrepancy between performance and goals is a crucial part of a manager's experience because it provides a signal that is used to guide future behavior (Lant, 1992). Tushman and Romanelli (1985) argue that a sustained period of poor performance is one of the most potent forces counteracting the strong persistence pressures organizations face. Poor performance calls into question the effectiveness of an organization's prior strategy and interpretive scheme (Greenwood and Hinings, 1988), particularly among external constituents such as an organization's shareholders or creditors. To the extent that managers are learning from their experience, failure should increase the likelihood of changes in strategic direction. In addition, external constituents can be expected to pressure an organization to change following periods of poor performance. Thus, organizations that have performed poorly are more likely to reorient than organizations that have experienced success with their prior strategy (Fombrun and Ginsberg, 1990; Ginsberg, 1988). [. . .]

Hypothesis 3: An organization's past performance relative to the industry average will be inversely related to the likelihood of strategic reorientation.

However, because of the inherent difficulty in learning accurately and because of the persistence forces that act on organizations, we expect even poor performers to be more likely to persist than to change strategic direction. Thus, while poorly performing companies will be more likely to reorient than successful ones, we expect that the frequency of reorientations even among poor performers will be lower than the frequency of persistence.

THE ROLE OF MANAGERIAL INTERPRETATIONS A key factor in organizational learning is managerial interpretations of cause and effect relationships. Interpretive models of strategic decision-making [. . .] emphasize the idea that managers are information processors who must not only interpret information about an organization's environment but who must also interpret information about an organization's past performance outcomes and their likely causes. We hypothesize that these interpretations influence the likelihood of strategic reorientation.

[. . .] Tushman and Romanelli (1985: 178) suggest that a major force for organizational change occurs when 'major changes in competitive, technological, social and legal conditions of the environment . . . render a prior strategic orientation, regardless of its success, no longer effective.' However, in order for such organization-environment incongruencies to create the needed momentum for change, managers must be paying sufficient attention to their environment to recognize such changes. When managers fail to notice important environmental changes, they are unlikely to make needed adjustments to an organization's strategy or structure [. . .]. Thus, the more managers are aware of changes in their environmental context, the more likely they are to make strategic reorientations.

Hypothesis 4: The more aware managers are of environmental changes, the greater the likelihood of strategic reorientation.

In addition, we expect that within the subset of poorly performing organizations, those whose managers are aware of environmental changes will be more likely to reorient than those whose managers appear to lack such an awareness.

[. . .] Researchers have also suggested that the nature of the attributions managers make for their recent performance history may be an important determinant of their strategic decisions (Ford and Baucus, 1987; Milliken and Lant, 1991). [. . .] Prior research suggests that managers' attributions for the organization's previous performance may be biased, such that poor performance outcomes are attributed to external events and good performance outcomes are attributed to the organization's strategy [. . .]. We predict that [. . .] managers who make external attributions for poor performance outcomes will be less likely to decide to change strategies. We believe this [. . .] prevents managers from learning about the impact of their behavior on organizational outcomes. [. . .]

Hypothesis 5: The more managers make external attributions for poor performance outcomes, the lower the likelihood of strategic reorientation.

[. . .]

THE ROLE OF TOP MANAGEMENT TEAM CHARACTERISTICS [. . .] Several researchers (e.g. Hambrick and Mason, 1984; Tushman and Romanelli, 1985) have argued that the composition of a top management team will affect the strategy formulation process. Specifically, the diversity of backgrounds and ages represented on a top management team have been hypothesized to affect the likelihood of innovation and the likelihood of strategic change [. . .]. The heterogeneity of a top management team is likely to influence strategy formulation through its effect on the diversity of perspectives brought to bear on strategic questions. Such a diversity of perspectives can create disagreements and equivocal experiences that result in more extensive discussion of strategic options, more learning opportunities, and thereby, reduce the likelihood of a groupthink-type phenomenon occurring (Janis, 1982). [. . .]

Hypothesis 6: The greater the heterogeneity of a top management team with respect to functional backgrounds, the higher the likelihood of strategic reorientation.

[. . .] Although heterogeneity in the top management team may mitigate persistence pressures, a management team that has shared similar experiences still may be subject to biases in their interpretations which result in strategic persistence. Experimental evidence suggests that groups as well as individuals are subject to various decision-making biases [. . .]. Actual turnover in the membership of the top management team, therefore, may be necessary for reorientation to occur (Virany et al., 1992).

Nystrom and Starbuck (1984) suggest that top management team turnover is one of the most effective ways of breaking down an organization's natural inclination to persist with prior strategies. Introducing a new top management team, they argue, enables poorly performing organizations to engage in the 'unlearning' processes that are necessary for strategic reorientations to occur. One reason why top management team change may be such an important factor in mitigating organizational persistence forces is that the newly appointed managers were not the architects of the prior strategy and so they have a lower level of psychological investment in the strategy (Milliken and Lant, 1991). [. . .]

Hypothesis 7: CEO and top management turnover will be associated with an increased likelihood of strategic reorientation.

The effects of past performance on top management team characteristics and managerial interpretations

[. . .] While theories of trial-and-error learning predict that poor performance feedback will be associated with a high likelihood of change, we predict that the effects of performance feedback may be considerably more complex. We predict that performance feedback will also indirectly influence the probability of strategic change through its effects on factors such as top management team characteristics and managerial interpretations. Hypotheses 8 through 12 make specific predictions about the possible effects of past performance on top management team characteristics and managerial interpretations.

[. . .] One reason why poorly performing companies may be more likely to reorient than successful ones is that poor performance is likely to be associated with a greater probability of CEO and top management team turnover [. . .], both of which tend to mitigate persistence forces and increase the likelihood of reorientation.

Hypothesis 8: Past performance will be inversely associated with CEO turnover; high past performance will decrease the likelihood of CEO turnover, and low past performance will increase the likelihood of CEO turnover.

Hypothesis 9: Past performance will be inversely associated with top management team turnover; high past performance will decrease the likelihood of top management team turnover, and low past performance will increase the likelihood of top management team turnover.

[. . .] Poor performance may not only cause change in the individuals on the top management team; it may also affect the mix of skills and experience on the team. Poor performance may lead the CEO and the other top managers to believe that the organization lacks certain types of skills and experience on the top management team. Thus, they may act to put individuals on the team who increase the heterogeneity of the team.

Hypothesis 10: Past performance will be inversely associated with top management heterogeneity; high past performance will be associated with low levels of top management team heterogeneity, and low past performance will be associated with high levels of top management team heterogeneity.

The effects of poor performance on top management turnover and top management heterogeneity will increase the likelihood of change. However, past performance might also have an indirect effect on the likelihood of reorientation through its effects on managerial interpretations. [. . .]

[. . .] An organization's recent performance history is likely to affect the level of awareness managers have about an organization's environmental context. In particular, poor performance is likely to reduce the resources available for environmental scanning. Further, a recent period of poor performance may pre-occupy managers and cause them to redirect cognitive energy that might otherwise be devoted toward environmental scanning towards solving the immediate performance crisis (Bourgeois, 1985). On the other hand, high levels of past performance will provide the resources that are necessary for environmental scanning and analysis. Thus, we predict that past performance will be positively related to managers' level of awareness of their environmental context; higher levels of past performance increase environmental awareness, while lower levels of past performance decrease environmental awareness.

Hypothesis 11: Past performance will be positively associated with managers' environmental awareness.

[. . .] Substantial research has demonstrated that individuals in general (Fiske and Taylor, 1984), and managers specifically (Bettman and Weitz, 1983; Staw et al., 1983), tend to make internal attributions for positive outcomes and external attributions for negative outcomes. Research also suggests that external attributions are common after periods of poor performance (Salancik and Meindl, 1984; Staw, et al., 1983). The desire to avoid dissonance (Festinger, 1957) may cause managers to seek excuses or external explanations for their failures, particularly when they are responsible for the strategies that are associated with failure. Thus, we expect that the motivation to make external attributions for negative outcomes will increase when the overall performance outcomes of an organization are poor.

Hypothesis 12: Past performance will be inversely associated with the likelihood that managers will make external attributions for any negative performance outcomes an organization has experienced; low past performance will increase the likelihood that managers will make external attributions for negative performance outcomes, and high past performance will decrease the likelihood that managers will make external attributions for negative performance outcomes.

Thus, the effects of past performance on environmental awareness and external attributions will work against the direct effect of past performance on the likelihood of reorientation. While trial-and-error learning predicts that poor performance will increase the likelihood of change, the effects of poor performance on managerial interpretations may generate actions that inhibit change.

The empirical study

Sample

We chose to study firms from two industries that differed significantly in their degree of turbulence in order to investigate possible differences in the process of strategic reorientation across different contexts. The furniture industry represents a stable environment and computer software represents a turbulent environment. The difference in the degree of turbulence was verified using the coefficient of variation on sales (Tosi et al., 1973). [. . .] All firms in the sample are publicly held. Firms with fewer than 2 years of past performance data were excluded from the sample. This selection process yielded 40 furniture companies and 63 computer software companies. A sample of 40 computer software firms was randomly chosen from the 63.

Data sources

Performance data were gathered from the COMPUSTAT Industrial Data Base. Interpretation variables, CEO and top management team variables, and the measure of reorientation were obtained through content analysis of 10K and annual reports. All content coding was conducted by two coders in order to check for reliability. Intercoder reliability before discussion was 88 per cent, on average; prior work using content analysis to study organizational strategy suggests that this is an acceptable level of intercoder reliability (Jauch et al., 1980; Miller and Friesen, 1984). [. . .]

Operational definitions

The major dependent variable in this study is strategic reorientation. Tushman and Romanelli (1985) define reorientation as change in four critical organizational dimensions: business strategy, organizational structure, power distribution, and control systems. Operationally, Virany et al. (1992) define reorientation as change in at least three of these dimensions: fewer than three changes is considered evidence of convergence. We define strategic reorientation somewhat differently. First, since we are interested specifically in *strategic* reorientations, we define strategic reorientation as a change in business strategy coupled with change in other key organizational dimensions. Thus, a change in business strategy is a necessary but not sufficient condition for strategic reorientation. Secondly, because we believe that the number of changes chosen to distinguish between convergence and reorientation is somewhat arbitrary, for most of the research propositions we use a measure of reorientation that reflects a count of the number of organizational dimensions that changed in the same time period that strategy changed.

We looked for change over a 2-year time period, from 1984 to 1986. [. . .] We coded all the strategies a company mentioned as a means of competing. A company was coded as having changed strategies when they either did not mention a strategy they had indicated in 1984, or when they mentioned a new strategy that had not been indicated in 1984. [. . .]

Change in organizational structure was coded when there was evidence of a major change in structure, such as a change from a functional to a divisional organization, between the 1984 and 1986 10K reports. [. . .] Change in control systems was coded when there was evidence of new control systems being put into place or of old systems being changed. [. . .] Change in power distribution was measured as the proportion of change in functional backgrounds such as finance, marketing, manufacturing, or research and development, represented on the top management team. The distribution of functional backgrounds was conceptualized as reflecting the distribution of power on the top management team; this is based on the assumption that individuals are members of different coalitions depending on their functional background and, thus, the organizational departments that they represent (Cyert and March, 1963). [. . .]

This study includes three categories of independent variables: past performance, managerial interpretations, and top management team characteristics. The specific performance measure used in the analysis was return on assets. [. . .]

Return on assets data were collected for the 5-year period from 1980 through 1984. Managerial interpretations of the environment were coded from the 1986 10K and annual reports. The specific variable created was an indication of whether or not a firm mentioned changes or their expectations of changes in environmental contingencies. A firm's managers were coded as being aware of environmental contingencies if they indicated explicitly that they had observed or were predicting a specific change in their organization's environment. [. . .]

Attributions for past performance were obtained from content analysis of the management discussion in the 10K reports and the president's letter in the annual reports in 1986. [. . .]

CEO and top management team turnover were measured in the period 1982-84. [. . .]

Results

Table 10.1 presents descriptive statistics for both industries. Tables 10.2 and 10.3 present Spearman correlation coefficients for the variables examined in the hypotheses. Hypothesis 1 predicts that, in general, organizations will be more likely to persist with past strategies than to reorient. Table 10.4 shows the relative frequencies of strategic reorientation and convergence for the entire sample. Seventy-one per cent of the firms were classified as converging, while only 29 per cent were classified as reorienting. Hypothesis 2 predicts that organizations in turbulent environments are more likely to reorient than organizations in stable environments. This pattern can be seen in the contingency table in Table 10.5 which compares the relative rates of strategic reorientation in the furniture and software industries. Approximately 85 per cent of the furniture firms were classified as converging, as against 15 per cent that were classified as reorienting. In the software industry, 58 per cent of the firms converged, as against 42 per cent that reoriented. The Chi-square test indicates that software firms were significantly more likely to reorient than furniture firms.

Hypotheses 3-7 explore the impact of past performance, managerial interpretations, and top management team characteristics on the likelihood of reorientation. Strategic reorientation is a count variable of the number of

Table 10.1 *Descriptive statistics*

Variable	Mean furniture	Standard deviation furniture	Mean software	Standard deviation software
Strategic reorientation	1.00	1.39	1.94	1.37
Past performance	0.00	0.02	-0.05	0.24
CEO turnover	0.32	0.47	0.18	0.39
Top management turnover	0.36	0.29	0.35	0.25
Heterogeneity	0.61	0.25	0.62	0.23
Environmental awareness	0.67	0.48	0.75	0.44
External attributions	0.46	0.51	0.31	0.47

Table 10.2 *Furniture industry: Spearman correlation coefficients*

	Reorientation	CEO turnover	External attributions	Environmental awareness	Top management turnover	Heterogeneity
CEO turnover	0.324 (0.038)					
External attributions	0.297 (0.046)	0.250 (0.068)				
Environmental awareness	0.229 (0.100)	−0.216 (0.100)	0.240 (0.074)			
Top management turnover	0.008 (0.483)	0.286 (0.045)	−0.086 (0.313)	−0.062 (0.362)		
Heterogeneity	0.184 (0.152)	−0.161 (0.167)	−0.193 (0.120)	−0.119 (0.235)	0.089 (0.303)	
Past performance	−0.603 (0.000)	−0.364 (0.012)	−0.183 (0.133)	0.145 (0.180)	−0.102 (0.277)	0.192 (0.118)

Significance levels in parentheses.

Table 10.3 *Software industry: Spearman correlation coefficients*

	Reorientation	CEO turnover	External attributions	Environmental awareness	Top management turnover	Heterogeneity
CEO turnover	0.062 (0.362)					
External attributions	−0.373 (0.015)	0.209 (0.110)				
Environmental awareness	0.380 (0.011)	−0.061 (0.356)	−0.182 (0.148)			
Top management turnover	0.249 (0.082)	0.211 (0.105)	0.183 (0.158)	0.068 (0.344)		
Heterogeneity	0.311 (0.037)	−0.085 (0.312)	−0.247 (0.083)	0.163 (0.168)	0.299 (0.040)	
Past performance	−0.139 (0.209)	0.356 (0.013)	0.061 (0.364)	0.325 (0.020)	−0.068 (0.344)	0.225 (0.091)

Significance levels in parentheses.

Table 10.4 *Relative frequency of reorientation*

	No reorientation	Reorientation
Number of firms	49	20
Percentage of firms	71	29

Based on entire sample

Table 10.5 *Relative frequency of reorientation by industry*

	No reorientation	Reorientation
Furniture	28 84.8%	5 15.2%
Software	21 58.3%	15 41.7%

Chi-squared = 5.88; p = 0.015

organizational dimensions that have changed. For this type of dependent variable, Maddala (1983) recommends a Poisson regression model. In addition, tests for structural differences in the constants and slope coefficients across the two industries are conducted using the dummy variable technique suggested by Johnston (1984). This procedure is similar to testing for interaction effects between the industry and each of the independent variables. The difference is that these tests not only determine if the effect of an independent variable is different across the two industries, but also provide separate coefficient estimates for each industry. Table 10.6 presents the separate sets of coefficients for each industry and a test for significant differences across the two industries. Table 10.7 presents the coefficients based on combined samples for variables that did not have significantly different effects on reorientation across the two industries.

Table 10.6 *Poisson regression analysis of the determinants of strategic reorientation by industry*

| Independent variable | Furniture industry | | Software industry | | Difference between industries |
	Standardized coefficient	T-ratio	Standardized coefficient	T-ratio	T-ratio
Constant	−3.969	−2.846**	−2.912	−2.388*	0.571
Past performance	−0.639	−4.347**	−0.335	−2.293*	3.419**
Environmental awareness	0.576	2.282*	0.603	2.474**	−0.018
External attributions	0.196	1.354	−0.192	−2.213*	−2.336*
Heterogeneity	0.688	1.824*	0.653	1.821*	−0.067
CEO turnover	0.171	1.157	0.207	2.152*	0.455
Top management turnover	−0.165	−0.920	0.099	0.912	1.275

N = 59, *p <0.05, **p <0.01, Chi-squared = 47.993**

Table 10.7 *Poisson regression analysis of the determinants of strategic reorientation pooled across industries*

Independent variable	Standardized coefficient	T-ratio
*Constant – furniture	−4.171	−4.285**
*Constant – software	−2.761	−2.979**
*Past performance – furniture	−0.593	−3.708**
*Past performance – software	−0.277	−2.216*
Environmental awareness	0.550	3.459**
*External attributions – furniture	0.166	1.226
*External attributions – software	−0.175	−2.060*
Heterogeneity	0.312	2.627**
CEO turnover	0.225	2.132*
Top management turnover	0.004	0.042

N = 59, Chi-squared = 55.171**, *p <0.05, **p <0.01
(*Separate coefficients are reported for variables with significantly different coefficients as determined in Table 10.6 @ p <0.05)

Hypothesis 3 predicts that organizations with performance below the industry average will be more likely to reorient than those that have above average performance. This hypothesis is supported in both industries. Table 10.6 shows that the coefficient on past performance is negative and highly significant in the furniture industry, and negative and somewhat smaller in the software industry. The coefficients are significantly different across the two industries. In the pooled analysis shown in Table 10.7, the standardized coefficient of past performance in the furniture industry is approximately twice as large as the coefficient in the software industry. Although poor performers are more likely to reorient than good performers, we also predicted that the rate of reorientation among poor performers would be less than their rate of convergence. We find support for this prediction. In the furniture industry, 23 per cent of poor performers were classified as reorienting as against 77 per cent that were classified as converging. In the software industry, 42 per cent of poor performers were classified as reorienting whilst 58 per cent that were classified as converging.

Hypothesis 4 predicts that those firms whose managers indicate an awareness of environmental changes will be more likely to exhibit reorientation. This prediction is supported in both industries. The coefficients are not significantly different between the two industries, and thus a coefficient based on the pooled sample is given in Table 10.7. This coefficient is positive and highly significant. We also expected that poorly performing companies whose managers indicated an awareness of environmental changes would be more likely to reorient than poorly performing companies whose managers do not indicate this awareness. We find support for this prediction within the subsample of poorly performing firms. The number of reorienters among failing firms that indicated an awareness of potentially important environmental changes (40 per cent) was significantly greater than the number of reorienters among failing firms that did not indicate environmental awareness (18 per cent) ($z = 1.28; p < 0.05$).

Hypothesis 5 predicts that organizations whose managers tend to make external attributions for negative outcomes will be less likely to reorient. In the furniture industry, the coefficient is positive but not significant. The effect in the software industry is significant and negative as predicted. The coefficients are significantly different across the two industries. Table 10.7 indicates the separate coefficients for this variable in the pooled analysis; the direction and significance of the coefficients in each industry are the same as in Table 10.6. We also predicted that Hypothesis 5 would hold true for the subsample of failing firms. We do not find this to be the case. In the furniture industry, failing firms that made external attributions for poor performance outcomes were, in fact, more likely to reorient than failing firms that did not make external attributions ($z = 1.28, p < 0.05$). This result is consistent with an impression management argument. There is no significant difference in the rate of reorientation between failing software firms that either made external attributions or did not. Interestingly, it is successful software firms where external attributions make a difference. Successful software firms that make external attributions for poor performance outcomes are less likely to reorient than successful software firms that do not make external attributions for poor performance.

Hypothesis 6 predicts that firms with more heterogeneous top management teams will be more likely to reorientation. In Table 10.6, we see that this hypothesis is supported. The coefficients for each industry are not significantly different. Table 10.7 presents the coefficient on the pooled sample, which is significant in the predicted direction. Hypothesis 7 predicts that organizations with CEO and top management team turnover will have higher rates of reorientation. Table 10.6 indicates that the coefficient for CEO turnover in the furniture industry is positive but not significant. In the software industry, the coefficient of CEO turnover is positive and significant. There is no significant difference between the coefficients for the two industries. Table 10.7 presents the coefficient for the pooled sample, which is significant in the predicted direction. The coefficient for top management team turnover is not significant in either industry, or in the pooled analysis in Table 10.7.

Hypotheses 8-12 explore the impact of past performance on managerial interpretations and top management team characteristics. The results of testing these hypotheses appear in Tables 10.8 and 10.9.

Hypotheses 8 and 9 predict that poor performance will be associated with CEO and top management team turnover. Table 10.8 presents the logistic regression analysis for the CEO turnover dummy variable. Structural change analysis indicated that the coefficients across the two industries were different; thus, two separate coefficients are reported. The results suggest, however, that past performance does not have a significant impact on CEO turnover in either industry. Table 10.8 also presents the ordinary least squares regression analysis for top management team turnover. The coefficients for the two industries are not significantly different; the coefficient for the pooled industries is marginally significant in the predicted direction.

Hypothesis 10 predicts that poor performance will tend to increase the heterogeneity of the top management team. Table 10.8 presents the ordinary least squares regression for this hypothesis test. The coefficients for the two industries were not significantly different; the coefficient based on the pooled sample is not significant.

Hypothesis 11 explores the effect of past performance on managers' environmental awareness. The result of this hypothesis test is presented in Table 10.9. Since environmental awareness is a dummy variable, the hypothesis test is based on a logistic regression. Structural change analysis indicated that the co-efficients were not significantly different across the two industries. Thus, this

Table 10.8 *Logistic regression analysis of CEO change*

Independent variable	Standardized coefficient	T-ratio
Constant	−1.107	−3.653**
Past performance – furniture	−0.014	−0.016
Past performance – software	8.504	1.509

$N = 77$, Chi-squared = 4.224, **p <0.01
(Furniture and software coefficients are significantly different)

OLS regression analysis of TMT turnover pooled across industries

Independent variable	Standardized coefficient	T-ratio
Constant	0.345	10.896**
Past performance	−0.155	−1.323+

$N = 73$, $F = 1.749$, +p <0.10, **p <0.01

OLS regression analysis of TMT heterogeneity pooled across industries

Independent variable	Standardized coefficient	T-ratio
Constant	0.615	22.454**
Past performance	0.055	0.476

$N = 77$, $F = 0.227$, **p <0.01

Table 10.9 *Logistic regression analysis of environmental awareness pooled across industries*

Independent variable	Standardized coefficient	T-ratio
Constant	1.090	4.019**
Past performance	6.004	2.198*

N = 79, *p <0.05, **p <0.01, Chi-squared = 9.318**

Logistic regression analysis of attributional bias pooled across industries

Independent variable	Standardized coefficient	T-ratio
Constant	−0.457	−1.899+
Past performance	0.304	−0.626

N = 74, +p <0.10, Chi-squared = 0.397*

hypothesis test is based on the pooled sample. Hypothesis 11 predicts that good organizational performance will increase managers' environmental awareness. The coefficient of past performance is positive and significant as predicted.

Hypothesis 12 explores the effect of past performance on the tendency to make external attributions for poor performance outcomes. The logistic regression results for the pooled sample are presented in Table 10.9. We hypothesize that poor performance will increase the likelihood that managers will make external attributions for negative outcomes; however, the coefficient of past performance is not significant.

Discussion

In this research, we built and tested a model of the determinants of strategic reorientation that was derived from past research on strategic change [. . .] as well as from the literature on organizational learning processes [. . .]. The process of strategy formulation, we argued, is fundamentally a process of managerial learning that is affected by an organization's performance history, the nature of an organization's context, and managers' interpretive or sensemaking processes. Our findings support prior organizations research, which suggests that organizations are more likely to persist with their past strategic orientations than to reorient, due to structural inertia (Hannan and Freeman, 1984) and other persistence forces (Miller and Friesen, 1980; Milliken and Lant, 1991; Tushman and Romanelli, 1985). Our results also suggest that firms in our sample differed in their likelihood of reorientation as a function of their industry context, past performance, managerial interpretations, and top management team characteristics.

The determinants of strategic reorientation

INDUSTRY CONTEXT Our results suggest that although the tendency to converge occurred in both stable and volatile industry contexts, it was significantly more pronounced in the stable industry context. This finding is in keeping with the logic of contingency theorists who argue that organizations survive by 'fitting' their strategies and structures to the nature of their environmental context.

PAST PERFORMANCE We also found, as we had hypothesized, that although a history of poor performance increased the likelihood of changes in an organization's strategic orientation, the majority of poorly performing companies in our sample persisted with their past strategic orientations despite negative performance feedback. In addition, past performance had a significantly larger effect on reorientation in the furniture industry than in the software industry. One reason may be that the signalling value of past performance differs across different environmental contexts. In a relatively stable environment, such as the furniture industry, past performance over a 5-year period may be a relatively valid indicator of the effectiveness of a firm's strategic orientation. Therefore, a period of poor performance would be a strong signal of the need to consider reorientation as a means to achieve a performance turnaround. In a turbulent environment, however, past performance may be a less valid indicator of the long-term effectiveness of the current strategic direction. These firms may weigh the validity of the past performance signal against other information, such as environmental forecasts and trends. In addition, the computer software industry was at an early stage in its industry life cycle during the time period in which we collected data. Such a rapidly growing, immature industry may exhibit greater instability in performance outcomes than a mature industry such as the furniture industry, making past performance a relatively unreliable indicator of future success.

The finding that periods of poor performance (even 5 years worth) may not be sufficient to motivate a strategic reorientation is interesting because it suggests that simple trial-and-error learning models, which predict that organizations will persist when successful and change when past strategies yield poor performance outcomes, may be inadequate for predicting an organization's strategic choices. Trial-and-error models may have to be amended to include a consideration of factors, such as the predominance of persistence pressures, that complicate the learning process in organizational settings.

MANAGERIAL INTERPRETATIONS We believe that a key contribution of our model is its recognition of the role of managerial interpretations in predicting the likelihood of strategic reorientation. Our results indicate that managerial interpretations of their environmental context and of their past performance outcomes are important predictors of the likelihood of strategic reorientation.

Managerial awareness of environmental changes was an extremely significant predictor of the likelihood of strategic reorientation in both industry contexts. Further, we found that within the subsample of firms whose performance was below the industry norm, companies whose managers expressed an awareness of changes in their organization's environment were more likely to reorient than companies whose managers did not indicate such an awareness. The coupling of this result with the finding that poor performers were more likely to persist than to change suggests that awareness of environmental contingencies may be a necessary factor for motivating change in poorly performing organizations. Although these findings are not especially surprising given the obvious need for managers to attend to environmental contingencies, they do suggest that we need to develop our understanding of the factors that influence managerial perceptions, interpretations, and attention allocation with respect to the environmental context.

Our results also suggest that the attributions managers make about the causes of their poor performance outcomes may be an important predictor of the likelihood of strategic reorientation. However, the effect of the external attribution bias we studied appears to vary by industry. In the software industry, managers who made external attributions for negative performance outcomes were less likely to engage in strategic reorientations. The finding of a negative relationship between attributional bias and change, which we had predicted, is consistent with the interpretive view of the role that causal attributions have in influencing the likelihood of reorientation. To the extent that managers see external forces as the cause of their poor performance, they may be less likely to perceive a need to change their strategies, particularly if they view these changes as temporary (Ford, 1985). In the furniture industry, in contrast, the tendency to make external attributions for negative performance outcomes was not significantly associated with the likelihood of strategic reorientations.

TOP MANAGEMENT TEAM CHARACTERISTICS In our effort to explore the factors that influence the likelihood of strategic reorientation, we also examined the effects of top management team characteristics on the likelihood of strategic reorientation. We argued, along with Nystrom and Starbuck (1984), that turnover of managers may enable organizations to unlearn patterns of behavior that are no longer functional, and thus, would increase the likelihood of reorientation. Further, we had anticipated that increased levels of heterogeneity on the top management team would further enable organizational learning and subsequent strategic change. We found that although CEO turnover increased the likelihood of reorientation, top management turnover had no significant effect on reorientation. One possible explanation for the latter finding is that top management team turnover is associated with a greater likelihood of strategic reorientation only under certain conditions. For example, top management turnover may enhance the likelihood of reorientations only when it is accompanied by CEO change. Alternatively, it is possible that it is not turnover *per se* that increases the likelihood that an organization will reorient, but rather, it is only when turnover introduces heterogeneity or fresh perspectives into the top management group that the likelihood of reorientation increases. By this logic, it may be important to look at the effects of turnover on top management team heterogeneity. We found, in fact, that companies with more heterogeneous teams were more likely to reorient than companies with less diverse top management groups, a finding that is consistent with the results of other research (Bantel and Jackson, 1989; Wiersema and Bantel, 1992).

Speculating about processes

THE EFFECT OF PAST PERFORMANCE ON MANAGERIAL INTERPRETATIONS If managers' interpretations of their environment and of the causes of their past performance outcomes are important factors in understanding managers' strategic choices, then it becomes important to try to understand the variables that influence these interpretive processes. Our findings suggest that managers of organizations with a history of good performance were more likely to be aware of the organization's environmental context. We explain the positive effect of past performance on environmental awareness with the argument that companies that are performing well are likely to have more resources to devote to environmental scanning and thus, their managers are more likely to be aware of changes in their organization's environmental context. In addition, managers of poorly performing companies may become preoccupied with attempts to improve the efficiency of their organizations, and thus pay less attention to trends in the environment that may signal potential, but not immediate, problems. Thus, while our results suggest that poor performance has a direct effect of increasing the likelihood of reorientation, the effect of poor performance on environmental awareness may result in a lowered likelihood of reorientation.

Contrary to our expectations, past performance did not have a significant effect on the tendency to make external attributions for poor performance outcomes. There was a general tendency among firms in our sample to attribute specific outcomes to external causes if the outcome was undesirable.

THE EFFECT OF PAST PERFORMANCE ON TOP MANAGEMENT TEAM CHARACTERISTICS Prior research has suggested that poor performance often results in turnover of the CEO and top management team (Allen et al., 1979; Brown, 1982; Pfeffer and Davis-Blake, 1986). We had also speculated that past performance might have an impact on the heterogeneity of the top management team as well as on the turnover of individuals. In our study the only significant effect of past performance on top management characteristics was the finding that poor performance was associated with higher levels of top management turnover. Performance did not affect CEO turnover or heterogeneity. One possible explanation for this set of relationships may lie in the respective decision-making power of the CEO and the top management team. CEOs may replace individuals on their top management team when their organization experiences poor performance; this replacement of individuals may not, however, result in a mix of individuals that brings a larger variety of experience to the team. This result has an interesting implication when coupled with our earlier finding that top management team turnover alone did not increase the rate of reorientation, while increased heterogeneity of the management team did increase the rate of reorientation. If poor performance increases turnover in the top management team, but does not subsequently increase the heterogeneity of the team, then poor performance does not increase the likelihood of reorientation through its effect on top management team characteristics.

Summary

Figure 10.2 summarizes the results of our study by indicating which relationships in our model were found to be significant, and the direction of these relationships. This research suggests that environmental turbulence, poor performance, CEO turnover, top management team heterogeneity, and managerial awareness of environmental changes are associated with strategic transformation. Managers' explanations of their past performance outcomes also appear to affect the likelihood of reorientation, but the direction of the effect tends to change depending on an organization's environmental context. We also found that poor past performance is associated with a decreased level of environmental awareness and with a greater likelihood of top management team turnover.

Conclusions and implications for future research

Our model suggests that organizational learning may be more complex than the trial-and-error process often emphasized in the organizational learning literature (Cyert and March, 1963; Levinthal and March, 1981; March and Olsen, 1976; March and Simon, 1958). Our model considers the role that managers' interpretations of their experience play in influencing a firm's strategic actions in

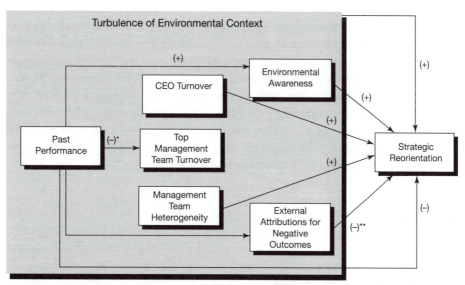

* Significant at p<0.10; significance level for other relationships is at least p<0.05.
** This relationship is significant in the software industry only.

Figure 10.2 *Summary of significant relationships in the model*

addition to the role played by past performance information. We believe that our finding that managers' level of environmental awareness and attributions for performance outcomes influenced the likelihood of strategic reorientation attests to the importance of developing our understanding of managers' interpretive processes and their antecedents. Further, our model also allows for the recognition that managers may become psychologically invested in the strategies they have designed, creating the tendency to persist with past strategies despite negative performance outcomes. The finding that CEO turnover and top management team heterogeneity increase the likelihood of reorientation suggests that either leadership change or a diversity of perspectives may be necessary to counteract persistence forces. Further, our model suggests that poor performance may have not only a direct effect on the likelihood of strategic reorientation, consistent with the prediction of trial-and-error learning, but also indirect effects that occur through the influence of past performance on manager's interpretations of their environment and their past performance results. In particular, our finding that poorly performing firms have lower levels of environmental awareness may be one explanation for the overwhelming persistence of poorly performing firms.

We believe these findings, although preliminary, reinforce the importance of understanding the processes that underlie strategy formulation if we are to understand and predict managers' choices [. . .]. Specifically, our findings suggest that in order to understand the strategy formulation process, we not only need to have objective information about a firm's performance and environment, but we also need to have data on manager's perceptions and interpretations of this 'objective' information. There is a growing body of work in the strategic management literature that suggests that managers' interpretations matter [. . .]. Our findings offer further empirical evidence for this argument. However, our understanding of what factors influence how managers interpret information is limited. For instance, we have only a limited understanding of the factors that influence the degree to which managers perceive contingencies in their environment and interpret these accurately. We also do not fully understand when and why managers will interpret performance information in such a way that they escalate their commitment to prior strategies. Systematic investigation of perception and interpretation can be found in the social and cognitive psychology literatures [. . .]. What is needed is more systematic integration of this empirical research into the strategy literature [. . .].

References

Allen, M. P., Panian, S. K. and Lotz, R. E. (1979) 'Managerial succession and organizational performance: A recalcitrant problem revisited', *Administrative Science Quarterly*, 24: 167–80.

Bantel, K. A. and Jackson, S. E. (1989) 'Top management and innovations in banking: Does the composition of the top team make a difference?', *Strategic Management Journal*, 10: 107–24.

Bettman, J. R. and Weitz, B. A. (1983) 'Attributions in the boardroom: Causal reasoning in corporate annual reports', *Administrative Science Quarterly*, 28: 165–83.

Bourgeois, L. J. III. (1985) 'Strategic goals, perceived uncertainty, and economic performance in volatile environments', *Academy of Management Journal*, 28: 548–73.

Brown, M. C. (1982) 'Administrative succession and organizational performance: The succession effect', *Administrative Science Quarterly*, 27: 1–16.

Burns, T. and Stalker, G. M. (1961) *The Management of Innovation*. London: Tavistock.

Cyert, R. M. and March, J. G. (1963) *A Behavioral Theory of the Firm*. Englewood Cliffs, NJ: Prentice-Hall.

Festinger, L. (1957) *A Theory of Cognitive Dissonance*. Stanford, CA: Stanford University Press.

Fiske, S. T. and Taylor, S. E. (1984) *Social Cognition*. Reading, MA: Addison-Wesley.

Fombrun, C. and Ginsberg, A. (1990) 'Enabling change in corporate aggressiveness', *Strategic Management Journal*, 11: 297–308.

Ford, J. D. (1985) 'The effects of causal attributions on decision-makers' responses to performance downturns', *Academy of Management Review*, 10: 770–86.

Ford, J. D. and Baucus, D. A. (1987) 'Organizational adaptation to performance downturns: An interpretation-based perspective', *Academy of Management Review*, 12: 366–80.

Ginsberg, A. (1988) 'Measuring and modelling changes in strategy: Theoretical foundations and empirical directions', *Strategic Management Journal*, 9: 559–76.

Greenwood, R. and Hinings, C. R. (1988) 'Organizational design types, tracks and the dynamics of strategic change', *Organization Studies*, 9(3): 293–316.

Hambrick, D. C. and Mason, P. M. (1984) 'Upper echelons: The organization as a reflection of its top managers', *Academy of Management Review*, 9: 193–206.

Hannan, M. T. and Freeman, J. (1984) 'Structural inertia and organizational change', *American Sociological Review*, 49: 149–64.

Janis, I. (1982) *Groupthink: Psychological Studies of Policy Decisions and Fiascoes*. Boston, MA: Houghton Mifflin.

Jauch, L. R., Osborn, R. N. and Glueck, W. F. (1980) 'Short-term financial success in large business organizations: The environment-strategy connection', *Strategic Management Journal*, 1: 49–63.

Johnston, J. (1984) *Econometric Methods*, 3rd edn. New York: McGraw Hill.

Kiesler, S. and Sproull, L. (1982) 'Managerial responses to changing environments: Perspectives on problem sensing from social cognition', *Administrative Science Quarterly*, 27: 548–70.

Lant, T. K. (1992) 'Aspiration level adaptation: An empirical exploration', *Management Science*, 38: 623–44.

Lant, T. K. and Mezias, S. J. (1992) 'An organizational learning model of convergence and reorientation', *Organization Science*, 3: 47–71.

Lawrence, P. R. and Lorsch, J. W. (1969) *Organization and Environment*. Homewood, IL: Irwin.

Levinthal, D. A. and March, J. G. (1981) 'A model of adaptive organizational search', *Journal of Economic Behavior and Organization*, 2: 307–33.

Levitt, B. and March, J. G. (1988) 'Organizational learning', in B. Bacharach (ed.), *Annual Review of Sociology*, 14: 319–40.

Maddala, G. S. (1983) *Limited-dependent and Qualitative Variables in Econometrics*. Cambridge, MA: Cambridge University Press.

March, J. G. (1981) 'Footnotes to organizational change', *Administrative Science Quarterly*, 26: 563–77.

March, J. G. and Olsen, J. P. (1976) *Ambiguity and Choice in Organizations*. Bergen, Norway: Universitetsforlaget.

March, J. G. and Simon, H. (1958) *Organizations*. New York: Wiley.

Miller, D. and Friesen, P. (1980) 'Momentum and revolution in organizational adaptation', *Academy of Management Journal*, 23: 591–614.

Miller, D. and Friesen, P. (1984) *Organizations: A Quantum View*. Englewood Cliffs, NJ: Prentice-Hall.

Milliken, F. J. and Lant, T. K. (1991) 'The effect of an organization's recent performance history on strategic persistence and change: The role of managerial interpretations', in J. Dutton, A. Huff and P. Shrivastava (eds), *Advances in Strategic Management*, 7. Greenwich, CT: JAI Press. pp. 125–52.

Nystrom, P. C. and Starbuck, W. H. (1984) 'To avoid organizational crises – unlearn', *Organizational Dynamics*, 12(4): 53–65.

Pfeffer, J. and Davis-Blake, A. (1986) 'Administrative succession and organizational performance: How administrator experience mediates the succession effect', *Academy of Management Journal*, 29: 72–83.

Porter, M. E. (1981) *Competitive Strategy*. New York: The Free Press.

Salancik, G. R. and Meindl, J. R. (1984) 'Corporate attributions as strategic illusions of management control', *Administrative Science Quarterly*, 29: 238–54.

Staw, B. M., McKechnie, P. I. and Puffer, S. M. (1983) 'The justification of organizational performance', *Administrative Science Quarterly*, 28: 582–600.

Terreberry, S. (1968) 'The evolution of organizational environments', *Administrative Science Quarterly*, 12: 590–613.

Thompson, J. R. (1967) *Organizations in Action*. New York: McGraw-Hill.

Tosi, H., Aldag, R. and Storey, R. G. (1973) 'On the measurement of the environment: An assessment of the Lawrence and Lorsch environmental uncertainty scale', *Administrative Science Quarterly*, 18: 27–36.

Tushman, M. L. and Romanelli, E. (1985) 'Organizational evolution: A metamorphosis model of convergence and reorientation', in L. L. Cummings and B. M. Staw (eds), *Research in Organizational Behavior*, Vol. 7. Greenwich, CT: JAI Press. pp. 171–222.

Virany, B., Tushman, M. L. and Romanelli, E. (1992) 'Executive succession and organization outcomes in turbulent environments: An organizational learning approach', *Organization Science*, 3: 72–91.

Wiersema, M. F. and Bantel, K. A. (1992) 'Top management team demography and corporate strategic change', *Academy of Management Journal*, 35: 91–121.

C HAPTER 11

The Cognitive Perspective on Strategic Decision-making

CHARLES R. SCHWENK*

[. . .]

The cognitions of key decision-makers are receiving increased research attention in strategic management. This is due to the increased recognition of the importance of key decision-makers' perceptions in studying the links between the environment, strategy, and structure as well as a greater awareness of the role of cognitions in strategic issue diagnosis and problem formulation.

Several studies illustrate this recognition [. . .]. In a longitudinal study of strategic change in a retail chain, Mintzberg and Waters (1982) suggest that in the entrepreneurial mode of strategy-making the development of a new strategy is typically carried out 'in a single informed brain'. They conclude that that is why the entrepreneurial mode is at the centre of the most glorious corporate successes (Mintzberg and Waters, 1982: 496). The study of strategists' cognitions provides information about the workings of these informed brains, and therefore the factors which contribute to some glorious corporate successes (as well as some dismal strategic failures).

Hambrick and Mason (1984) note that strategic decision-making is influenced by the cognitive frames and decision processes of members of organizational 'upper echelons'. Anecdotal evidence in the business press supports this view. Business ventures (particularly if they fail) are often described as being the result of the predispositions and thought processes of key upper-level decision-makers.

Finally, [. . .] Dutton et al. suggest that the concepts, beliefs, assumptions, and cause-and-effect understandings of strategists determine how strategic issues will be framed (1983: 310). Lyles notes that subjectivity is involved in the process of problem definition and suggests that strategists' problem definitions will be guided by their past experiences (1981: 62).

* Blackwell Publishers for Schwenk, C. 'The cognitive perspective on strategic decision-making', *Journal of Management Studies*, 25(1). Copyright © Blackwell Publishers 1988.

Recognizing the importance of cognitions, strategic management researchers have begun to explore their role in strategic management. This research focuses not on individuals and individual differences in cognition but on *cognitive structures and processes* which may in some cases be shared by multiple strategists.

In this article, recent research on four specific topics in strategic cognition will be summarized. These topics include: cognitive heuristics and biases, cognitive frames, strategic assumptions, and analogy and metaphor. [. . .] In the author's judgement they represent those topics which are the most potentially useful in understanding the ways decision-makers understand and solve strategic problems. [. . .]

Research on strategic cognition

A useful starting point in a discussion of cognitive processes is the concept of cognitive simplification. Simon (1957, 1976) laid the groundwork for the treatment of cognitive simplification in his discussion of 'bounded rationality' which suggests that decision-makers must construct simplified mental models when dealing with complex problems (1976: 79–96). Further, they can only approximate rationality in their attempts to solve these problems (Simon, 1976; Taylor, 1975). They may be subject to selective perception since they are unable to evaluate comprehensively all variables relevant to a decision (Hogarth, 1980; Mason and Mitroff, 1981). Further, when *groups* are making strategic decisions, they may be subject to perceptual biases associated with groupthink (Janis and Mann, 1977: 129–33).

Mason and Mitroff (1981) and others have observed that strategic problems are, almost by definition, extremely complex. How do strategists with limited information processing capacities deal with this complexity in order to make sense of strategic problems? The material in the next section deals with this question.

Attempts by strategists to understand complex problems may introduce *biases* into their *strategic assumptions*. Strategic assumptions then form the basis for the frames of reference or *schemata* through which decision-makers represent complex strategic problems. Finally, *analogy and metaphor* may be the means by which cognitive maps and schemata from other problem domains are applied to new strategic problems. If new strategic problems cannot be dealt with through analogy, then a complex diagnosis may have to be done. Heuristics and biases may then come into play in developing new strategic assumptions. These points will be elaborated in the research reviews which follow.

Cognitive heuristics and biases

The behavioural decision theory literature provides material for the study of cognitive heuristics and biases in strategic management. Researchers have recently begun to suggest that the decisional biases identified in laboratory contexts may affect strategic decision-making as well [. . .].

Extensive lists of heuristics and biases have already been developed [. . .]. Researchers have identified a number of heuristics or 'rules of thumb' which decision-makers use to simplify complex problems and a number of decisional biases which may have an impact on strategic decisions. Tversky and Kahneman (1974), and other behavioural decision theorists have pointed out that the heuristics may provide efficient short cuts in processing information. As Tversky and Kahneman (1974: 1125) state, 'in general, these heuristics are quite useful, but sometimes they lead to severe and systematic error'. [. . .] Those which seem most likely to affect strategic decisions are listed in Table 11.1.

To illustrate the nature of heuristics and biases, one example of each will be discussed here. Strategic decisions are often influenced by judgements about the probability of certain types of changes in the environment. One heuristic which may affect such probability judgements is the availability heuristic (Barnes, 1984; Tversky and Kahneman, 1974). Using this heuristic, decision-makers judge a future event to be likely if it is easy to recall past occurrences of the event. In other words, judgements of the likelihood of an event are based on the availability of past occurrences in memory. Generally, frequently occurring events are easier to recall than infrequently occurring events so availability is a good way of judging probability.

However, other things besides frequency can increase the availability of certain types of events in memory. Dramatic vivid events may be easy to recall even if they occur infrequently. Also, recent events may be easier to recall. For this reason, the availability heuristic may distort judgements of probabilities.

One bias which may affect strategic decisions is the illusion of control (Duhaime and Schwenk, 1985; Langer, 1983; Schwenk, 1984, 1986). This bias may affect people's assessments of their chance of success at a venture. Langer reports on six studies which show that subjects making a variety of decisions expressed an expectancy of personal success higher than the objective probability would warrant. They tend to overestimate their skill or the impact it will have on the outcome (Langer, 1983: 59–90).

Table 11.1 *Selected heuristics and biases*

Bias	Effects
Availability	Judgements of probability of easily recalled events distorted.
Selective perception	Expectations may bias observations of variables relevant to strategy.
Illusory correlation	Encourages belief that unrelated variables are correlated.
Conservatism	Failure sufficiently to revise forecasts based on new information.
Law of *small* numbers	Overestimation of the degree to which small samples are representative of populations.
Regression bias	Failure to allow for regression to the mean.
Wishful thinking	Probability of desired outcomes judged to be inappropriately high.
Illusion of control	Overestimation of personal control over outcomes.
Logical reconstruction	'Logical' reconstruction of events which cannot be accurately recalled.
Hindsight bias	Overestimation of predictability of past events.

Langer suggests that we are subject to this illusion of personal control because of the way we collect information. She notes that as people constantly seek ways to control outcomes in the environment, they form hypotheses about the effects of their actions on these outcomes. In her words, they then 'tend to seek out information that supports their hypotheses while innocently ignoring disconfirming evidence' (1983: 24). This type of information search tends to reinforce the illusion of personal control.

Most of the heuristics and biases have been identified in laboratory experiments using relatively structured tasks. Therefore, strategic management researchers have attempted to identify examples of the operation of the biases in actual strategic decisions. The focus on simplification processes for which laboratory and field support exists should increase the chance of identifying cognitive processes which really do affect organizational decisions rather than processes produced only by the artificiality of the laboratory context or the political processes in organizations.

In summary, there is some evidence from the laboratory and the field that availability, the illusion of control, and other biases identified in this research may affect strategic decisions by restricting the range of strategic alternatives considered and the information used to evaluate these alternatives.

It is likely that multiple biases affect strategic decisions. Schwenk (1986) has shown how some of the biases may interact and reinforce each other. For example the availability bias might increase the illusion of control in successful executives. These executives' past experiences of success might be salient to them and therefore more easily recalled when they are assessing their chances of success with a new strategy. Researchers are now attempting to describe the ways individual biases interact to affect such decisions.

Strategic assumptions, cognitive maps, and schemata

The effects of cognitive heuristics and biases may be seen in decision-makers' assumptions about strategic problems. Mason and Mitroff (1981) suggest that assumptions are the basic elements of a strategist's frame of reference or worldview. According to Mason and Mitroff, strategic problems involve organized complexity; in other words, problem variables are interdependent in such a way that solutions to some problems create others (1981: 3–21). Assumptions about such problems are necessary because policy-makers must often take action in the absence of certainty (Mason and Mitroff, 1981). In strategic decisions, many of the most important assumptions deal with the behaviour of groups or individuals who are important to the success of the strategy and who have a *stake* in the outcome of the strategy. Freeman (1984) calls such individuals and groups *stakeholders*.

Since assumptions form the basis of strategies, it is important that they are consistent with the information available to strategists. This requires careful examination of assumptions. However, this is difficult because most policy-makers are unaware of the particular set of assumptions they hold and of methods that can help them in examining and assessing the strength of their assumptions (Mason and Mitroff, 1981: 18). The accuracy of these assumptions may be affected by the cognitive biases previously discussed.

Strategic assumptions form the basis of top managers' frames of reference. Shrivastava (1983), and Shrivastava and Mitroff (1983) suggest that analysis of these frames of reference is helpful in understanding how strategic problems are formulated. Two concepts from the cognitive psychology literature, cognitive maps and schemata have been discussed in connection with strategic problem frames.

The term 'cognitive map' was first used by Tolman (1948) in discussions of learning in laboratory animals and human beings. These cognitive maps consist of concepts about aspects of the decision environment and beliefs about cause-and-effect relationships between them. Such maps serve as interpretive lenses which help decision-makers select certain aspects of an issue as important for diagnosis.

Axelrod (1976) has developed methods for representing cognitive maps diagrammatically. Though they are often used to represent individual worldviews, they may be used to represent shared assumptions among a group of strategic decision-makers which makes them useful in the study of strategic problem formulation. Axelrod notes that the purpose of cognitive mapping is not to represent a person's entire belief system. Rather, it represents the causal assertions of a person with respect to a particular policy domain (Axelrod, 1976: 58). [. . .]

Bougon et al. (1977) and Weick (1979) suggest that cognitive maps may direct information search in organizations and that cognitive maps may exist at the organizational level. They are discovered or inferred by organization members and used as a basis for action (1979: 52). [. . .]

Strategic choices are determined by the way strategists conceptualize their environment and industry. [. . .] Cognitive mapping may help researchers to describe more effectively the ways executives understand relations among industry factors and to determine which factors are taken most seriously by executives in formulating their strategies. Research using cognitive mapping may also help clarify the processes by which industry factors affect strategies. Therefore, this type of analysis might supplement research based on 'objective' assessment of industry factors as determinants of strategy. [. . .]

The term *schemata* is sometimes used in connection with cognitive maps. From the definitions of the two terms in the literature, the distinction between cognitive maps and schemata is not completely clear. In general, however, 'schemata' is a broader term. A cognitive map may be defined as a particular type of schema or a part of a broader schema (Weick, 1979: 48–53). Schemata have been defined as cognitive representations of attributes and the relationships between them which constitute commonsense social theories (Rumelhart and Ortony, 1977), and as active cognitive structures which frame problems (Neisser, 1976: Ch. 6).

Taylor (1982: 72–3) and Taylor and Crocker (1983), suggest that schemata are abstract conceptions people hold about the social world, and that previously developed schemata may be applied to new problems. Chittipeddi and Gioia (1983:

6) state that schemata are evoked by cues in a problem-solving setting and they provide frames for problems which makes it unnecessary for decision-makers to expend the mental effort necessary to diagnose completely each element of a new strategic problem.

In conclusion, human cognitive limitations introduce biases into the development of strategic assumptions and may lead to simplification in strategic schemata. These biases and simplifications affect strategic decisions when decision-makers' existing schemata are used in diagnosing and framing new strategic problems. Analysis of executives' strategic schemata helps explain strategic choices in response to environmental and industry forces. The use of existing schemata in diagnosing new problems can be better understood through the discussion of analogy which follows.

Analogy in diagnosis

In some ways, each strategic problem is unique. However, when diagnosing or framing a new strategic problem, decision-makers may draw on their experience of situations which seem to be similar. These 'similar situations' may come from relatively straightforward sources like previous strategic decisions, or from relatively imaginative sources like athletic contests. Research on analogy and metaphor in strategic decision-making deals with the transfer of schemata from one domain to another.

Isenberg (1983: 17) has given some interesting examples of the use of metaphor and analogy in defining organizational missions and framing strategic problems. He found that managers created new meanings by comparing a current strategic issue with an issue that a prototypical organization dealt with in a particular manner. For example, a bank CEO frequently used MacDonald's hamburgers as a way of understanding how standardization of branches could be a very powerful marketing tool. When discussing the bank's ability to compete with other banks and its ability to rally its employees around a common goal, he would frequently draw an analogy to the army. The CEO of the same company would sometimes compare and contrast his control systems with those of ITT.

Isenberg also found that in order to make sense of dramatic events, managers in a pharmaceutical company likened these events to experience that they had already had, such as rushing at a fraternity. The process of drawing analogies seems to be very common when organizational actors are trying to understand an ambiguous or novel situation (Louis, 1980).

Analogies are more likely to shape strategic problem formulation when they are *shared* by organizational members. Sapienza (1983) has discussed the development of shared analogies which help frame strategic decisions. The process involves the creation of a shared vocabulary among the decision-makers through discussion of problems and the emergence of shared images among the group to define the problems.

Researchers who study governmental decision-making have insights into the uses of analogy which may be helpful to strategic management researchers.

Steinbruner (1974) has discussed reasoning by analogy in foreign policy-making. This involves the application of simple analogies and images to guide complex problem definition. This process helps to reduce the uncertainty perceived in the environment. Since both foreign policy and business strategy decisions are complex, ill-structured, top-level decisions, analogy may affect business strategy as well. The use of analogy affects decision-makers' problem diagnosis and generation of potential solutions in ways which may increase or decrease the quality of strategies.

Reasoning by analogy has been shown to be effective in generating creative solutions to a variety of problems (Gordon, 1961). However in strategic decisions which involve a great deal of uncertainty and complexity, the use of simple analogies may mislead the decision-makers into an over-simplistic view of the situation (Steinbruner, 1974: 115). When decision-makers use analogies to define problems, they may not recognize that there are critical differences between their analogies and the decision situations they face.

The past often provides a ready source of analogies. Present decisions may be viewed as similar to past decisions (Huff, 1982: 123). May (1973) [. . .] notes that foreign policy decision-makers frame present problems by using analogies to the past. They sometimes select the first analogy which comes to mind rather than searching more widely, or pausing to analyse the analogy and ask in what ways it might be misleading (May, 1973: xi). Gilovich (1981) demonstrated that analogies to the past influenced decision-makers' recommendations about how to resolve a hypothetical international relations crisis in a laboratory experiment. Subjects developed different recommendations depending on whether the scenario they received had information suggesting similarities to the Second World War or to Vietnam.

Huff (1982) notes that a firm may also draw on the analogous experiences of other firms in the industry. She suggests that this may account for the similarities in strategic concepts and frames among firms in a single industry.

In summary, diagnosis of a strategic problem sometimes involves the application of a relevant schema from another domain. Essentially, the decision-maker draws an analogy between the causes and solutions for the current problem and those of past problems. Analogies then specify the ways the problem should be solved, particularly if they are shared by organizational members. Individuals' past experiences of other companies in the industry provide the most common sources of analogy.

Integration and questions for future research

The previous sections summarize four major streams of research on strategic cognitions. These have yet to be integrated into an overall theory of cognition in strategic choice. In this final section, an integrative model is proposed and a number of hypotheses for future research are developed from this model.

Though the relationships between the research streams within the cognitive perspective have not yet been articulated, they can be integrated around two basic concepts; the development of schemata and the application of schemata to the diagnosis of particular strategic problems. Figure 11.1 describes the relationships between the four types of strategic cognitions and the two processes of schemata development and application.

This model is based on the assumption that there are two ways in which understanding of strategic problems is achieved. First, in order to comprehend some types of strategic problems, data may be carefully analysed and a new schema may be developed. For other types of problems, understanding may be achieved by *applying* a previously developed schema to the current strategic problem. This involves less diagnosis and information search.

Mintzberg et al. (1976) have discussed similar ideas in connection with the development of *solutions* to strategic problems. They suggest that in some cases solutions are designed to deal with very new strategic problems. In other cases, pre-existing solutions which were developed for other problems are sought out and applied to the problem. Mintzberg et al. suggest that two fundamentally different thought processes underlie the activities of design and search (1976: 255–6).

In the model in Figure 11.1, heuristics and biases affect the development of strategic assumptions and cognitive maps, which in turn affect the development of strategic schemata. The term schemata, being a broader term than cognitive maps, is used to describe the basic cognitive structures through which strategic problems are understood. Schemata may contain cognitive maps as well as assumptions about the strength of the relationship between variables, assessments about decision-makers' degree of confidence, and so forth. Cognitive heuristics and biases may affect the development of cognitive maps. Analogy is the means by which previously

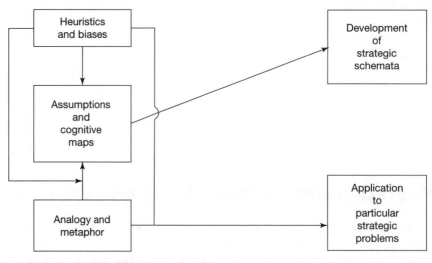

Figure 11.1 *Strategic problem comprehension*

developed schemata are applied to new strategic problems. These processes are described in more detail in the following discussions of the development and application of schemata.

The development of schemata

Simon's work (1957, 1976) suggests that schemata are *simplified* models of the relationships between variables relevant to a strategic problem. Given the complexity of strategic problems and the cognitive limitations of strategists, some types of simplification are needed. Heuristics and biases may enter into this simplification process.

Researchers have not yet dealt explicitly with the *types* of biases which might affect the development of strategic assumptions and cognitive maps. However, work on the availability heuristic suggests that strategists' judgements about the causal relationships between variables in their cognitive maps would be distorted by their recollections of vivid events. Research on the illusion of control suggests that the causal role of key individuals would be exaggerated in strategists' assumptions and cognitive maps. The role of environmental variables which are difficult to control would be underestimated.

The previous speculations on the effects of cognitive heuristics and biases on strategic assumptions and cognitive maps provide the basis for several hypotheses to guide future research:

1 Decision-makers subject to the illusion of control will overestimate the causal role of their own actions in constructing their cognitive maps. Since this bias causes decision-makers to overestimate their level of personal control, it should be reflected in their assessments of the number of variables within their cognitive maps which can be influenced or determined by their own actions.

2 Cognitive heuristics and biases will reduce the number of variables included in decision-makers' cognitive maps. Since heuristics and biases serve to simplify strategic problems, they should reduce the number of variables in cognitive maps related to strategic problems.

3 Heuristics and biases will lead to a smaller number of conflicting strategic assumptions in cognitive maps. Conflicting assumptions are possible when dealing with complex problems. Under the influence of heuristics and biases decision-makers may abandon plausible assumptions which conflict with more deeply held assumptions in order to simplify their cognitive maps for dealing with these problems.

4 Decision-makers who report greater numbers of recent successful business decisions will assign a larger causal role to their own actions in their cognitive maps. Langer's (1983) work suggests that recollections of recent successes may increase the illusion of control

which should lead decision-makers to overestimate the causal role of their own actions.

Analogy and metaphor may affect the development of cognitive maps dealing with strategic issues. Cognitive maps deal with variables and the causal relationships between them. Analogy and metaphor may suggest causal relationships to decision-makers developing new cognitive maps. For example, referring to Figure 11.1, strategists attempting to determine the effect of new product introduction on competitors' behaviour may draw on analogies to other industries with which they are familiar (Huff, 1982). Or, they may draw on analogies to the past (May, 1973) or to competitive games and sports or other personal experiences (Isenberg, 1983).

These considerations form a hypothesis for future research on the effects of analogy and metaphor on cognitive maps.

5 Differences in strategists' personal experiences and industry experience will affect their choice of analogies in constructing cognitive maps. Strategists with different personal or industry experience will have different analogies to draw upon. This should influence the type of analogies chosen in constructing cognitive maps.

The application of schemata

If a broad definition of the term 'analogy' is adopted, it could be said that *any* application of a previously developed schema to a new strategic problem involves analogy. Analogy and metaphor may be the basic processes by which schemata are transferred from one domain to another.

Those writing on analogy and metaphor have not clearly specified the cognitive processes by which they affect strategic problem comprehension. However, it appears that cognitive heuristics and biases may be involved in this process. For example, the *availability* heuristic might cause decision-makers to use dramatic and vivid events as the basis for their problem-defining analogies, even though these events may bear little resemblance to the problems they are attempting to understand. The *illusion of control* bias may lead decision-makers to use analogies to situations in which they had a great deal of control over outcomes, even though this may not be true of the present situation. Further, this bias may draw decision-makers' attention to aspects of the strategic problem over which they have control. These aspects of the problem then provide the *cues* which are used in selecting an analogy.

These points lead to two final hypotheses:

6 Decision-makers who report greater numbers of recent successful business decisions will be more likely to define new strategic problems using analogies to situations in which they had a high level of personal control. As suggested in the comments on hypothesis 4,

the illusion of control is more likely in decision-makers who have experienced success. This should lead them to define new problems in terms of past situations in which they had personal control.

7   Differences in strategists' personal experiences and industry experience will determine which cues are used in selecting analogies to define new strategic problems. Strategists with different backgrounds are likely to attend to different features of new problems when attempting to define them. Therefore, it is likely they will focus on different cues when selecting a problem-relevant schema as a framework for defining the new strategic problems.

[. . .]

Conclusion

In general, researchers in strategic management have not paid sufficient attention to strategists' cognitions in the past. As was pointed out earlier in the paper, the study of cognition may improve our understanding of industry and competitive strategy and the ways environmental factors affect strategic decisions. In this chapter, I have surveyed recent research on four specific topics related to strategic cognitions. I have also developed a model which shows the interrelationships between these topics and I have provided an example to illustrate the features of this model.

As was stated at the beginning of the chapter, interest in strategic cognitions is growing because of increased awareness of their role in strategic issue diagnosis and problem formulation. Research on cognitive structures, processes, and biases gives insights into the ways decision-makers with limited cognitive capacities comprehend and solve very complex strategic problems. It may also give insights into the types of errors they make in strategic decision-making. However, no one has yet shown how these separate streams of research relate to each other. Such integration is necessary in order for future research to provide a complete understanding of strategic problem-solving.

A better understanding of strategists' cognitive structures and processes will also provide a basis for better recommendations for improving strategic decision-making. Strategic decision aids can be developed which are more consistent with the ways decision-makers represent strategic problems. Also, once the most important biases are identified, decision aids can be designed to reduce these. Decision aids may also be developed to help decision-makers to examine more carefully the analogies they use to define new problems.

References

Axelrod, R. (1976) *The Structure of Decision: Cognitive Maps of Political Elites*, Princeton, NJ: Princeton University Press.

Barnes, J. (1984) 'Cognitive biases and their impact on strategic planning', *Strategic Management Journal*, 5: 129–38.

Bougon, M., Weick, K. and Binkhorst, B. (1977) 'Cognitions in organizations: an analysis of the Utrecht jazz orchestra', *Administrative Science Quarterly*, 22: 606–39.

Chittipeddi, K. and Gioia, D. (1983) 'A cognitive psychological perspective and the strategic management process'. Paper presented at the National Academy of Management Meetings.

Duhaime, I. D. and Schwenk, C. (1985) 'Conjectures on cognitive simplification in acquisition and divestment decision-making', *Academy of Management Review*, 10: 287–95.

Dutton, J., Fahey, L. and Narayanan, V. (1983) 'Toward understanding strategic issue diagnosis', *Strategic Management Journal*, 4: 307–23.

Freeman, R. (1984) *Strategic Management: A Stakeholder Approach*. Boston: Pitman.

Gilovich, T. (1981) 'Seeing the past in the present: the effect of associations to familiar events on judgements and decisions', *Journal of Personality and Social Psychology*, 40: 797–808.

Gordon, W. (1961) *Synectics*. New York: Harper & Row.

Hambrick, D. and Mason, P. (1984) 'Upper echelons: the organization as a reflection of its top managers', *Academy of Management Review*, 9: 193–206.

Hogarth, R. M. (1980) *Judgement and Choice: The Psychology of Decision*. Chichester: Wiley.

Huff, A. (1982) 'Industry influences on strategy reformulation', *Strategic Management Journal*, 3: 119–31.

Isenberg, D. (1983) 'How senior managers think (and what about)'. Unpublished manuscript, Harvard University.

Janis, I. and Mann, L. (1977) *Decision-Making*. New York: Free Press.

Langer, E. J. (1983) *The Psychology of Control*. Beverly Hills, CA: Sage.

Louis, M. R. (1980) 'A cultural perspective on organizations'. Paper presented at the National Academy of Management Meetings.

Lyles, M. (1981) 'Formulating strategic problems: empirical analysis and model development', *Strategic Management Journal*, 2: 61–75.

Mason, R. O. and Mitroff, I. I. (1981) *Challenging Strategic Planning Assumptions*. New York: Wiley.

May, E. (1973) *'Lessons' of the Past*. New York: Oxford University Press.

Mintzberg, H. and Waters, J. (1982) 'Tracking strategy in the entrepreneurial firm', *Academy of Management Journal*, 25: 465–99.

Mintzberg, H., Raisinghani, P. and Theoret, A. (1976) 'The structure of "unstructured" decision processes', *Administrative Science Quarterly*, 2: 246–75.

Neisser, U. (1976) *Cognition and Reality*. San Francisco, CA: Freeman.

Rumelhart, D. and Ortony, A. (1977) 'The representation of knowledge in memory', in R. Anderson, R. Spiro and W. Montague (eds), *Schooling and the Acquisition of Knowledge*. Hillsdale, NJ: Lawrence Erlbaum.

Sapienza, A. M. (1983) 'A cognitive perspective on strategy formulation'.

Paper presented at the Academy of Management National Meetings, Dallas, August.

Schwenk, C. (1984) 'Cognitive simplification processes in strategic decision-making', *Strategic Management Journal*, 5: 111–28.

Schwenk, C. (1986) 'Information, cognitive bias, and commitment to a course of action', *Academy of Management Review*, 11: 298–310.

Shrivastava, P. (1983) 'A typology of organizational learning systems', *Journal of Management Studies*, 20: 7–28.

Shrivastava, P. and Mitroff, I. I. (1983) 'Frames of references managers use: a study in applied sociology of knowledge', in R. Lamb (ed.), *Advances in Strategic Management*, V: 1, Greenwich, CT: JAI Press.

Simon, H. A. (1957) *Models of Man*. New York: Wiley.

Simon, H. A. (1976) *Administrative Behavior* (4th edn) New York: Free Press.

Steinbruner, J. D. (1974) *The Cybernetic Theory of Decision*. Princeton, NJ: Princeton University Press.

Taylor, R. N. (1975) 'Psychological determinants of bounded rationality: implications for decision-making', *Decision Sciences*, 6: 409–29.

Taylor, S. (1982) 'The interface of cognitive and social psychology', in J. Harvey (ed.), *Cognition, Social Behavior and the Environment*. Hillsdale, NJ: Lawrence Erlbaum.

Taylor, S. and Crocker, J. (1983) 'Schematic bases of social information processing', in E. Higgens, C. Herman and J. Zauna, *Social Cognition: The Ontario Symposium*. Hillsdale, NJ: Lawrence Erlbaum.

Tolman, E. (1948) 'Cognitive maps in rats and men', *Psychological Review*, 1(55): 189–208.

Tversky, A. and Kahneman, D. (1974) 'Judgement under uncertainty: heuristics and biases', *Sciences*, 185: 1124–31.

Weick, K. (1979) 'Cognitive processes in organizations', in B. Staw (ed.), *Research in Organizational Behavior*. Greenwich, CT: JAI Press.

CHAPTER 12

The Impact of Organizational Culture on Approaches to Organizational Problem-solving

PAUL BATE*

Organizational culture is a subject which until recently has failed to capture the serious attention of researchers. [. . .] ....
The three research studies which form the basis of this chapter [. . .] were all 'action research' projects in the field of organizational change and development. The main focus of change in the three companies was their decision-making processes, and more particularly the issue of wider employee participation in them. [. . .]

One general conclusion reached repeatedly during the course of the work was that organizational change was substantially different in practice from the theory of change – and more difficult. One strand of this theory states that change will take place if and when the following 'preconditions' are present: a problem or problems and a desire or felt need to resolve them; an awareness of the existence and basic nature of the problem; and available information which allows the parties to the problem to define it and make appropriate choices between alternative courses of action (Lippitt et al., 1958; Schein, 1969). In practice it was discovered – initially in the footwear company and later in the others – that change did not always occur even when all of these conditions were in evidence. Something – whatever it may be – was enmeshing people in their problems in a persistent and repetitive way.

Increasingly attention became focused on the question: why were situations allowed to persist when they were accepted by the parties themselves as problematical and undesirable? Gradually a fascinating notion began to emerge that the parties were actively *colluding* in a process which effectively removed all

* Bate, P. (1984) 'The impact of organisational culture on approaches to organisational problem solving', *Organisation Studies*, 5(1). Copyright © Paul Bate 1984.

possibility of a resolution to their problems. Closer investigation suggested that at the heart of this collusion process lay the organizational culture. The thesis that resulted from this line of inquiry provides the basis of this chapter. It can be summarized as follows: people in organizations evolve in their daily interactions with one another a system of shared perspectives of 'collectively held and sanctioned definitions of the situation' which make up the culture of these organizations. The culture, once established, prescribes for its creators and inheritors certain ways of believing, thinking and acting which in some circumstances can prevent meaningful interaction and induce a condition of 'learned helplessness' – that is a psychological state in which people are unable to conceptualize their problems in such a way as to be able to resolve them. In short, attempts at problem-solving may become culture-bound.

This chapter looks at that 'something' about organizational culture that has the power to lock people in with their own problems.

What is organizational culture?

[. . .] The first important point is that culture is predominantly *implicit* in people's minds; it is not something that is 'out there' with a separate existence of its own; neither is it directly observable. The components of organizational culture are really internalized social constructs – socially produced definitions of the situation that are part of and inseparable from a person's definition of him or herself. These constructs form the basis of that person's 'commonsense' view of her organizational world, something that is notable for its unconscious and unreflecting character. As Silverman (1970: 133) observes in this context, this world is 'a taken-for-granted world governed by what we understand as the laws of nature'.

The deeply embedded nature of culture partly explains why people have difficulty describing it in precise and critical terms. But this is not the only reason: culture forms the very foundation stone of our social existence; it gives meaning in a very literal sense to our social and organizational lives by providing us with a relatively self-contained 'order' or rationale – what Kluckhohn and Kelly (1945) call a design for living. To have this questioned can be both threatening and upsetting, and it is because of this that we defend ourselves by hiding alien values behind stereotypes, restricting our information to selective sources (reading only our 'colour' of newspaper), and limiting our interactions to those with other people of roughly similar outlooks [. . .].

Another key feature of culture is that it is *shared* – it refers to the ideas, meanings and values people hold in common and to which they subscribe collectively. [. . .] While not denying the existence of differences – sometimes numerous and fundamental – in people's outlooks, motivation and interests, the culture concept tends to focus on the commonalities which give a work organization, for example, a recognizable personality and unity – shared perspectives which constitute what Baker (1980: 8) calls 'the social glue holding the company together'. [. . .]

A third important characteristic of organizational culture, (is) that it is *transmitted* by a process of socialization. People are required to acknowledge and, to a degree at least, conform to patterns of thinking and acting that might stretch far back into an organization's history. [. . .] It is organizational culture which acts as the vehicle for transmitting and giving continuity to the past – the 'living history' as Malinowski (1945) graphically describes it.

An issue around which there is a good deal of debate is what culture actually consists of. Some writers [. . .] emphasize its normative dimension by drawing attention to established organizational taboos, folkways, mores and formal rules, all making up a set of expected behaviours which regulate the behaviour of different groups. [. . .] Others choose to focus on the values dimension of culture – the morality (Marcuse, 1969) or collective conscience (Durkheim, 1952) of the society or organization. [. . .] My view is that both of these dimensions are not so much the elements of culture as its product. This view is sustained if one considers organizational culture from the perspective of 'interactionism' (Mead, 1964; Blumer, 1965). The basis of symbolic interactionism is that humanity, from a process of observation, self-interaction, and social interaction, symbolizes or attributes 'meanings' to the surrounding world, and acts in accordance with these meanings. Just as the way that people act arises out of these meanings, so too can values and norms be regarded as having the same derivative. The term 'meaning' thus refers to something which includes but is much wider than actions, values and norms – a conceptual structure of generalizations or contexts, postulates about what is essential, assumptions about what is valuable, attitudes about what is possible, and ideas about what will work effectively. In the organizational context this conceptual structure will encompass one's own roles, the roles of others, rules and institutions, traditional ways of acting, and specific issues such as the nature of authority, leadership and democracy, and many more.

Thus the term 'culture' can be defined as the meanings or aspects of the conceptual structures which people hold in common and which define the social or organizational 'reality'. [. . .]

Methodology

A number of instruments purporting to 'measure' culture were found in the literature [. . .]. While many of the concepts contained in these were useful, it was decided that the actual instruments were usually too general to be used in an organizational context, or, more seriously, too culture-bound themselves to have much credibility. It was therefore decided, in the case of this piece of research, to begin the approach from the opposite end first by focusing on the minutiae of culture specifically within the organizational context, and secondly by seeking to describe and understand organizational culture from the viewpoint of the parties to it. The task was to build up a picture from the data of how individuals defined aspects of their work situation, to ascertain from this which meanings or definitions were widely shared in the organization, and finally to try to establish some connections between such observed cultural meanings and human actions (for example, approaches to problem-solving). [. . .]

The main source of data has been what Pettigrew (1979) calls the 'symbols' of the organization – the myths, legends, rituals and displays which contain, as encoded messages, some of the most sacrosanct of the organization's cultural meanings. Myths and legends permeate, in varying degrees, different levels and groups, and emerge quite naturally in conversations and interviews (particularly with self-confessed 'deviants'). [. . .]

Language itself is perhaps the most important symbolic offering of culture, containing a wealth of information about social meanings. [. . .] To use Pettigrew's (1979: 575) phrase:

> The study of organizational vocabularies is long overdue. The analysis of their origins and uses and in particular their role in expressing communal values, evoking past experiences, providing seed beds for human action, and legitimating current and evolving distributions of power represent key areas of inquiry in research on the creation and evolution of new organizations.

[. . .]

Summary of findings

My main concern was to identify those aspects of each culture that had a strong impact on organizational problem-solving, and it gradually became clear that certain characteristics were present, to a greater or lesser extent and in different forms, in all three organizations. They have been labelled as follows:

Unemotionality

Depersonalization

Subordination

Conservatism

Isolationism

Antipathy

Unemotionality: 'Avoid showing or sharing feelings or emotions'

In two of the companies studied – the footwear manufacturer and the chemicals multinational – and to a lesser degree in the third, there appeared to be a hidden dictate that displays of feeling and emotion were not permitted or were somehow 'bad' for the individual and bad for the organization. This was well captured in the phrase 'civil service mentality' used by one junior manager, who then went on to define it:

> Everything is handled in a formal, stiff-upper-lip way. Problems are sterilized and laundered in the company washing machine, and come out whiter than white. One never need get one's hands wet or dirty. Our meetings are all the same – brisk, businesslike and to the point.

Unemotionality was also reflected in the apparent superficiality of work relationships. 'Work' and 'personal' relationships were separately defined: 'There are none of them personal friends. The word personal is watered down at work. One's judgement is a bit bland because one is talking about a work rather than total relationship' (senior manager). And, 'I don't think it's part of one's work to form likes or dislikes. I don't find many people sympathetic, nor do I want them to be' (middle manager). And, 'I would rather not have close, socially intimate relationships with people either on whom I depend or who conceivably depend on me as part of their job. I would find that quite difficult' (director).

Such a definition of the work relationship did appear to affect people's ways of dealing with each other:

> I suppose on those occasions when I have tried to get close to someone and actually speak my mind, I've sort of sensed the barriers coming down. You know, sort of seen a blank look coming over their face. You see this as a warning signal against getting too close, and begin to back off. (operator)

The reasons given for playing down feelings and emotions were that it was somehow impolite, embarrassing, or just 'plain useless' to do otherwise: 'Nobody wants to hear about my feelings and problems. And it's not for me to burden others with them' (foreman). And another, 'When somebody blows off steam, everyone else is made to feel uncomfortable. It doesn't really get anyone anywhere at all' (operator). When a female worker was asked why she had not brought her long-standing complaints to the attention of her supervisor, she replied: 'It would cause more trouble than it would solve – a bit like being sick over the floor: first it would upset me, second it would upset him, and third it might lead to me getting a black eye!'

In the case of managers, showing feelings and emotions was construed as a sign of unprofessionalism – a sign of weakness or inefficiency: 'If I blow my top, people will start to brand me an "hysterical woman" and suggest maybe I was working too hard' (female personnel officer). Another said,

> You soon learn how to be seen as good at your job – you keep your head down and above all you keep your cool; always keep that little bit of distance; be inscrutable. If you remember this you don't actually have to do anything outstanding to be a high-flier.

Then there was the issue of vulnerability: 'Once you show that something means a great deal to you people can begin to use it against you. You dare not risk getting personally involved' (senior manager). Unemotionality in this sense is therefore closely connected with the issue of low trust. It is also a protection: a person can 'hide behind his office' when under attack or when having to deal with some volatile or embarrassing issue. A case of being able to say 'I'm only doing my job. I'm sure you appreciate there is nothing personal in this', words which preface announcements of redundancies, strike action, cut-backs in budgets, and so on. What this adds up to is an abdication of personal responsibility in the face of the demands of one's office.

The evidence suggests that, as a result of this orientation, differences between people tended to be repressed (and allowed to smoulder on) or dealt with unsatisfactorily at a 'distance'. There was a fear of bringing true feelings about a problem into the open in case tempers would fray and the situation would become 'unmanageable' (a likely enough outcome in view of people's inexperience of confrontation and openness). Instead, people would tend to 'chew' on their problem for as long as they possibly could, even though this obviously produced a lot of tension and frustration. When the problem could no longer be ducked, the next stage was to approach it in a way that deterred people from opening it up too far. One way in which some senior managers in the footwear company did this was to use junior managers as the first line of defence, and then to issue a written memorandum to the parties involved (the tone of this being vague but firm and conclusive) – in both cases avoiding face-to-face contact. Failing that, one-to-one meetings were held, at which some kind of secret deal was struck – a 'Spanish custom' as it is widely known in the footwear company. Larger meetings were studiously avoided whenever possible except for routine, non-emotive business.

It is not difficult to understand why, in such an environment, joint attempts to deal effectively and creatively with problems often failed miserably. The culture, while having a rationale of sorts, made people inflexible and overcautious. Attempts at exploring issues and using others to collaborate in this would have been regarded – in sensitive areas – as highly dangerous, a case of (to use people's actual words) 'turning over stones and finding the worms' or of 'poking your nose into something that you would do better to keep out of'. People's concern, therefore, was to cope with the situation – *not* to change it – by avoidance and repression strategies, all of which added up to a failure to get to grips with the problems.

People's lack of ability to engage in meaningful interaction was painfully obvious in meetings that did take place: 'We all want to discuss common problems but when we actually get there most of us are fairly mute' (junior manager). And, 'Our meetings? In a word – weak. Lukewarm affairs' (shop steward). 'People never really open up about their concerns. It means that our meetings are pretty dry affairs . . . I suppose we are all fairly reluctant to bring our dirty washing into the open' (personnel officer).

Depersonalization of issues: 'Never point the finger at anyone in particular'

In all three organizations I found a tendency for people at all levels to be publicly vague about the source of their problems or grievances, even when they clearly had in mind a 'blacklist' of culprits and privately discussed this with one or two close colleagues. Confronting or 'naming' individuals was regarded (if regarded is the best word for an unreflecting and natural way of seeing things) as completely out of the question – ungentlemanly, unkind, unnecessary, and often dangerous. The corollary of this was that few people appeared to accept personal responsibility for things that were going wrong: collective responsibility on the lines of a government cabinet was considered to be the order of organizational life.

The following extracts from conversations illustrate the range of different ways people tended to generalize and externalize the sources of their problems: 'You ask why we get upset about things. Well, it's that lot up there – the people at head office up there in London. What do they know about our problems?' When asked whether he was referring to anyone in particular this man – a shop-floor worker – replied, 'No, not really. All them buggers are the same. There's nothing to choose between them.' When pressed further he said that it would not be right to pick out individuals. Employees in the footwear company frequently picked on the 'family' owners as the cause of their difficulties:

> It's one thing they all seem to bring with them – a sort of insincerity and lack of positive support . . . no, no one in particular; you've got to remember that they have all come out of the same mould. (manager)

Only on rare occasions did people differentiate between members of the family. In the case of the chemicals company it was often the parent company in Germany that was behind a problem:

> The trouble with that lot is that they can't tell the difference between a safety committee and a participation committee. No wonder we're not getting support in what we want to do. (director)

> We're not really getting on top of things. We respond to changes in the market far too slowly. We are not abreast of new technology, and we are not developing enlightened policies. But you tell me where there's any hope when they are now insisting that even buying a new flag pole requires head office approval. (manager)

If it was not 'head office' or the 'family' then it was 'the workers', 'the unions', or 'the managers' who were to blame, depending on your standpoint. Even more widely it was often 'the government', 'the recession', or 'the strength of the pound' which were the cause of the problem – but rarely any one individual.

To try to explain this attitude, one must begin with the moral aspects. Widespread in the three organizations was a strong professed belief that to name names was wrong; that there was something uncouth about confronting or even talking about an individual in public. It was, however, a rather odd morality in that it was acceptable to engage in gossip or even smear campaigns behind someone's back. A typical example was a director in the chemicals company who insisted that 'names' should not be put to problems, but who admitted in private that he was keeping secret dossiers on people who weren't pulling their weight – managers and workers whose *bosses* would be shown the contents of such files when the time was ripe!

Several other factors contributed to this attitude: fear, for example – not many people would dare to go to their boss and blame him for any difficulties being experienced; then the view that 'speaking up for yourself' was 'forgetting your place'; it was also regarded as unprofessional to question or criticize individuals (or for individuals to break the party line and take a personal stand on things), and such a course of action was unquestioningly seen to be destructive rather than constructive.

As a result, attempts to resolve problems frequently dissolved into vague discussions which skirted the real issues, or hurried attempts to move on to easier, less contentious ones. In meetings, one would often see the chairman intervening with, 'I really think we should accept that we're not going to get far on this one. I don't think the brief for this meeting is to talk about individuals or individual cases.' Or, 'I'm sure we all know *who* is being referred to here but I'm equally sure we'd all agree that it is better to let sleeping dogs lie.' What is notable – and what emphasizes the collusive side of a culture – is that on these occasions people rarely challenged the chairman on this. There was a conspiracy of silence in a literal and very powerful sense.

An alternative strategy often involved the attribution of a technical (i.e. non-human) cause to the problem under discussion, thereby setting in motion the less threatening search for a technical solution. The weaknesses, failings or mistakes of a person or group of people would thus be transformed into 'outdated machinery', 'production pressures', 'design difficulties', and so on.

The evidence suggests that both unemotionality and depersonalization reflected and perpetuated a situation where people were incapable of directness in diagnosing and dealing with their problems. The requirement for diagnostic activities, 'valid information about the status quo, current problems and opportunities, and effects of actions as they relate to goal achievement' (French and Bell, 1973), was not met. 'Valid' information was neither gathered nor discussed; such information as existed was never really evaluated or put to the test – people were allowed to go around with semi-private opinions which might or might not have stood up to public scrutiny. The system also worked in such a way that no one needed to own up to a problem and no one needed to accept responsibility for doing anything about it.

Subordination: 'Never challenge those in authority and always wait for them to take the initiative in resolving *your* problems'

A member of staff in the footwear company pointed out how totally dependent his colleagues had become upon their bosses at the head office: 'All my colleagues now rely on "Mecca" speaking – so if nobody speaks from there nothing happens.' Some of these colleagues to whom he referred also had something to say on this issue: 'X is my boss in the Centre. He should be coming along and saying what needs to be done, and we should be listening to that.'

Leadership was defined – by many leaders and subordinates – as providing the initial impetus for change and problem resolution. The legitimacy of a subordinate doing this was questionable, since 'subordinate' connoted 'following', 'responding', 'carrying out instructions', and similar things. Subordination also symbolized not taking responsibility for solving problems – even if they were your own problems. When resolution was not forthcoming people would tend to suffer in silence or grumble quietly amongst themselves, oblivious to the fact that one of the reasons for the persistence of their problems was their own definition of their role.

Challenging this ingrained way of seeing things, as I encouraged people to do in newly established participative processes, can be an unnatural and painful experience. This was captured well in a comment made by a chargehand-foreman to some of his colleagues:

> I would agree that to begin with we accepted things too easily in our participation committee. It's just a thing you naturally do – you know, there is this feeling that they reserve the final right to say yes or no. You have got to learn how to challenge. You have to get into a way of keeping issues alive. But all this is very embarrassing at times: in meetings the management have tried to get things taken off the agenda. So you have to raise things again and again. It can make the atmosphere pretty icy. It does take a lot of nerve and a very thick skin.

As with other aspects of culture this subordination was reinforced by sanctions of various kinds applied to deviants. If, for example, someone did challenge authority or take it upon himself to seek a resolution of his own problems, pressures would be applied to make him 'back off'. Such pressures – as evidenced by the following extract from a conversation with some of the workers in the chemicals company – can be very great indeed:

> *First worker*: It's all very well and good you telling us to speak up for ourselves at the meetings, but it wouldn't really be worth our while. Our life wouldn't be worth living.
>
> *Researcher*: What do you mean?
>
> *First worker*: You would know what I mean if you worked here.
>
> *Second worker*: Take the people in the warehouse. They have a reputation for sticking up for themselves. And look what happens. If they see you've got views – are a bit bolshie – they pick on you. You get all the bad jobs.
>
> *First worker*: And black eyes into the bargain.
>
> *Second worker*: People need protection.
>
> *First worker*: It pays to keep your mouth shut.

In all three companies many of the relationships that were observed between the shop-floor workers and the management were characterized by counter-dependence. Workers defined themselves as powerless (which they sometimes were) and grudgingly submitted to management authority. This had the effect of reinforcing the managerial view of this authority, thereby producing a situation where decisions were made without consultation and explanation, and only minimal input was made by workers themselves concerning their problems and anxieties. Consequently, managers were often blissfully unaware that these problems existed and therefore did nothing to search for a solution.

Conservatism: 'Better the devil you know'

Managers and workers alike often had an ingrained conservatism about organizational life that partly stemmed from an underlying scepticism either that 'things will never change', or that if they did the situation might actually become worse than it currently was. The result was that problem-solving was often approached in a half-hearted way, and tended to be superficial or marginal in content. 'What it boils down to is a question of personalities. You'll never change these. What is the point in trying?' (factory manager). And, 'What's the use? Participation is a load of rubbish. If we were to put anything forward it would be squashed – a case of you can't have it, goodbye. There's no point is there?' (operator).

The following example from a recent experience (Bate and Mangham, 1981: 119) shows that such a frame of mind can completely deactivate a change effort. A colleague and I were meeting a group of workers in the chemicals company for the first time to ascertain their views on 'more' participation:

> The operators on the whole were fairly indifferent and off-hand about the whole thing – yes, that would be nice, yes, it sounds a good idea, but well, you know, nothing much will come of it . . . etc. 'What's the supervision like round here?' we asked, trying to stir them into some kind of action. 'Oh, not bad', they replied with a yawn. And taking another tack, 'Do you find things you raise get blocked?' 'Yes', came the reply – followed by another yawn. 'Well, would you like to enlarge on that?' 'Yes, things do get blocked.' 'Oh, thank you. Are there any issues you could raise at the new meetings?' (Yawning) 'Yes, hundreds, but there's not much point, is there?' 'Why not?' 'Well, things get blocked, don't they?'

Similar pockets of scepticism were encountered in the other two organizations, with broadly similar consequences for the change programme.

Isolationism: 'Do your own thing and avoid treading on other people's toes'

In all three companies there was a widely shared belief that one should be able to stake out a personal territory in the organization in which one could 'do one's own thing'. In return one was expected to let others do likewise. This belief had found institutional expression through a highly differentiated organizational structure: each of the three companies was divisionalized, each division was strongly departmentalized, and each department sectionalized. Horizontal and vertical links between people in these areas tended to be weak, and there was little evidence of people working in teams that actually came to decisions. Any approach to problem-solving was highly individualistic: only when a person failed to make progress would he approach his superior for guidance and support, usually on a one-to-one basis. When meetings were held, those who had not been involved would be *informed* of the one-to-one deal that had been struck, but would be discouraged from influencing the matter further. Other people, on the whole, tended to be regarded as more of a hindrance than a help, an obstruction rather than a resource to be tapped, a problem to be 'managed' or avoided. They were also a threat, in so far as they were seen to be competing to take away some of your territory.

> I'm trying to involve myself as much as I can. I'm really like a child sitting on the floor with all his toys around him. And I'm trying to do two things. I'm making sure nobody pinches *my* toys, and if any toy passes close to me belonging to somebody else, I'll pinch that if I can. We're all doing the same. (manager)

And, 'Everyone is fairly jealous of his area – a bit prickly if he feels people are trespassing' (engineer). And, 'I think we all like to run our own thing because the fewer people there are interfering in what you do the easier it is to do it' (manager).

The evidence suggests that the problematical consequences of extreme isolationism are numerous. Information may be withheld, leaving others to piece together a picture of what is happening or to invest considerable energy in 'teasing out' information by various means. Rumour systems may be working overtime to plug the gaps in direct information. Decisions may be made which reflect only one view of a problem and fail to take into account different perceptions of that problem. Available expertise may not be fully utilized. Perhaps more important, long-standing differences between people remain a running sore so long as isolationism is used as a way of avoiding conflicts: 'I for one don't seek criticism or conflict. In fact I'm quite happy if we can actually avoid airing our differences, and establish non-conflicting roles for ourselves' (director). And,

> I suppose the main reason why we haven't sorted out the problems between engineering and ourselves is that we haven't got together and had a good free-for-all. Yes it would clear the air but I'm not sure who is going to take the initiative in setting that up. (manager)

Antipathy: 'On most things people will be opponents rather than allies'

In view of what has already been said about the superficiality of relationships, low trust, and isolationism, it is not surprising that all three companies – though, in fairness, some factories less than others – were characterized by a particular brand of extreme pluralism. Not only were they, according to the pluralist tradition, 'fractured into a congeries of hundreds of small interest groups, with incompletely overlapping memberships and widely differing power bases' (Polsby, 1963: 25), but many of these groups were engaged in protracted hostilities with each other. Relationships between them were belligerent, distant and untrusting. Meanings attached to intergroup relations were firmly rooted in a 'them' and 'us' tradition. Antipathy was the order of the day.

The multitude of shared meanings that had grown up around such intergroup relations had found expression in the 'adversary principle' of industrial relations and problem-solving. It was assumed by the parties involved – notably (but not exclusively) managers and shop stewards – that all or most of the important issues were of a win–lose nature. Any gains would have to be at the expense of the other party. It was further assumed that there were conflicts of interest over most of the major issues. Even when this was clearly not the case, the parties – ritually and almost instinctively – took up their opposing positions and flatly refused to budge from them. Problems were 'solved' by brinkmanship and confrontation. In one or two factories, relationships had reached a particularly low ebb: nearly all issues were fought over, neither 'side' was prepared to move or look for compromise, and even the most trivial of matters was bitterly contested.

What the parties did have in common was the belief that pluralism of this kind was inevitable – a fact of industrial life:

> The fact is that you can't trust the management an inch. If you turn your back for a moment they'll get you. (shop steward)

> Frankly, it's essential that I keep my distance. If I lose my independence I lose my integrity – and I'm left with nothing. (shop steward)

> You have to fight them all the way – fight them as they fight you. It's like a tug-of-war. You all heave like hell, dig your heels in. If you can't win you make sure you don't lose. (shop steward)

Managers tended to convey the same sentiments in different metaphors:

> It's a bit like a chess game. They're black, you are white! The name of the game is simply to win. Clobber the opposition. (factory manager)

> It's called 'playing the Italian defence' – you hack down the opposition before they get too near your goal, or you run them out at the corner. (director)

What was not said, but was nonetheless patently obvious, was that this 'way of going about things' actually suited the interests of the parties concerned. A point made by Barbash (1979: 456) is relevant in this regard:

> Management prefers the adversary relationship, because it fears that union collaboration will dilute management authority and thereby impair efficiency. The union prefers it that way, because the adversary relationship is most consistent with the maintenance of the union as a bargaining organization, and bargaining is what the union is all about.

However, while pluralist conceptions have developed chiefly to preserve the survival interests of the parties this is a very different issue from – and one which may well work against – the need to develop effective problem-solving processes.

Discussion

The findings from the three studies described in this chapter lend support to the view that organizational culture can shape patterns of organizational behaviour [. . .], and in particular that certain cultural orientations can constrain problem-solving behaviour [. . .]. How does this occur? In what areas does organizational culture exert influence and what processes are involved? One explanation implied throughout this chapter [. . .] is that the culture affects the type and quality of interpersonal relationships, which in turn affect the approach to joint problem-solving processes. To be more precise, certain shared cultural meanings, once established, define what are acceptable, natural, desirable and effective ways of relating and acting. Taken together, they constitute people's 'dominant relational orientation' to work and to each other (Kluckhohn and Strodtbeck, 1961; Kluckhohn, 1963).

From this we can see that culture has a social consequence, in shaping relationships and interactions. It therefore directly affects the *activity* of joint problem-solving. But this is not the entire picture: my research findings suggest that certain cultural orientations have an important psychological impact, producing a sense of futility and pessimism in people long before they enter the problem-solving arena. The culture induces a condition similar to Seligman's 'learned helplessness' (1975) – a psychological state which results when a person perceives that he can no longer control his own destiny. If this perception finds confirmation in experience – if one learns from trying that one is indeed helpless – 'this saps the motivation to initiate responses' (Seligman, 1975: 74). In other words one simply gives up trying; the energy and will to resolve problems and attain goals drains away.

There is a good deal of data in this chapter to support Seligman's theory: the quotations offer many variations on the theme 'there is no point in trying; there is nothing I can do to change the situation', and in practice there were few if any actual attempts to do so. There is, however, an important difference: whereas Seligman stated that helplessness resulted when a person tried and failed, my findings suggest that an organizational culture can transmit to its members, a priori, the assumption that they are powerless – without them actually having to experience this at all. A state of *socialized* helplessness results, and this becomes an internalized, unquestioned 'fact'. Its reality is never tested and the resulting lack of change reinforces the initial cultural assumption. The culture is confirmed, and the circuit between no action and no motivation is closed. The one predicts the other.

An example of this was mentioned earlier, in the section on subordination where two workers were explaining why they did not air their long-standing problems at meetings. They believed that, as a result, they would end up with all the bad jobs, 'and black eyes into the bargain'. Perhaps this was a realistic assumption but more to the point is that they had never really put it to the test. Helplessness had been socialized, by peers and managers, and had come to be taken for granted. When we challenged them, they confirmed our suspicions:

Self: Can I ask you, Maggie, whether in fact anyone has been given a black eye?

Maggie: I can't recall any specific instances – I suppose it's this fear of getting one that prevents it happening.

[. . .]

Kluckhohn and her contemporaries regarded culture as a society or organization's *solution* to the basic 'life problems', implying that the culture has somehow 'got it right'.

I prefer the term '*attempted* solution', since the data in this chapter clearly suggest that the culture has, to some extent, got it wrong, at least with regard to interpersonal relations and problem-solving in organizations. This is perfectly understandable, given the complexity of the issues involved, the resistance of culture to change, and the fact that a culture often merely represents a solution to the 'life problems' of the small number of powerful groups who created it. (Crozier [1964, 1969] similarly claims that French organizations invariably get it wrong – that their cultures have brought about total rigidity and paralysis.)

Thus we come to a vital question: if, to some degree, an organization's culture has 'got it wrong', what are the alternatives? What are the basic organizational 'life problems' to which a solution has to be found? In Table 12.1 I have suggested six basic organizational issues, in the form of questions, to which my six cultural orientations are the seemingly imperfect solutions.

My argument [. . .] is that these six basic issues represent an unavoidable and important range of choices facing people in organizations everywhere: every organization has to find *some* cultural 'solution' to each of the problems. Thus, *some degree* of unemotionality, depersonalization, and so on will be present in every organization. [. . .] The choices facing organizations are universal, the solutions are infinitely variable. What exactly do these choices involve, and what are the consequences? Lack of space prevents a detailed discussion here, but some examples will suffice: the first of the basic issues (affective orientation) requires evaluations about how emotionally bound up people will become with each other – the degree of intimacy, disclosure of 'self' and feelings. [. . .]

The data show that the six cultural orientations appear to be linked with the following range of problematical predispositions: a low commitment to and

Table 12.1

Basic organization issues	Cultural responses
1 How emotionally bound up do people become with others in the work setting? (Affective orientation)	Unemotionality
2 How far do people attribute responsibility for personal problems to others, or to the system? (Animate-inanimate orientation to causality)	Depersonalization
3 How do people respond to differences in position, role, power and responsibility? (Hierarchical orientation)	Subordination
4 How far are people willing to embark with others on new ventures? (Change orientation)	Conservatism
5 How far do people choose to work alone or with and through others? (Individualist-collectivist orientation)	Isolationism
6 How do people in different interest groups relate to each other? (Unitary-Pluralistic orientation)	Antipathy

involvement in the change process; a disowning of problems and an abdication of responsibility for the search for solutions; a lack of openness in confronting and dealing jointly with issues; avoidance of data-gathering on the causes of problems; overcaution and a lack of decisiveness and creativity in problem-solving; erection of barriers to change; and a taking of adversary positions on all issues regardless of whether any potential measure of agreement between the parties exists.

Clearly the degree to which some or all of the six cultural orientations is present will greatly affect issues such as problem-solving and an organization's willingness or resistance to change. Argyris (1965: 11) has noted that some relational orientations are more conducive than others to 'interpersonal competence in problem-solving', and suggests that the latter will be low in organizations where the degree of subordination is high and the culture is highly cognitively rational. Arguably we can now include depersonalization, conservatism, isolationism and antipathy in this list. Can change agents therefore be optimistic if they find an organization that is 'low' on some or all of these? Generally speaking, from the results of our studies I feel this to be the case. [. . .]

The evidence remains that the three companies studied showed a leaning towards the same cultural 'solutions' to each of the basic organizational issues, that is a preference for the adversary brand of pluralism, individualism rather than collectivism, and so on. Perhaps, then, there are cultural approaches as yet largely untried which might provide more effective solutions to the problems described above. Perhaps the 'alternative organization' – the commune, the co-operative, the co-partnership – has already begun to experiment with alternative cultural solutions (emotionality, personalization, power equalization, and so on). The scope for alternatives is unquestionably great, but whether the existing cultural preferences will allow this scope to be explored is quite another matter.

References

Argyris, C. (1965) *Organization and Innovation*. Homewood, IL: Irwin.

Baker, E.L. (1980) 'Managing organizational culture', *Management Review*, 69(7): 8–13.

Barbash, J. (1979) 'The American ideology of industrial relations', *Proceedings of Industrial Relations Research Association Spring Meeting*, 30(8): 453–7.

Bate, S.P. and Mangham, I. (1981) *Exploring Participation*. Chichester: Wiley.

Blumer, H. (1965) 'Sociological implications of the thought of George Herbert Mead', *American Journal of Sociology*, 71: 535–48.

Crozier, M. (1964) *The Bureaucratic Phenomenon*. Chicago: University of Chicago Press.

Crozier, M. (1969) 'The cultural determinants of organizational behavior', A.R. Negandhi (ed.), in *Modern Organizational Theory*, pp. 220–8. Kent, Ohio: Kent State University Press.

Durkheim, E. (1952) *The Rules of Sociological Method*. Chicago: Free Press.

French, W.L., and Bell, C.H. (1973) *Organization Development*. Englewood Cliffs, NJ: Prentice-Hall.

Hofstede, G. (1978) 'National cultures and work values', Paper read at XIXth International Congress of Applied Psychology, Munich.

Kluckhohn, C. and Kelly, W.H. (1945) 'The concept of culture', in R. Linton (ed.), *The Science of Man in World Crisis*. New York: Columbia University Press.

Kluckhohn, F.R. (1963) 'Some reflections on the nature of cultural integration and change', in E.A. Tiryakian (ed.), *Sociological Theory, Values and Sociocultural Change*. New York: Free Press.

Kluckhohn, F.R. and Strodtbeck, F.L. (1961) *Variations in Value Orientations*. New York: Row, Peterson.

Lippitt, R., Watson, J. and Westley, B. (1958) *The Planning of Change*. New York: Harcourt Brace.

Malinowski, B. (1945) *The Dynamics of Culture Change*. New Haven, CT: Yale University Press.

Marcuse, H. (1969) *An Essay on Liberation* London: Methuen.

Mead, G.H. (1964) *Selected Writings* (ed. A. J. Peck). New York: Bobbs-Merrill.

Pettigrew, A.M. (1979) 'On studying organizational cultures', *Administrative Science Quarterly*, 24: 570–81.

Polsby, N.W. (1963) *Community Power and Political Theory*. New Haven, CT: Yale University Press.

Schein, E.H. (1969) *Process Consultation: Its Role in Organization Development*. Reading.

Seligman, M.E.P. (1975) *Helplessness: On Depression, Development, and Death*. San Francisco: Freeman.

Silverman, D. (1970) *The Theory of Organizations*. London: Heinemann.

The Societal Context of Organizational Decision-making

This section moves the focus from the internal working of organizations to the relationship between organizations and the wider society. It addresses the question: what determines what is taken for rationality? What are the standards by which rationality is identified and measured in a society or in an organization at a particular historic moment?

Section 4 completes our analysis. It consists of four articles, each of which in different ways returns to the starting point of the book: what is rationality and how are standards of rationality determined and applied? It identifies some widely accepted organizational standards of rationality and shows their location within and dependence upon a certain cognitive and political context which renders these ideas and assumptions natural and powerful. This makes truth relative. It suggests that the standards used by members of organizations to assess the adequacy of means to ends themselves derive from the larger society. Actually writers on organizations have always been aware of this crucial connection. Weber for example recognized that bureaucracy was only possible and could only develop in societies where there was what he called a 'rational-legal' basis for authoritative power. What people may regard as true is relative, and the ideas that organizational members may apply or pursue almost un-thinkingly may owe their strength not to their objective truthfulness but to their origin in bodies of ideas and values pervasive, popular and dominant within the wider society. Furthermore, these variations are not simply culturally variable, they also vary with the dominance of different bodies of knowledge. Stuart Hall (1997) has argued that the perceived 'truth' of a body of ideas does not follow from its correspondence with objective reality or other truth tests but from its dominance within a particular regime. *In organizational matters ideas are not powerful because they are true: they are true because they are powerful.*

The final chapter by Laroche speculates about the limitations of a focus on decisions, and the difficulties surrounding the identification and assessment of decisions. His solution to this difficulty is an intriguing one: it is to argue that decisions are indeed important but possibly not in the way we originally thought.

Reference

Hall, S. (1997) 'The Work of representation', in S. Hall (ed.), *Representation: Cultural Representations and Signifying Practices*. London: Sage, pp. 13–74.

Organizational Forms: Can we Choose them?

NILS BRUNSSON AND JOHAN P. OLSEN*

Formal organizations are important realities of our time. They appear in great numbers and penetrate almost every aspect of life. Organizations have also been getting larger, more professionalized, more differentiated and wealthier, all of which has made the question of controlling them a crucial issue. In a world dominated by formal organizations it is generally hoped that the behaviour and achievements of these organizations can be controlled not only by other organizations but also by individuals. It is often assumed that they can be controlled by their leaders: by top management, by politicians or by others to whom we have assigned the task of controlling them.

If organizations can be controlled from above, it would seem to follow that leaders control and change the forms of organizations, i.e. their structures, working methods or ideologies, thereby improving their results. And indeed, large organizations today are often the subject of what we will refer to here as administrative reforms, that is to say expert attempts at changing organizational forms. Departments or whole organizations are frequently merged or split. Organizational charts are rewritten. Changes are often introduced in the systems for delegating authority, disseminating information or distributing responsibility. And leaders try to convince their subordinates of new ideas and ideologies. Reform projects have become a commonplace, in many organizations almost a matter of routine.

Administrative reform and change

The concept of reform brings a special perspective to bear on the processes of organizational change and the way organizations function, as well as on internal leadership and power. In a reform perspective administrative change is assumed to

* Routledge for Brunsson, N. and Olsen, J. P. 'Organisational forms: can we choose them?', *The Reforming Organisation* (1993). Copyright © Routledge 1993.

be the result of deliberate goal-directed choices between alternative organizational forms. The structures, processes and ideologies of organizations are shaped and altered, to help the organizations operate more functionally and efficiently. (Re)organization is a tool used by the reformer or reformers. There is a continuous chain of cause and effect starting from the intentions of the reformers and proceeding through decisions, new structures, processes and ideologies to changes in behaviour and improved results. At the same time experience leads to learning. If results do not correspond to intentions, or if the conditions for action change, the process of reform begins anew.

The reforms we shall be discussing below are those instigated by politicians or other elected representatives, owners or corporate executives, or people supported by such groups. Reform can also be triggered from lower levels in an organization or from the broader mass of the people, but such changes can even verge on the revolutionary. Although they are naturally important they are no part of our subject here.

In a reform perspective organizations are regarded as instruments or means. Two qualities are seen to distinguish formal organizations from other types of social arrangement: they are set up to accomplish specific tasks and to advance quite precise objectives, and they have a formalized structure which determines the distribution of authority and the division of labour. An inequitable and undemocratic distribution of labour and working conditions, of authority, status, power and resources, is justified by reference to its role in promoting efficiency and achieving the objectives of the organization. The structure of the organization with its system of rewards and punishments encourages some types of behaviour and inhibits others. Looked at in this way, the organizational structure can be said to create a system that is rational in terms of its own previously determined goals, by channelling behaviour and resources in the direction of these goals. Organization and co-ordination allow for action and problem-solving far beyond what any individual members could achieve on their own.

This interpretation of change in terms of rational choice and of organizations in terms of instruments, stems from a hierarchical view of leadership and power. It is thus assumed that reformers have the right to organize, i.e. to make authoritative, binding decisions about organizational change, and that they have the power to crush any resistance, which means we can concentrate on the question of how correct decisions are made. Once decided, the implementation of reforms is fairly straightforward. A distinction is made between thought and action, between making a decision to reform and implementing that decision. The first is a task for the few, the leaders, and the second a task for the many, the non-leaders.

The reform perspective belongs to a rational, instrumental tradition in organizational research. Despite persistent criticism of the fundamental principles of this tradition over the years, it is still strong. [. . .] The rationality norm is also held in high esteem in political and economic life. To many people formal organizations represent the very incarnation of their belief in control, rationality, leadership, power and order. This belief in the virtue of controlling social arrangements and societal development parallels man's aspirations to exert control over nature. Its models are the industrial process and the efficient machine, its catchwords are clear goals, design, implementation, efficiency and optimization, and its key actors are the social engineers.

How free is the choice?

This chapter is based on several studies of reform processes in a variety of formal organizations. From these it appears that in practice it may actually be difficult for reformers to make decisions on reform, to implement reforms once decided, to achieve the desired effects, or to profit from the experience of earlier reforms. This means that we shall be questioning the fundamental assumptions about rational calculation and social control (Dahl and Lindblom, 1953) on which the rational-instrumental approach rests.

Instead of assuming that changes in formal organizations are the result of reforms and deliberate choices, we ask how much freedom of choice the reformers actually enjoy when they decide that a reform should or should not take place, when they determine its content and direct its implementation and its consequences. In raising this question we are associating ourselves with the classical debate on political control and the design of institutions. This was the issue launched in 1861 by John Stuart Mill, when he published his *Considerations on Representative Government*. In this book he also summed up years of discussion by distinguishing between two main standpoints, both of which are easily discernible in contemporary organization theory.

On the one hand Mill (1861/1962) identifies a school which sees institutional development as a practical matter, geared to the finding of effective instruments. A 'good' institution must have clearly defined objectives; the effects that different organizational forms will have on the chosen objectives must be assessed, and the alternative chosen that will best achieve them. Mill then identifies another school which sees the evolution of institutions as a natural and spontaneous process. Institutions are neither designed nor chosen. They emerge in a historical process, and represent a cultural development that is neither directed nor controlled by any particular group of reformers.

It is important to keep in mind the possibility that reforms account for a limited part only of the changes which occur in formal organizations. If it is true that the connection between change and attempted reform is a weak one, in the sense that many changes are not the result of reforms and many reforms never result in change, then there are two questions which must be considered.

One concerns the way in which an organization's structures and processes change, when the changes are not the result of reforms. What factors, other than the intentions of the reformers, affect the occurrence, the implementation and the consequences of change? An analysis of this question would also help to identify the conditions which influence the reformer's freedom of choice. The second point concerns the reform projects themselves: what do they mean and why are they so abundant in formal organizations if they are not associated with change? It is this last issue which will chiefly engage our attention in the present book.

Once we acknowledge the problematic nature of the relationship between change and reform, we can no longer assume that organizations are (always) instruments, and that the power relationship is (always) hierarchical between those attempting to reform – 'the reformers' – and those who are to be reformed – 'the reformees'. Many factors can affect the freedom that the reformers actually enjoy, but we will limit ourselves here to the institutional element in their situation. Thus, if formal organizations are perceived not as instruments but as institutions in environments which are also institutionalized, what implications does this have for the reformers' freedom of action?

Institutionalized organizations

Organizations can be said to be institutionalized insofar as their behaviour is determined by culturally conditioned rules which manifest themselves in certain routines for action and which give meaning to those actions. They reflect relatively stable values, interests, opinions, expectations and resources (March and Olsen, 1984, 1989). Every organization has a history, and in the course of time it evolves its own accepted ideas about what work is important and what results are 'good', and about how such results can be achieved. Some ways of thinking and behaving come to be seen as self-evident, thus excluding other interpretations and behaviours (Meyer and Scott, 1983). Structures and processes also acquire an intrinsic value (Selznick, 1957), and cease to be regarded simply as a way of achieving the variable objectives of the leaders.

Seeing organizations as having institutional environments means emphasizing that many of the rules in individual organizations are part of a wider rule-system in society. There are many norms for how organizations should behave that are not formulated or controlled within the local, individual organizations but are produced on a more general level and have a more general applicability (Meyer and Scott, 1983; Thomas et al., 1987).

A well-developed institution generates a capacity for action. It facilitates effective co-ordination. But it also creates inertia or friction in face of attempted reforms. This phenomenon is well known in political theory. Wolin (1960), for example, compared classical Greek and Roman political philosophies, and tried to identify the types of leadership that are possible in an institutionalized world. Greek political philosophy saw the leader as hero. Individuals could leave their mark on institutions and even society as a whole. The conditions of leadership in ancient Rome were quite different: leaders had to adapt to existing institutions, with all the rules and expectations this implied. The individual – the 'great statesman' – thus had less impact and the institutions had more, as regards creating the capacity for action as well as setting the limits for its exploitation.

[. . .]

Institutionalized environments

Not only do people inside organizations have specific ideas of how their organization's operations should be organized. Also people external to the organization display the same interest. They are not simply or sometimes even primarily interested in the services or goods produced by organizations. Organizations are also judged by the use they make of the structures, processes and ideologies which significant groups in their environment consider to be rational, efficient, reasonable, fair, natural or up to date. Organizations live in partly institutionalized environments (Meyer and Scott, 1983).

Companies not only have to grapple with legislation regarding structure, such as the Joint Stock Company Act, or laws about employee representation on company boards: they are also exposed to the quirks of fashion in organizational structure. To win the respect of shareholders, banks, clients, suppliers or government, it may be advisable on some occasions to boast a centralized organization and on others a decentralized, divisionalized or matrix organization. The way the organization spends money can also affect its external support. It might be wise to invest a decent sum in in-house training, environmental protection or cultural sponsoring, regardless of whether the outlay has any effect on production.

Similarly there are norms dictating the processes which organizations are expected or even obliged to use. For instance, ever since the 1970s large companies have been expected – by banks and other finance institutes, by the business schools and consultancy firms – to draw up budgets. They have also been exposed to strong pressure to base their investment decisions on increasingly numerous and sophisticated financial calculations [. . .].

The organization's ideology, the opinions it expresses, may also influence its external support. It can lay claim to numerous positive qualities such as efficiency, service-mindedness and public spirit. Objectives are even more useful in this connection: if the organization falls short of the norms in some respects it may be a good idea to emphasize how hard it is striving to achieve certain goals that society or important sections of it hold in high esteem (Brunsson, 1989).

All these norms are external to a particular organization in the sense that they are formed outside and apply to a larger set of organizations. But this does not necessarily mean that people within an organization consider the norms to be external. People in organizations, perhaps in particular at the management level, often share the norms: their ideas of what is decent, rational, etc. do not differ from those of important people outside the organization. This makes the norms particularly strong.

But whether reformers share external norms or not, such norms will restrict their choice of reform content. It is difficult to propose reform ideas that are generally considered as unfashionable, unfair, irrational or inefficient. Society may be convinced that theatres should in principle be governed by administrative managers rather than public meetings, or that universities should be run by bodies drawn from many groups in the community and not just by professors. Theatres and universities often go along with such normative preconceptions, regardless of whether they make for better theatre, research or education. Sometimes the norms are even acknowledged when the people who work at the theatres and universities are convinced that they will impair the quality of their results.

Reformers may also find it difficult to propose reforms which would involve creating new norms and institutions. Grønlie (1989) has shown, for example, how an institutionalized organizational form long established in private industry, namely the joint stock company, became predominant in the organization of state-owned companies in Norway after the Second World War, although the reformers were always dissatisfied with this arrangement. A model was available, ready for use, while it was proving difficult to develop new forms of organization. Similarly, the organization of the Norwegian National Petroleum Administration reflected traditional principles of the organization of government departments and agencies rather than the particular nature of petroleum operations. Once again the joint stock company form was adopted, albeit with some modifications (Olsen, 1989).

Finally, the existence and change of external norms may be the very reason for reform. When fashion swings, organizations must change their forms if they are to be considered normal and up to date.

Decoupling

The demands imposed from outside on the organization's structures, processes and ideologies are often justified on the grounds that they will increase its efficiency and adaptability. But it cannot be taken for granted that what powerful groups in society consider to be good administrative forms will actually lead to good results in practice.

When environmental norms and perceptions do not coincide with what is required for effective action and production, we can expect organizations for which effective actions are important to develop two sets of structures, processes and ideologies – one for each set of demands. For the organization it is important that these parallel sets do not disturb one another, and they therefore tend to be decoupled, separated and isolated (Meyer and Rowan, 1977).

In practice, the result is two organizational structures. The formal organization is the more visible one, and it is thus particularly important that it should be adapted to the institutionalized norms of society. It is relatively easy – basically with a couple of strokes of the pen on an organizational chart – to adapt the formal organization to changes in norms or new laws or fashions. At the same time the organization can use a completely different structure for co-ordinating its activities. This is often referred to as the informal organization.

Similarly, two sets of organizational processes also evolve, one concerned with the production of goods and services, and one which is displayed to the rest of the world but has little or no effect on production. These second processes can be described as rituals. For example, a company may abide by the rules of industrial democracy, obediently consulting its employees before making important decisions, but the consultations will not necessarily have any effect on the content of the subsequent decisions. Increasingly, numerous and complex routines are used in investment calculations, but they have little impact on the ultimate investment decisions (Jansson, 1987). It is perfectly possible to draw up a budget, and not to follow it (Högheim et al., 1989). It is possible to collect huge amounts of information, and not use it when decisions are made (Feldman and March, 1981).

Organizations may also develop double standards, one ideology for internal and one for external use. The picture of the organization and its objectives that corporate management presents to the outside world does not necessarily have to agree with the signals they send out to their employees.

These differences between formal and informal organization, these rituals and double standards can all be very important, if not essential, to a modern organization which wants to live up to society's demands for respectability and rationality, while also effectively producing co-ordinated action (Brunsson, 1989).

The existence of decoupling means that organizations influence the strength of external support, or the amount of resources, freedom or criticism that will come their way, by altering their structures and processes and ideologies, regardless of whether such changes increase their production or improve their efficiency. Similarly, it is possible to affect people's picture or perception of an organization by talk, changing a name or projecting an image through symbols without (necessarily) changing any structures or processes or altering productivity or efficiency.

In this light reform projects can be seen as one step in moulding public opinion, and the very fact that reform is being attempted tells the outside world that the organization is open to change and renewal. A visible willingness to change may then make it easier for the organization to acquire resources and support, and to shield itself from criticism and external intervention. Such an interpretation helps to explain why so many reforms are attempted, even though they have little effect on structures and processes, let alone on results.

Modernity and fashion

The institutional environments of an organization may have been profoundly affected by long-term historical and cultural processes, significant trends which, although not answering the intentions of any specific group of reformers, nonetheless determine developments. 'Modernization' is an example of such a trend, and we can expect that any reform accepted as 'modern' will have a greater chance of success than many others. Being 'modern' is associated in our culture with improvement, progress and development, which makes it extremely difficult to argue against reforms aimed at modernizing an organization. But these profound and long-term trends do not only block the opponents of reform: they also determine in part what the reformers can include in their reforms, thus restricting their freedom of choice.

Institutionalized environments are also affected by other shorter-term fluctuations, the swings of fashion. Democracy and efficiency are certainly values central to economic and political life, but the balance between them can vary greatly, often within a short time. During the 1970s, for example, many reforms were aimed at making organizations more democratic. In all kinds of organizations in many countries, campaigns were launched to extend participation and representation, to make information more available and to extend rights of control to more members. Then during the 1980s the normative framework changed radically: reforms associated with democracy and co-determination became increasingly rare. The focus switched to efficiency, instead, and the model for attempts at reorganizing the public sector was an idealized picture of private enterprise. The aim of most reform attempts was to improve efficiency by adapting to market forces and encouraging competition.

Such fluctuations in fashion also affect the content of reform proposals, as well as limiting the number of acceptable arguments and choices available to both advocates and opponents. During the 1980s it was easier than it had been ten years before to justify and win support for reform proposals implying an improvement in efficiency, and more difficult than it had been in the past to argue for increasing democracy.

The creation of meaning

The idea of the institutionalized environment, characterized by significant long-term trends and short-term fluctuations in fashion, provides an alternative or complement to the rational-instrumental perspective when it comes to interpreting the effects of attempted reforms or trying to explain why changes occur without their being the result of reform. When the environment is institutionalized, the primary effect of attempted reforms may be the creation of meaning and the moulding of public opinion. Attempted reforms can then be regarded as part of a cultural struggle for norms, worldviews, symbols and legitimacy. Reform processes are characterized more by the creation and reshaping of aims and preferences than by the transformation of predetermined aims into new structures and processes.

In such situations attempts at reform are only loosely connected with any direct improvements in structures, processes or results. Both reformers and observers may see the reform as successful, even though it results in few material changes. The participants are not even particularly interested in implementing the reform. Nor are they especially interested in following up any effects it may subsequently have on behaviour or results.

The perception of institutionalized environments and attempted reforms as elements in the creation of meaning and norms in a society also gives us an alternative approach to the question of why changes occur in formal organizations. It is less a matter of sudden big changes stemming from explicit choices and reforms, and more one of gradual transitions resulting from changes in worldviews and norms.

A gradual redefinition of an organization, of its objectives and the criteria on which outsiders should assess it, may also help reformers to create a crisis, a major discrepancy between ambitions and performance, which in turn motivates a call for sweeping reforms. The tendency in the late 1980s to describe all kinds of organizations, including government agencies and universities, in terms previously reserved for industry, and to cite economic efficiency as the paramount criterion, can be seen as just such an attempt to launch a process of redefinition.

The redefinition of the tasks, the objectives and the performance of an organization can be brought about by rational discourse, involving argument and the development of ideas (Wagner and Wittrock, 1989). But worldviews and norms can also be changed in a process involving slogans and propaganda, myths and symbols. In formal organizations the production of ideology and attempts to change organizational cultures by influencing norms and ideas, are being used deliberately and increasingly as a management technique (Czarniawska-Joerges, 1988a, 1988b).

Challenging a hegemony

[. . .]

An important task for organizational research is to try to understand to what extent organizational forms can be chosen, and how far reformers can achieve their goals with the help of deliberate, directed changes in administrative structures and processes. Our analysis starts from the recognition that formal organizations and their environments are often institutionalized, which means that ways of thinking and acting are governed by culturally determined rules. Consequently organizational research needs to explore the question of how institutional factors affect change processes and attempts at reform, and how far they account for the weakness that sometimes exists in the links between reform and change. [. . .]

The insight that institutionalized organizations and environments will restrict the reformers' choices has some paradoxical consequences. On the one hand, it might help to scotch the illusion of the reformers' freedom of choice and the myth that the future can be fairly easily influenced by designing rational, efficient organizations today. On the other hand, this view may help reformers and others to see more clearly just how much freedom of choice they actually have. And this should make it easier for all parties to make sensible choices. People would also be better equipped to defend their interests and achieve their goals if they based their actions on realistic institutional conditions, instead of ignoring the institutional framework within which they nonetheless have to act.

At the same time an institutional perspective draws attention to the fact that attempted reforms are largely about things other than making decisions and changing structures, processes and behaviour with a view to raising the efficiency of production. Institutions are the bearers of meanings, norms and ideas. Reforms and institutional change processes are thus part of a historical–cultural definition process which gives meaning and order to our perceptions of society and social development. Reform processes can affect what participants and observers regard as possible, true and right. They can contribute to the creation and alteration of objectives and preferences. The study of reform can thus help us to understand who has the power to mould public opinion in individual organizations and in society as a whole. [. . .]

References

Brunsson, N. (1989) *The Organization of Hypocrisy: Talk, Decisions and Actions in Organizations*. Chichester: Wiley.

Czarniawska-Joerges, B. (1988a) *Att handla med ord: Om organisatoriskt prat, organisatorisk styrning och företagsledningskonsultering*. Stockholm: Carlsson Bokförlag.

Czarniawska-Joerges, B. (1988b) *Reformer och ideologier: Lokala nämnder på väg*. Lund: Doxa.

Dahl, R.A. and Lindblom, C.E. (1953) *Politics, Economics, and Welfare*. New York: Harper & Row.

Feldman, M.S. and March, J.G. (1981) 'Information in organizations as signal and symbol', *Administrative Science Quarterly*, 26: 171–86.

Grønlie, T. (1989) *Statsdrift*. Oslo: Tano.

Högheim, S., Monsen, N., Olsen, R. and Olson, O. (1989) 'The two worlds of management control', *Financial Accountability and Management*, 5: 163–78.

Jansson, D. (1987) *Investeringskalkyler i empirisk investeringsforskning*. Stockholm: EFI Forskningsrapport.

March, J.G. and Olsen, J.P. (1984) 'The New Institutionalism: organizational factors in political life', *American Political Science Review*, 78: 734–49.

March, J.G. and Olsen, J.P. (1989) *Rediscovering Institutions: The Organizational Basis of Politics*. New York: Free Press.

Meyer, J.W. and Rowan, B. (1977) 'Institutionalized organizations: formal structure as myth and ceremony', *American Journal of Sociology*, 83: 340–63.

Meyer, J.W. and Scott, W.R. (1983) *Organizational Environments: Ritual and Rationality*. Beverley Hills, CA: Sage.

Mill, J.S. (1861/1962) *Considerations on Representative Government*. South Bend, IN: Gateway Editions.

Olsen, J.P. (1989) *Petroleum og politikk*. Oslo: Tano.

Selznick, P. (1957) *Leadership in Administration*. New York: Harper & Row.

Thomas, G.M., Meier, J.W., Ramirez, F.O. and Boli, J. (eds) (1987) *Institutional Structure: Constituting State, Society, and the Individual*. Beverley Hills, CA: Sage.

Wagner, P. and Wittrock, B. (1989) 'Social science and the building of the early welfare state: transformations of discourse and institutions interlinked',

Uppsala: The Swedish Collegium for Advanced Study in the Social Sciences, manuscript.

Wolin, S. (1960) *Politics and Vision: Continuity and Innovation in Western Political Thought*. Boston: Little, Brown.

C

The Cult[ure] of the Customer

PAUL DU GAY AND GRAEME SALAMAN*

[. . .]

In this chapter we explore the nature, origins and consequences of a major aspect of current managerial thinking and theorizing about the structure and direction of work organization and the employment and governance of staff. Our subject matter is the managerial attempt to reconstruct work organizations in ways which are defined as characteristically commercial and customer focused. A fundamental aspect of managerial attempts to achieve this reconstruction involves the re-imagination of the organization. Frequently this means the supplanting of bureaucratic principles by market relations.

In this first section we describe some of the major initiatives in work and organizational redesign which explicitly or covertly centre around the managerial attempt to restructure organizational systems and relationships in terms of market relations. These restructuring programmes are located in the context of key environmental developments, also outlined in this first section.

However we do not argue that the supplanting of bureaucratic structures and relationships by market relations ('the sovereign consumer') is causally *determined* by environmental developments. The restructuring of work and work relations is as much supported by the discourse of enterprise (within and without the employing organization) as it is determined by environmental pressures. [. . .]

The second section thus moves beyond developments in and at work to an analysis of the language which informs and supports these developments: the language of enterprise. In this section this discourse is addressed at the level of the corporation, and the corporation's customers, with particular attention being paid to the construction and redefinition of employees. In the third section we examine the role this discourse plays in reimagining the 'social' and the 'political' in contemporary Britain. One of the key arguments is the importance of mapping the resonances between the levels and spheres represented by the three constituent

* Blackwell Publishers for du Gay, P. and Salaman, G. 'The cult(ure) of the customer', *Journal of Management Studies*, 29(5). Copyright © Blackwell Publishers 1992.

sections of the chapter. The chapter moves progressively through these three levels and offers an attempt to trace these connections.

'Close to the customer'

Current emphasis on the customer as a means of analysing and defining work performance and work relations represents a highly significant addition to management attempts to understand and explain the nature of the enterprise. [. . .] Recent emphasis on a clearly defined notion of the the key dynamic of market relations has become a central feature of work reorganization, and critically, of attempts by managers and their advisers to delineate and intervene into the organization of paid work.

We must start with a brief overview of the environmental developments which supply the justification for enormous emphasis on the consumer, whereby 'meeting the demands of the "sovereign" consumer becomes the new and overriding institutional imperative' (Keat and Abercrombie, 1990: 3). We shall find that one of many advantages of the emphasis on the customer as a method of understanding and directing organizational change is that it allows a conflation of external developments and pressures (the market) and internal relationships and strategies whereby both can be conceptualized in the same terms as if they were the same phenomenon, that is, in terms of a discourse of enterprise.

Many researchers have identified a cluster of related environmental developments which put pressure upon organizations to find new ways of enhancing their competitiveness and their market share: 'increased competition from foreign industry, a more quality-conscious consumer population, rapidly changing product markets, deregulation and new technologies' (Fuller and Smith, 1991: 1). Most important of these developments is the increasing differentiation of demand.

The fragmentation and differentiation of demand for goods and services is a conspicuous and widely accepted feature of modern Western economic life. 'The changing nature of product markets is a significant determinant of contemporary economic restructuring' (Hill, 1991: 397). 'Neo-Fordism arose out of "new constraints on the realization of value" stemming from the growth of product market variability' (Smith, 1989: 209). [. . .]

This view of shifts in the nature of consumer demand is supported by analyses of consumption which stress its insatiability and striving for novelty. Consumption occurs in anticipation of actual use or consumption, for reality brings anti-climax: 'consumption is dynamic, for disillusionment (and moving on) is the necessary concomitant of the acquisition of goods that have been longed for in fantasy' (Abercrombie, 1991: 178).

Furthermore, as Abercrombie notes, the current consumer/customer is also active, enterprising: searching, innovating, forcing change and movement upon producers in marked contrast to the passive, easily pleased customer of Fordism.

These pressures, particularly the differentiation of demand, have forced change on work organizations. Radical organizational change in response to these pressures is becoming the norm. [. . .]

The value placed on the customer in current programmes of organizational change represents an attempt to recreate within the organization types of relationship which normally occur on the interface of the organization with its customers.

[. . .] This emphasis is usually closely related to changes in market – i.e. customer – behaviour. And these changes are frequently conceptualized in terms of the differentiation of markets.

That demand is now highly differentiated, with consumers being both knowledgeable, and *demanding* is not simply an important *fact* of modern economic life, it is, more significantly, an important *idea* in modern economic life which plays a critical role in attempts to restructure organizations. [. . .]

The expression 'customer' has displaced other ways of describing those who are served by the organization. Those who travel by British Rail are no longer passengers; they are customers. The term has become paradigmatic, and represents a major shift in the ways in which the purpose and structure of work organizations is defined. However, the idea of the paradigmatic customer depends upon, and closely relates to, other arguments and developments.

First, it assumes 'an actual or at least achieveable relationship between the conduct of commercial enterprises in a free market economy and the display of enterprising characteristics by those involved in the process of production' Keat and Abercrombie, 1990: 6). That is, it is possible and desirable to reproduce, within the organization, relationships which resemble those between the organization and its clients. In this way, current emphasis on customer-focused behaviour and relationships relates directly to attempts to restructure work.

Secondly, managerial emphasis on the significance of the customer assumes a high degree of control over what is produced being exercised by the freely made choices of 'sovereign' consumers (Keat and Abercrombie, 1990: 7). This overlooks the extent to which consumers' preferences are generated and structured by the producers themselves.

Nevertheless, although there is evidence that this emphasis on customer sovereignty is exaggerated, there is no doubt that managerial representations of the customer as a means of restructuring organizations, and of influencing employees' behaviour and attitudes, are of real importance.

The importance of managerial discussions of the paradigmatic sovereign consumer lies in the ways in which this idea and its associated language and assumptions relates to current programmes of organizational change. These programmes focus on the redesign of organizational structures, work structures and practices. The common element of these programmes is that they argue the need to impose the model of the customer–supplier relationship on internal organizational relations, so departments now behave as if they were actors in a market, workers treat each other as if they were customers, and customers are treated as if they were managers.

[. . .]

The traditional view of the merits of bureaucratic structures is entirely opposed by the current language of the sovereign consumer; for this asserts that in order to compete successfully against competitor suppliers, and to achieve adequate profit margins, organizations must be able to satisfy customers. And in order to do this, internal organizational relations must resemble – indeed even become – market relations. Thus, in a curious inversion of what was for many years the received wisdom, that the inadequacies of the market should be ameliorated by the bureaucratic method of controlling transactions, market co-ordination is imposed on administrative co-ordination. 'A central feature of current attempts to construct "an enterprise culture" in Britain has been a series of institutional reforms designed to introduce market principles and commercially modelled forms of organization into a wide range of activities previously conducted upon different principles' (Keat, 1990: 216).

Thus a major thrust of current programmes of organizational change is to replace management hierarchical control with simulated market control: divisions, regions, become quasi-firms, and transactions between them become those of customer or supplier or even competitor. Corporations are decentralized into a number of semi-autonomous business units or profit centres, each of which is required to achieve a given level of financial contribution to head office. This policy is seen to remove obstructive and expensive bureaucratic controls; liberate innate entrepreneurship and to make local management '. . . more sensitive to the satisfaction of product market requirements in order to meet . . . performance targets' (Hill, 1991: 402). It is argued that by this means, sub-unit goals will necessarily become clearer, as each sub-unit pursues its own self interest within the context of head office policy and financial constraints.

This form of organizational restructuring is not confined to those organizations which literally operate with a clearly defined market; it is also apparent within the public sector – the National Health Service and local authorities – where the notion of a market, and of customers exercising choice is not an obvious one. In these cases the imposition (or creation) of customer sovereignty is forced through central government legislation requiring competitive tendering of services previously supplied by hierarchies, not markets; by service level agreements between separate functional specialities or by patients' charters. The interesting point here is the way in which the emphasis on the sovereign consumer as a method of restructuring organizations gains a further level of reality and conviction by becoming enshrined in legislation covering those organizations which are furthest removed from market and consumer pressures. Paradoxically, we thus find that the adaptation of market relations and structures in organizations is frequently a result of formal, centralized and bureaucratic compulsion.

Another important area where management conceptions of the value of customer-type relations have been pervasively applied is in the sphere of work restructuring. [. . .] 'The changing nature of product markets is a significant determinant of contemporary economics restructuring' (Hill, 1991: 397). It is possible to trace [. . .] direct and detailed connections between new work forms and management emphasis on the customer as a paradigm of internal organizational relationships. Two key mechanisms of work restructuring both frequently associated with work (functional) flexibility programmes, total quality management (TQM) and just-in-time (JIT) systems, both require the redefinition of the relationship between workers in terms of the customer model: workers become each others' customers.

[. . .]

The third way in which the language of the paradigmatic custom is focused and applied in work restructuring occurs when customers – as constructed by management through customer survey technologies – are made to exert control over employees. [. . .] In the case of service industries with significant employee/customer interaction, customers are made to function in the role of management. In this sector, customer satisfaction is now defined as critical to competitive success, because of its importance in achieving high levels of customer retention. Quality is thus defined as usual, in terms of giving customers what they want, yet at the same time traditional methods of control (i.e. bureaucratic control) are too overtly oppressive, too alienating and too inflexible to encourage employees to behave in the subtle ways which customers define as indicating quality service, many of which – subtleties of facial expression, nuances of verbal tone, or type of eye-contact – are difficult to enforce through rules, particularly when the employee is out of sight of any supervisor.

[. . .]

Furthermore, bureaucratic control may achieve compliance with the letter of the regulation but may also allow the minimal performance standard to become the norm, and to stifle individual spontaneity and responsiveness. The 'solution' is to seek to change behaviour, values and attitudes through culture change rather than structural change, and to measure the success of these programmes through customer feedback. It is of course possible to see the use of elaborate and sophisticated customer feedback data as a method of measuring, monitoring and ultimately managing service employees as a new solution to a traditional managerial dilemma: achieving sufficient control and direction without destroying the very behaviour that is required. (Fuller and Smith, 1991, document this aspect of the managerial use of customer feedback very thoroughly.) But our interest in this is less in the development of new managerial forms of control, and more in the ways in which the language of the sovereign customer is increasingly embedded in a wide-ranging series of organizational structures, practices and technologies.

In the following section we describe and analyse this language in terms of a consideration of the discourse of enterprise. This discourse both sustains and is supported by the restructuring initiatives described earlier. [. . .]

The enterprising cult[ure] of the customer

As the language of 'the market' becomes the only valid vocabulary of moral and social calculation, 'civic culture' gradually becomes 'consumer culture', with citizens reconceptualized as enterprising 'sovereign consumers'.

In the public sector, for example, [. . .] there can hardly be a school, hospital, social services department, university or college in the UK that has not in some way become permeated by the language of enterprise. Enterprise has remorselessly reconceptualized and remodelled almost everything in its path. Ostensibly different 'spheres of existence' have fallen prey to its 'totalizing' and 'individualizing' economic rationality (Foucault, 1988b; Gorz, 1989) – from the hospital to the railway station, from the classroom to the museum, the nation finds itself translated. 'Patients', 'parents', 'passengers' and 'pupils' are reimaged as 'customers'.

While this process of relabelling may appear as a totalitarian attack on diversity and difference it is never conceived of or represented as such. Rather, the enterprising customer consumer is imagined as an empowered human being – the moral centre of the enterprising universe. Within the discourse of enterprise customers/consumers are constituted as autonomous, self-regulating and self-actualizing individual actors, seeking to maximize the worth of their existence to themselves through personalized acts of choice in a world of goods and services.

[. . .]

While the enterprising language of the customer structures political debate, providing the rationale for programmes of intervention and rectification in the public domain – such as the delivery of health care, the provision of local government services and the delivery of education – it is also linked to a transformation in programmes and technologies for regulating the internal world of the business enterprise. In other words, although private enterprise provides the model for the reconstruction of social relations in the public domain, this does not mean that there are not varying degrees of enterprising enterprise.

Enterprising enterprises

Within the discourse of enterprise, private sector corporations are not considered to be inherently enterprising. Certainly the free market system provides the inherently virtuous model through which all forms of social relation should be structured, but in order to guarantee that maximum benefits accrue from the workings of this intrinsically virtuous system it is the moral obligation of each and every commercial organization, and each and every member of such an organization, to become obsessed with 'staying close to the customer' and thus with achieving 'continuous business improvement'. To put it simply: commercial organizations must continually struggle to become ever more enterprising. Thus the discourse of enterprise also envisages a new type of rule and imagines new ways for people to conduct themselves within the private business enterprise, as well as in public sector institutions.

The notion of 'Total Customer Responsiveness' (Peters, 1987), in this sense, appears as both symptom of and answer to, the problems thrown up by the increasingly dislocated ground upon which globalized capitalism operates. The more dislocated the ground upon which business organizations must operate, the less they are able to rely upon a framework of stable social and political relations and the more they are forced to engage in [. . .] constant 'creativity' and [. . .] less on inherited objective forms (bureaucracy) [. . .]. The only way to 'run a tight ship' in the inherently 'chaotic' global economy, it is argued, is through 're-enchanting' the work organization around the figure of the 'customer':

> the focus on the outside, the external perspective, the attention to the customers, is one of the tightest properties of all . . . it is perhaps the most stringent means of self-discipline. If one really is paying attention to what the customer is saying, being blown in the wind by the customer's demands, one may be sure he (sic) is sailing a tight ship. (Peters and Waterman, 1982: 32)

Reimagining the corporation through the culture of the customer means encouraging organizations and their participants to become more enterprising. In this sense enterprise refers to a series of techniques for restructuring the internal world of the organization along 'market' lines in order to anticipate and satisfy the needs and desires of the enterprising sovereign consumer, and thus ensure business success. Through the medium of various technologies and practices inscribed with the presuppositions of the 'enterprising self' – techniques for reducing dependency by reorganizing management structures ('de-layering'); for cutting across internal organizational boundaries (the creation of 'special project teams', for example); for encouraging internal competitiveness through small group working; and for eliciting individual accountability and responsibility through peer-review and appraisal schemes – the internal world of the business organization is reconceptualized as one in which customers' demands and desires are satisfied, productivity enhanced, quality assured, innovation fostered, and flexibility guaranteed through the active engagement of the self-fulfilling impulses of all the organization's members.

[. . .] Operating with a unitary frame of reference, enterprise projects the vision of a cohesive but inherently flexible organization where an organic complementarity is established between the 'greatest possible realization of the intrinsic abilities of individuals at work' and the 'optimum productivity and profitability of the corporation'. In this vision the 'no win' scenario associated with a mechanistic, bureaucratic lack of enterprise is transformed into a permanent 'win/win' situation through the active development of a flexible, creative and organic entrepreneurialism [. . .]. Enterprising corporations are those in which 'customer relations' mirror 'employee relations', where 'staying close to the customer' means gaining 'productivity through people' (Peters and Waterman, 1982: 166).

As the CBI (1988: 5) argues, enterprising enterprises are those which increasingly turn:

> to the people who work for them to develop . . . competitive advantage. The winners are those who can organize and motivate their people at all levels so that they give willingly their ideas, their initiative and their commitment to the continuous improvement that winning requires. . . . And it is up to those people as individuals to make the difference. They can no longer be treated as part of the collective mass . . . people want to do a good job, to have opportunities for self development, to contribute their thoughts as well as their physical skills to the teams and firms for which they work, and to be recognised and rewarded for their whole contribution.

Governing the business organization in an enterprising manner is therefore said to involve 'empowering', 'responsibilizing' and 'enabling' all members of that organization to 'add value' – both to the company for which they work and to themselves. 'Total customer responsiveness' inaugurates a 'new form of control – self control born of the involvement and ownership that follows from, among other things, training people . . . to take on many traditionally supervisory roles. Being fully responsible for results will concentrate the mind more effectively than any out of touch cop' (Peters, 1987: 363).

In this way the government of the enterprising firm can be seen to operate through the 'soul' (Foucault, 1988a) of the individual employee. These firms get the most out of their employees by harnessing the psychological strivings of individuals for autonomy and creativity and channelling them into the search for 'total customer responsiveness', 'excellence' and success. Enterprising companies 'make meaning for people' by encouraging them to believe that they have control over their own lives; that no matter what position they may hold within an organization their contribution is vital, not only to the success of the company but to the enterprise of their own lives. Peters and Waterman (1982: 76, 81), for example, quote approvingly Nietzche's axiom that 'he who has a why to live for can bear almost any how'. They argue that 'the fact . . . that we think we have a bit more discretion leads to much greater commitment'. The enterprising firm is therefore one that engages in controlled de-control. To govern the corporation in an enterprising fashion is to 'totalize' and 'individualize' (Foucault, 1988b) at one and the same time; or, to deploy Peters and Waterman's (1982: 318) terminology, to be 'simultaneously loose and tight' – 'organizations that live by the loose/tight principle are on the one hand rigidly controlled, yet at the same time allow, indeed, insist on, autonomy, entrepreneurship, and innovation from the rank and file'.

The key to 'loose/tight' is culture. According to Peters and Waterman, the effective management of meanings, beliefs and values (which accompanies the increasing 'capitalization' of all areas of human activity) can transform an apparent contradiction – between increasing central control while extending individual autonomy and responsibility – into 'no contradiction at all'. If an organization has an appropriate 'culture' of enterprise, if all its members adopt an enterprising relation to self, then efficiency, economy, autonomy, quality and innovation all 'become words that belong on the same side of the coin' (Peters and Waterman, 1982: 321).

[. . .]

Rather than being some vague, incalculable 'spirit', the culture of enterprise is inscribed into a variety of mechanisms, such as application forms, recruitment 'auditions', and communication groups, through which senior management in enterprising companies seek to delineate, normalize and instrumentalize the conduct of persons in order to achieve the ends they postulate as desirable. Thus governing the business organization in an enterprising manner involves cultivating enterprising subjects – autonomous, self-regulating, productive, responsible individuals – through the development of simultaneous loose/tight 'enabling and empowering vision' articulated in the everyday practices of the organization.

[. . .]

The discourse of 'enterprise'

Although the discourse of enterprise, and contemporary attempts to create an 'enterprise culture' in the UK, are virtually synonymous with the politico-ethical project of 'Thatcherism' they are not reducible to this phenomenon. [. . .] The development of an 'enterprise culture' must be located within the context of increasing globalization. [. . .] The 'entrepreneurial revolution' to which Thatcherism contributed with such passionate brutality is 'still working its way through the system' (Hall, 1991: 10).

In Britain attempts to construct a culture of enterprise have proceeded through the progressive enlargement of the territory of the market – of the realm of private enterprise and economic rationality – by a series of redefinitions of its object. Thus the task of creating an 'enterprise culture' has involved the reconstruction of a wide range of institutions and activities along the lines of the commercial business organization, with attention focused, in particular, on their orientation towards the customer. At the same time, however, the market has also come to define the sort of relation that an individual should have with him/herself and the 'habits of action' he or she should acquire and exhibit. [. . .]

In an 'enterprise culture' freedom and independence emanate not from civil rights but from choices exercised in the market: 'the sovereignty that matters is not that of the king or the queen, the lord or the white man, but the sovereignty of the consumer in the market-place' (Corner and Harvey, 1991: 11).

No longer simply implying the creation of an independent business venture, enterprise now refers to the application of 'market forces' and 'entrepreneurial principles' to every sphere of human existence. [. . .]

For Miller and Rose (1990: 24), the significance of enterprise as a discourse resides in its ability to act as a translation device, a cypher 'between the most general *a priori* of political thought', and a range of specific programmes for managing aspects of economic and social existence. Thus, enterprise can be seen to be more than a political rationality, it also takes a technological form: it is inscribed into a variety of often simple mechanisms – contemporary organizational examples could include quality circles, assessment centres, appraisal systems and personality profiling – through which various authorities seek to shape, normalize and instrumentalize the conduct of persons in order to achieve the ends they postulate as desirable. Inscribed with the presuppositions of the 'enterprising self', these technologies accord a priority to the self-steering and self-actualizing capacities of individuals. In other words, enterprise serves not only to articulate a diversity of programmes for making the world 'work better', but, in addition, it also enables these programmes 'to be translated into a range of technologies to administer individuals and groups in a way . . . consonant with prevailing ethical systems and political mentalities' (Miller and Rose, 1990: 24; Rose, 1990).

[. . .]

Enterprise has operated on many fronts at the same time, changing the world by rewriting the language, redefining the relation between the public and the private, the corporate and culture. Rather than viewing this process of translation as in some sense a side-show to, or 'ideological distortion' of, the realities of restructuring, it is important to recognize that if an activity or institution is redefined, reimagined or reconceptualized it does not maintain some 'real', 'essential' or 'originary' identity outside of its dominant discursive articulation, but assumes a new identity.

[. . .]

The success of neo-liberalism in the UK with its flagship image of an enterprise culture, 'operates within a much more general transformation in "mentalities of government", in which the autonomous, free, choosing self . . . has become central to the moral bases of political arguments from all parts of the political spectrum' (Rose, 1989: 14). The language of enterprise has established an affinity between the politico-ethical objectives of neo-liberal government in the UK, the economic objectives of contemporary business, and the self-actualizing, self-regulating capacities of human subjects.

References

Abercrombie, N. (1991) 'The privilege of the producer', in R. Keat and N. Abercrombie (eds), *Enterprise Culture*. London: Routledge. 171–85.

Confederation of British Industry (CBI) (1988) *People – the Cutting Edge*. London: CBI.

Corner, J. and Harvey, S. (eds) (1991) *Enterprise and Heritage*. London: Routledge.

Foucault, M. (1988a) 'Technologies of the self', in L. H. Martin, H. Gutman and P. H. Hutton (eds), *Technologies of the Self*. London: Tavistock.

Foucault, M. (1988b) 'The political technology of individuals', in L. H. Martin, H. Gutman and P. H. Hutton (eds), *Technologies of the Self*. London: Tavistock.

Fuller, L. and Smith, V. (1991) 'Consumers' report: management by customers in a changing economy', *Work, Employment and Society*, 5: 1–16.

Gorz, A. (1989) *Critique of Economic Reason*. London: Verso.

Hall, S. (1991) 'And not a shot fired', *Marxism Today*, December: 10–15.

Hill, S. (1991) 'How do you manage a flexible firm?', *Work, Employment and Society*, 5(3): 397–416.

Keat, R. (1990) 'Introduction', in R. Keat and N. Abercrombie (eds), *Enterprise Culture*. London: Routledge. pp. 3–10.

Miller, P. and Rose, N. (1990) 'Governing economic life', *Economy and Society*, 19: 1–31.

Peters, T. (1987) *Thriving on Chaos*. Basingstoke: Macmillan.

Peters, T. and Waterman, R. H. (1982) *In Search of Excellence*. New York: Harper & Row.

Rose, N. (1989) 'Governing the enterprising self'. Paper presented to a conference on 'The Values of the Enterprise Culture', University of Lancaster, September.

Rose, N. (1990) *Governing the Soul*. London: Routledge.

Smith, C. (1989) 'Flexible specialization, automation and mass production', *Work, Employment and Society*, 3(2): 203–20.

CHAPTER 15

Managerialism and Social Welfare

JANET NEWMAN*

There is nothing new about the idea of managing welfare services. There is always a need for activities to be co-ordinated, budgets allocated, staff supervised, control exercised. The focus of this chapter, however, is the change in the organization and delivery of social welfare that took place in the UK through the 1980s and 1990s. [. . .]

Bashing bureaucracy

Dismantling the old organizational settlement

[. . .] The organizational settlement was one of four settlements on which the old welfare state was built. It was based on the rather different principles of bureaucratic administration on the one hand, and professional expertise on the other. [. . .] It was characterized by compromise and accommodation rather than complete harmony and consensus. Bureaucratic administration was a rational, rule-bound and hierarchical approach to co-ordinating complex systems of people and resource processing. Bureaucratic administration provided the organizational context in which welfare professionals – doctors, teachers, social workers, etc. – exercised their professional judgement. This combination of administrative rationality and professional expertise guaranteed the neutrality of the welfare state and protected the exercise of professional judgement in the delivery of social welfare. Despite recurrent tensions between 'bureaucrats' and 'professionals', this form of organizational regime provided a stable institutional base for the growth of the welfare state in the post-war years.

* Routledge and The Open University for Newman, J. 'Managerialism and social welfare', in G. Hughes and G. Lewis (eds), *Unsettling Welfare: Reconstruction of Social Policy*. Copyright © The Open University 1998.

The regime was not without its critics. A variety of critiques from socialist, feminist and anti-racist perspectives were directed at professional and bureaucratic power through the 1970s and 1980s. Challenges emerged from the growing number of user movements among recipients of social welfare, notably among people with disabilities (Taylor, 1993; Williams, 1996). Challenges had also been emerging throughout the period from the political Right [. . .] A new set of critiques began to emerge in economic and political theory which were picked up by the government during the Conservative administrations of the 1980s and 1990s. [. . .]

The economic critiques were rooted in neo-liberal theories of the proper relationship between the state and the economy. Within this broad set of ideas, public choice theory articulated a set of concerns about the inherent waste and inefficiency involved in the provision of services through the public sector rather than the market (for example Niskanen, 1971). Walsh (1995) neatly summarizes the main elements of public choice theory:

> There are three basic sources of failure in government organizations identified by public choice theorists. First, it cannot be assumed that politicians will demand the pattern of public sector outputs that reflects the best interests of society as whole. They will have their own interests to pursue and they will be subject to conflicting demands and pressures from special interests. Second, the bureaucracy will not necessarily carry out the wishes of the politicians, even if the latter do express the public good, since it is likely not to be in the bureaucrats' interests to do so. Third, it is unlikely that bureaucrats will act efficiently in producing whatever it is decided should be produced, since it may be in their interests to be inefficient. These criticisms of politicians and bureaucracy lead to the conclusion that the public service will be characterized both by allocative inefficiency, the production of the wrong mix of services, and by X inefficiency . . . that is the production of less than it is possible to produce with the given inputs. (Walsh, 1995: 17)

These views shaped the critiques of bureaucracy and informed the development of market mechanisms for the delivery of welfare services through the 1980s and 1990s. However, these neo-liberal economic critiques articulated powerfully with a second strand of New Right thinking: neo-conservatism. Here the focus was on the social consequences of welfare provision rather than its economic inefficiencies. The social critiques focused on the paternalism of the old regime and the effects of what came to be called the 'nanny state', which supposedly encouraged a 'dependency culture'. The focus on needs and entitlements was seen to undermine self-reliance and, ultimately, the moral welfare of society. For example, the provision of housing and benefits to lone parents was seen by many commentators to offer 'perverse incentives' which encouraged unmarried women to have children in order to secure welfare provision, and disadvantaged 'normal' families (Parker, 1982; see also Lentell, 1998).

The third set of critiques were political: bureau-professional power was seen to threaten the project of political and cultural change. Professionals – especially the more powerful medical professionals – represented important power blocks in their own right, and were thus able to gain concessions in the process of reform. The institutional forms of welfare also created and sustained attachments between citizens and the organizational forms of social democracy, with, for example, local government acting as a focus of resistance to many central government agendas, and with citizens expressing continued loyalties to the National Health Service as a symbolic institution.

The different forms of critique served to legitimate the introduction of managerial techniques and the strengthening of managerial power. The critiques of the past and assumptions about what management could offer in its place are summarized in Table 15.1.

Table 15.1 *Critiques of the old and legitimations of the new: the claims of managerialism*

Bureaucracy is:	Management is:
rule-bound	innovative
inward-looking	externally oriented
compliance-centred	performance-centred
ossified	dynamic
Professionalism is:	Management is:
paternalist	customer-centred
mystique-ridden	transparent
standard-oriented	results-oriented
self-regulating	market-tested
Politicians are:	Managers are:
dogmatic	pragmatic
interfering	enabling
unstable	strategic

Source: Clarke and Newman, 1997: 65

Managerialism played a central role in the programme of reform and restructuring through the 1980s and beyond. It offered a set of prescriptions for producing economies in what was seen as a rising spiral of welfare expenditure. It was also highly compatible with the idea of a more self-reliant welfare consumer. The strengthening of managerialism was central to the general political project of unravelling the complex of bureau-professional power and diminishing the power of local government. Government reforms of the 1980s and 1990s can be seen in terms of a series of attempts to destabilize these regimes through direct intervention, or through the introduction of market mechanisms. Each area of social welfare underwent a profound process of transformation in which the dominance of professional and administrative modes of organization was challenged, and partially or substantially displaced by a new managerial mode.

These shifts were both underpinned by, and legitimated through, managerialism as the basis of a new organizational settlement. In this sense, managerialism can be understood as an *ideology*, not as a set of neutral techniques. It was not just a means of doing things – it formed a new set of principles which shaped the process of change itself by presenting answers to economic and social problems. Take, for example, *Reinventing Government*, one of the key texts of the early 1990s, which was closely associated both with the first Clinton administration in the USA, and with John Major and the Citizens' Charter in the UK (Osborne and Gaebler, 1992). The preface states:

> Our governments are in deep trouble today. This book is for those who are disturbed by that reality. It is for those who care about government – because they work in government, or simply want their governments to be more effective. It is for those who know something is wrong, but who are not sure just what that is; for those who have launched successful experiments, but have watched those in power ignore them; for those who have a sense of where government needs to go, but are not quite sure how to get there. It is for the seekers.

> If ever there was a time for seekers, this is it. The millennium approaches, and change is all around us. Eastern Europe is free; the Soviet Empire is dissolving; the cold war is over. Western Europe is moving towards economic union. Asia is the new centre of economic power. From Poland to South Africa, democracy is on the march . . . The emergence of a post-industrial, knowledge based, global economy has undermined old realities throughout the world, creating wonderful opportunities and frightening problems. Governments large and small, American and foreign, federal, state and local, have begun to respond. (Osborne and Gaebler, 1992: xv–xvi)

The idea of the need for 'reinvention' and 'transformation' is established by convincing the reader that there is a problem which it is important to address. Like all good ideologies, a logical sequence of ideas is established which together point to a seemingly unchallengeable conclusion – dramatic change. Different ideas (globalization, democracy, technological change) are juxtaposed to provide an overarching narrative which creates the necessity of dramatic changes to the forms and institutions of government. The reader is addressed directly, and offered a range of positive identifications: 'problem solver', 'radical thinker', frustrated 'change agent' and, above all, 'seeker'.

The promise of managerialism's ability to deliver radical change was a recurring theme. If you look at the business management section of any major library or bookshop, you are likely to find a series of titles on particular activities and techniques: strategic management, marketing, 'human resource' management, managing quality, managing change, managing for competitive success. The topics change to reflect the very rapidly shifting fads and fashions coming from an ever-changing cast of management 'gurus'. But there is something about the tone that remains constant. The books are not just outlining a set of techniques: they are extolling the virtues of change. New forms of competition, the new 'global' market-place, the new demands from consumers, the new need for flexibility and quality to respond to these demands – all, it is, argued, require a fundamental change of approach, new attitudes and new ideas.

In the 1980s there was an enormous growth in the rate of publication of management books. Some (for example Peters and Waterman's *In Search of*

Excellence, published in 1982) reached a level of worldwide sales unprecedented for management books. Management 'gurus' proliferated, and many leaders of business, from John Harvey Jones to Richard Branson, attained the status of national heroes (though rather fewer heroines gained this sort of public profile). Clarke and Newman locate this phenomenon in the context of deep-rooted economic problems, especially in the US economy:

> Managerialism was being revived, if not re-invented, by the emergence of new 'schools', of excellence, culture management, Human Resource Management, Total Quality Management, and re-engineering (to name but a few). Each of these promised a more or less coherent philosophy of and approach to managing and all testified to the potency and rewards of doing management. They changed the face of managers away from their previous image as dull organizational time-servers to those of entrepreneurial and inspirational change agents. Like all good discourses, the new managerialism announced the conditions of its own necessity – elaborating a tale of the failings of the old management and their dire consequences. The new manager was born out of a climate of crisis and disillusionment – located in the start of a long drawn out crisis of US capitalism in the late 1970s and more specifically in its competitive failure in the face of the industrialising Pacific Rim. This climate of American failure was the precondition for the new managerial literature's promise of salvation. It announced the possibility of a way forward which linked the fortunes of the individual manager, the corporation and the nation. The born-again manager could rescue the situation brought about by the old corporate mentality: the 'playing safe' organization man; the ossified corporation; and the over-regulatory state produced by the politics of 'corporate liberalism'. (Clarke and Newman, 1997: 35)

The success of this new managerialism was based on its vision of the power of management to transform rule-bound, inert and bureaucratic corporations into dynamic and competitive enterprises. This notion of managerial knowledge as the driver of change had close affinities with the New Right agenda of social and economic transformation. Both stood against excessive state regulation; both required individuals to be 'liberated' from bureaucracy in order to play their part as the dynamic agents of change. In addition, the neo-liberal agenda of the New Right explicitly looked to the business world – and to the techniques of business management in the private sector – to solve the problems of what was considered to be an over-large, bureaucratic and self-seeking state sector: 'Efficient management is the key to the [national] revival . . . And the management ethos must run right through our national life – private and public companies, civil service, nationalized industries, local government, the National Health Service' (Michael Heseltine, then Secretary of State for the Environment, 1980, quoted in Pollitt, 1993: vi).

The 1980s and 1990s saw a shift in the dominant ethos and style of public management – indeed, many have talked of the emergence of a 'new public management' (Hood, 1991). This offered a powerful set of ideas and techniques which have helped to establish the need to reform the institutions of social welfare. To understand the principles of this new regime, the following sections explore managerialism from a number of perspectives. The next section views managerialism as a *set of discourses* which offer individuals particular points of identification and which prioritize certain forms of knowledge and expertise. The following section explores managerialism as a *field of relationships* through which activities are co-ordinated – relationships which are shaped around a particular set of priorities, strategies and judgements.

Managerialism as discourse

Managerialism does not form a unified body of knowledge, but can be understood as a set of discourses, each of which draws on a different knowledge base, legitimates particular goals, and underpins a particular ordering of relationships. Each discourse is a structured set of ideas which has an internal coherence. The different discourses can be seen as a number of different languages of management. However, a discourse is more than just a language. As du Gay comments,

> Throughout the twentieth century a range of discourses have appeared, each of which has offered a certain way of drawing the map of the organizational world. These discourses . . . have all offered novel ways of 'imagining organization' and have played an active role in 'making up' new ways for people to conduct themselves at work. (du Gay, 1994: 130)

[. . .]

What du Gay is suggesting is that a discourse offers a particular set of identifications for those who speak it or are spoken by it. For example, the identification of being a 'leader' is rather different from that of being a 'senior social worker': it implies different relationships and priorities, and requires different skills and a new focus of expertise. Discourses, then, imply actions as well as identities. Of course, calling someone a leader rather than a social worker does not necessarily change their loyalties and identifications. However, studying the different discourses of managerialism can help us to unlock some of the changes in role, practices and purposes that accompanied the process of state restructuring discussed in this book. We begin with one which is rather confusingly titled 'neo-Taylorism'.

Neo-Taylorism

Pollitt (1993) viewed the initial period of change in the UK, characterized by cost control and decentralization, as a 'neo-Taylorist' form of managerialism. This referred to the scientific management principles set out by Frederick William Taylor in the early years of the twentieth century. Taylor argued that previously unmeasured aspects of the work process could and should be measured in order to fix and control the effort levels of workers. Neo-Taylorism was based on an assumption that workers were individual units responding directly to fairly simple incentives and punishments, and that managerial control of the workforce could be enhanced by the application of scientific principles of work design and organizational structure. As applied to public management, neoTaylorism referred to a strengthening of the control and measurement of work through mechanisms such as target-setting, performance indicators, and monitoring and control of the work process (through time recording and the use of information technology in a way which records the performance of individual workers). It was functional and mechanistic in its orientation:

> The central theme, endlessly reiterated in official documents, is to set clear targets, to develop performance indicators to measure the achievements of those targets, and to single out, by means of merit awards, those individuals who get 'results'. The strengthening and incentivizing of line management is a constant theme . . . In official terms, what seems to be required is a culture shift of a kind that will facilitate a more thorough-going functional/Taylorist management process. (Pollitt, 1993: 56)

This strengthening of control was linked to the drive for economy and efficiency in public management. Metcalfe and Richards (1990: 17) suggest that this emphasis in the early stages of civil service reform had led to an 'impoverished' concept of management whose implementation would 'drag British government kicking and screaming back into the 1950s'. Nevertheless, neo-Taylorism remained firmly in place. There were continual pressures to control costs, to increase productivity, to manage performance and above all to demonstrate 'value for money' through a focus on the three Es of economy, efficiency and effectiveness. This was encouraged by external bodies such as the Audit Commission which, through a series of reports, set out appropriate management arrangements for local government, the health service, the probation service and other bodies.

The discourse of neo-Taylorism offered roles based on the elimination of waste, cost control and performance management. The dominant language was based on calculation: counting, measuring, assessing. The focus was on inputs (the acquisition and deployment of resources) rather than outputs: that is, there was much greater focus on the first two of the three Es (economy and efficiency) rather than effectiveness. The setting of objectives and the close monitoring of performance strengthened central control within organizations. Rather than getting rid of bureaucracy, neo-Taylorism sometimes reproduced it, albeit in the rather different guise of formalized systems of planning and monitoring.

The excellence approach

Pollitt contrasted neo-Taylorism with the 'excellence' approach, so labelled because of the importance of Peters and Waterman's *In Search of Excellence*, first published in 1982. Peters and Waterman studied a group of successful US companies and identified the ingredients of their success, focusing particularly on the role of organizational culture: 'Without exception, the dominance and coherence of culture proved to be an essential quality of the excellent companies. Moreover, the stronger the culture and the more it was directed towards the market-place, the less need there was for policy manuals, organization charts, or detailed procedures and rules (Peters and Waterman, 1982: 75). The role of top managers was to build a strong, unified culture and to encourage workforce commitment rather than exert detailed control over the work process. The mode of control was *affective* rather than *directive*: that is, it was concerned with creating motivation through meaning and with sustaining attachments between managers-as-leaders and the workforce. As such, it has strong links with a set of related discourses: those of human resource management, leadership and staff 'empowerment'.

The ideas of the excellence school were of great significance in the process of transforming the organizations of social welfare. This significance stemmed from its critique of bureaucracy. As du Gay comments,

> The norms and values characterizing the conduct of 'excellent' organizations . . . were articulated in explicit opposition to those constituting the identity of 'bureaucratic' enterprises. Whereas bureaucratic organization encouraged the development of particular capacities and predispositions among its subjects – strict adherence to procedure, the abnegation of personal moral enthusiasms, etc. – the new discourses of work reform stressed the importance of individuals acquiring and exhibiting more market oriented', 'proactive' and 'entrepreneurial' attitudes and behaviours. 'Bureaucratic culture', it was argued, had to give way to 'new approaches that require people to exercise discretion, take initiative, and assume a much greater responsibility for their own organization and management' . . . . In other words, governing organizational life to ensure 'excellence' was deemed to necessitate the production of certain types of work based subject: 'enterprising', autonomous, productive, self regulating, responsible individuals. (du Gay, 1994: 130–1)

This antipathy to bureaucracy resonated with a range of existing critiques of the public sector, from those which saw bureaucracy as a source of waste and inefficiency to those who saw it as the source of unresponsive paternalism. Its paternalism was challenged by the emphasis in the excellence school on customer centredness and service quality, ideas which were picked up widely both by government and by service providers.

The different modes of control meant that these discourses gave rise to very different sets of injunctions for staff. For example, neo-Taylorism might hold 'meeting your financial targets' as the top priority, while the excellence approach might stress 'achieving service improvements' and 'satisfying customers'. [. . .] Despite differences between different managerial discourses, [. . .] both may be present in a single organization, giving rise to 'mixed messages' for staff [. . .]

Consumerism and quality

The idea of the recipient of welfare and other public services being a 'consumer' or 'customer', rather than a client or citizen, was a central reference point in the reform of welfare services from the mid-1980s onwards (see Hughes, 1998). It underpinned a range of market reforms in which the language of consumerism was used to legitimate the breaking up of the old welfare state monopolies and the introduction of competition as a means of increasing customer choice and improving service quality. The consumerist emphasis was welcomed by many modernizers within the welfare organizations because of its challenge to the paternalism of the 'old' systems of welfare delivery. Consumerism viewed the service user not as a passive recipient of bureau-professional decisions but as an active participant in the process of defining needs and wants. Thus although it was connected to the new managerial regime, the emphasis on customers was welcomed by many professionals seeking to 'empower' service users.

[. . .]

The language of the customer presents some difficulties in many areas of social welfare. Nevertheless, the ideas of customer centredness, quality and customer choice provided a new logic of legitimation for government reform, That is, changes were driven through in the name of the customer, and legitimated in terms of greater choice or increased consumer power. This can be contrasted with the efficiency-driven 'logic of legitimation' of neo-Taylorism, which is based on the presumed interests of the taxpayer rather than the welfare consumer.

The discourse of consumerism implied shifts in the roles, relationships and identities of welfare providers. They were to be 'responsive', 'enabling' and 'empowering' in their interaction with users; they were to measure levels of customer satisfaction; they were to be judged in league tables which ranked providers according to their performance: and they were to compete in the 'market-place' of public services (real or imaginary) for customers in order to survive. They were, in short, to model themselves more on the entrepreneurial images drawn from the business world than on the 'public servant' images of the old welfare state.

Business entrepreneurship

The fourth key discourse that informed welfare reform was the language of business, based on the notion that welfare services could be improved by modelling them on ideas and practices drawn from the private sector. This flowed across and interacted with both neo-Taylorism and the excellence discourse: sometimes it meant that organizations should be more efficient, with a firmer managerial grip on performance; sometimes it meant that managers should have more freedom to respond to the demands of customers. Underpinning both, however, was a more general valorization of the business world, and the search for solutions to the perceived problems of social welfare from the private sector. Key figures were imported from industry and commerce to help transform the institutions of government. For example, Sir Derek Rayner's move from Marks and Spencer to set up an 'efficiency strategy' for the civil service received wide press coverage:

> With a few honourable exceptions, the newspapers presented a picture of the Prime Minister's champion, bringing with him the good news from the private sector,

carrying her colours into the heartland of the enemy, the Civil Service, and there single handedly belabouring the inefficient and the wasteful . . . It says something about the lack of public understanding of top management styles in the private sector that the myth took hold. (Metcalfe and Richards, 1990: 6)

Models of management drawn from the business world (albeit often based on inaccurate understandings of how the business world actually operated) informed the practices of reform and restructuring. The training of public sector managers placed more emphasis on business management techniques. Competition was introduced as a stimulus to change, requiring managers to develop entrepreneurial skills and styles and challenging the professional paternalism of many providers [. . .].

These various discourses offer different kinds of subject positions and identifications for managers, with neo-Taylorism emphasizing managers as controllers, the excellence discourse emphasizing the role of managers as organizational innovators and transformers, and the business discourse locating managers as entrepreneurial actors. Some of the discourses represent managerial roles and practices as fundamentally rational (neo-Taylorism); others imply affective modes of engagement (leadership, culture and the excellence school). But together the new managerial discourses imply a fundamental shift in the institutions of social welfare, involving a reordering of relationships, shifts in power, and changes in the basis of decision-making.

Power, decision-making and the reordering of relationships

While the previous section explored differences *within* managerialism, the focus here is on the interaction *between* managerialism and bureau-professionalism. Each is the source of a different form of power; each orders relationships (internal and external) in a particular way; and each gives rise to different forms of judgement in the process of decision-making. The three different forms of power – bureaucratic power, managerial power and professional power – are likely to be present in most welfare organizations interacting in complex ways. To help understand the way in which these forms of power work, we want to look at each as an 'ideal type', abstracted from reality, before exploring ways in which they interact.

Power and decision-making: managerialism as a 'logic of decision-making'

As we have seen, managerial discourse partly redefined relationships with users, subordinating notions of clients and citizens to those of consumers and customers. This helped to dismantle the much criticized paternalistic effects of professional power by emphasizing customer choice, customer care and customer power, however shallow these turned out to be in practice. Professional power was largely based on the acquisition of specialist knowledge and the claim to expertise in making judgements within a defined field of decision-making. The forms of knowledge varied widely, but it typically enabled professionals to diagnose 'problems', identify and formulate 'needs', and categorize and treat 'clients'. These processes were allied to those of rational bureaucratic administration, in which formalized sets of rules underpinned the allocation of resources, including the resource of professional expertise itself. The knowledge basis of the professional bureaucracy therefore legitimated particular goals ('solving problems' and 'treating clients'). Professional power was derived from outside the organization (the professional body) and was organized through distinct sets of relationships within it (hierarchy and bureaucracy).

In professionally dominated organizations, such as health, decision-making was based on the exercise of professional judgement, and the basis of calculation was that of need (see Langan, 1998). For example, in the case of doctors in the NHS, decisions about treatment were made primarily on the basis of clinical need. Resources were allocated on this basis, though there was some prioritizing or targeting where particular groups were deemed to be 'at risk' (as in the case of flu inoculations for the elderly). Professional regimes accorded a great deal of discretion to the individual worker to define need and make judgements about the best allocation of resources.

In bureaucracies, such as those organizations concerned with the payment of welfare benefits, decision-making was based on the exercise of rules, and the basis of calculation was that of whether an applicant was entitled to the provision [. . .]. The much maligned bureaucratic structures and processes of many welfare services could be viewed as a means to ensure that decisions were made fairly on the basis of the equitable application of universal rules of entitlement. Unlike professional organizations, bureaucracies allowed discretion to the individual worker.

Neither professional nor bureaucratic organizations were particularly resource sensitive, in that decisions about the allocation of resources tended to be made separately from the control and management of budgets. Indeed, this was one of the criticisms levelled against the 'waste' and 'inefficiency' of public bureaucracies. The pursuit of economy and efficiency was a recurrent theme in social welfare as successive governments sought to manage the tensions between rising welfare demand and the drive to reduce public expenditure. 'Good management' lay at the heart of resolving this tension. It did so partly by the introduction of *economic* forms of knowledge and expertise as the basis for decision-making alongside the professionally derived and rule-based forms of knowledge enshrined in welfare bureaucracies. The 'logic of decision-making' of managerialism was based on predominantly economic criteria, with the bottom line of financial viability becoming of much greater significance.

This focus on financial criteria of success worked by instilling greater cost consciousness among both managers and front-line staff, leading to what Mackintosh

(1995) calls the rise of economic culture in both purchaser and provider organizations. Mackintosh (1995: 8) defines economic culture as a particular 'thought world' which is 'not just a set of ideas; it is also a way of making decisions, and hence a self-reinforcing way of individuals interpreting their own working worlds and making decisions in them'. For example, the devolution of care budgets to front-line staff in the social service departments she studied had the effect of sharpening competitive cost pressures on provider organizations as purchasers 'shopped around' for care provision. The effectiveness of managerialism in partly displacing professional bureaucracy as a mode of co-ordination can be traced in how far those who are not themselves 'managers' become subject to this new logic of decision-making. That is, how far professional decisions about 'needs' or administrative requirements of access and equity become subjected to the logics of resource management and to organizational goals and priorities. A key feature of managerial regimes is the partial assimilation of new logics of decision-making among all staff through, for example, the devolution of decisions about how to balance needs against available resources. Indeed, Mackintosh's study of the growth of 'economic culture' among staff in social services departments found that cost consciousness was higher among front-line staff (care assessors purchasing services) than among their managers.

Financial pressures also underpinned decisions about which groups services were targeted towards. Providers in a competitive field of relationships strove to control the conditions that affected their costs and performance. This produced two different, but related, strategies. The first, 'cream skimming', involved targeting a service towards particular groups of users (for example, schools seeking to exclude 'difficult' pupils and to attract pupils likely to achieve good exam performance to increase their success in the league tables of school performance). The second, 'boundary management', was concerned with shifting costs between organizations (for example, health and social services departments seeking to transfer the costs of 'expensive' patients to the budgets of other organizations). Both of these strategies helped define what or who should constitute a legitimate demand on an organization's resources. As such, they formed part of the managerial logic of decision-making.

Multiple and interacting regimes

The previous section outlined three different forms of decision-making – professional, bureaucratic and managerial – and the logics that underpin each. Some of the key words reflecting the logics of the different regimes are highlighted in Table 15.2.

Reality is, of course, more complex than charts like this suggest. Most organizations – and most managers – have to work within all of these frameworks and deal with the tensions and ambiguities that arise as different regimes interact. For example, let's take the case of a residential care establishment for the elderly seeking to minimize costs because of a squeeze on its financial resources. In doing

Table 15.2 *Modes of relationship*

	Bureaucratic	Professional	Managerial
Who has access	Citizens	Clients defined as having 'needs'	Customers or consumers
Gatekeeping mechanism	Legally defined entitlements	Professional needs assessment	Rationing or priority setting
Access shaped by	Extent of citizen knowledge of what is available	Gatekeeping by professional groups	'Cream skimming' and 'boundary management'
Basis of decisions	Application of universal rules (little workforce discretion)	Application of professional knowledge and expertise	Most efficient use of limited resources
Types of risk taken into account	Political	Clinical or social	Financial, organizational

so, it has made compromises on what, from a professional perspective, might be the best way of avoiding clinical or social risk. It has thus exposed itself to political risk (local scandals, headlines in the press, questions in the local council chamber, and so on). Such events may impact on the organization's reputation and therefore its capacity to attract new customers or win new contracts, thus reducing its competitive position. This takes us full circle back to the idea of managerial risk. In effect, the organization has to 'manage' multiple goals and success criteria. This is indeed a characteristic of most welfare and public service organizations, which have to respond to the requirements and interests of multiple groups and interests.

[. . .]

Despite the importance of understanding the ways in which different regimes interact, it was the knowledges and forms of expertise that managerialism laid claim to that shaped the restructuring of social welfare. In doing so it fundamentally changed relationships both within welfare organizations and within the field of social welfare as a whole.

Reordering relationships

Managerialism is based on the idea that managers must be given the right to manage – the freedom to make decisions about the use of organizational resources, unrestricted by over-burdening state regulation on the one hand, or trade union power on the other. The 1970s and 1980s saw significant changes in the forms and relations of management in the private sector; these were accompanied by changes in the social composition of the labour force, which entailed greater labour 'flexibility' and a reduction in labour costs. The place of managerialism in state restructuring was therefore more than simply a transfer of private sector practices into welfare services; managerialism as a field of relationships was itself undergoing significant transformations.

MANAGEMENT/WORKFORCE RELATIONS Enlarging the 'right to manage' meant displacing old forms of personnel management linked to bureaucratic regimes by a more strategic approach to human resource management. This focused on the development of direct relationships between managers and workforce in place of collective bargaining. The building of these relationships was based on a range of techniques from 'inspirational leadership' and culture change programmes to individual performance appraisals. New forms of employment contract were introduced in pursuit of greater workforce flexibility, and attempts were made to reduce labour costs by reorganizing work patterns (so that, for example, more of the work in some services was done by lower grade staff through a process of 'deskilling'). The activities of departments, groups and individuals became more closely tied to organizational goals through the mechanisms of funding, target setting and performance review.

[. . .]

ORGANIZATIONAL AND INTER-ORGANIZATIONAL RELATIONSHIPS The processes of decentralization and the introduction of market mechanisms produced an increasingly fragmented array of welfare services. This had the effect of diffusing decision-making responsibility for defining and meeting needs. While central government kept a tight hold on expenditure and set national frameworks and

DILBERT reprinted by permission of United Feature Syndicate, Inc.

standards, it also devolved and decentralized the management of implementation in complex ways. In some instances managerial responsibility was devolved from central government departments to executive agencies (for example the Benefits Agency); in others it passed to non-governmental organizations (such as training and enterprise councils and housing action trusts). Others involved passing responsibility to even more localized points of decision-making (headteachers and school governors, GP fundholders). In many cases the delivery of services passed to organizations in the private or voluntary sectors, controlled through an increasingly complex network of contractual relationships.

This fragmentation and localization of decision-making resulted in the problem of how welfare and other services were to be co-ordinated. Rather than hierarchical co-ordination, in which a line of direct control could be traced from ministerial policy to the point of service delivery, control mechanisms became obscured in a myriad array of contracts, framework documents, service level agreements, local business plans and devolved decision-making. Neither the complex rules of the bureaucratic regime nor the professional ethics and training of the professional regime could provide a coherent integrative framework. It is in this sense that managerialism might be said to form the 'glue' which co-ordinates the increasingly fragmented field of social welfare.

The processes of reform and restructuring, however, have had to address a number of tensions and paradoxes arising from the application of managerialism to welfare services. These are explored in the next section.

The paradoxes of managerialism

The idea that there has been a wholesale shift from 'old' public administration, characterized by bureaucracy and hierarchy, to a 'new' public management, characterized by efficiency, responsiveness and flexibility, has been challenged as an oversimplified view of change (Lowndes, 1996; Clarke and Newman, 1997). Narratives of change structured around clear oppositions between 'past' and 'present', or 'old and new', raise two important difficulties. First, there may be gaps between rhetoric and reality: that is, between what is described in textbooks or reports and what happens on the ground. When we talk about wholesale institutional change, we need to remind ourselves that we are talking about people who often have rather complex and ambiguous feelings about what is taking place. Sometimes change is welcomed because it is seen to bring benefits, perhaps to service users or groups of staff. Sometimes change is actively resisted. If the resistance is strong enough, a particular initiative may be modified (as happened when the introduction of general management met resistance from clinicians in the NHS). Another common response is for people to change the language they use and to adapt some of their practices to fit in with the new requirements, but to retain at least some of their old commitments and loyalties – for example to professional views of social work practice. This means that we can 'overread' the extent and embeddedness of change, and underestimate the important points of continuity with the old welfare regime.

The second reason why we should be suspicious of simple narratives of a wholesale shift from the 'old' to the 'new' is that they tend to tidy away some of the complexity and messiness of change. What is rather more interesting, but more difficult to describe, is how different elements of new and old are packaged and repackaged in ways which produce internal tensions, contradictions and paradoxes. [. . .] Different managerial discourses may not easily fit together since they require different management styles. They invoke different kinds of subject positions for managers (controller, leader, entrepreneur) and are based on different models of the subjects to be managed (neo-Taylorism assuming that workers require surveillance to perform effectively, the excellence school invoking the principle that workers want to use their creativity in the workplace, and market-based models of business entrepreneurship assuming that people work best when they are given incentives). In most organizations these different discourses are overlaid on each other in rather uncomfortable ways, giving rise to 'mixed messages'. There may be some tension between an approach based on winning commitment and giving staff responsibility for their own performance on the one hand, and the constant monitoring and checking by the centre on the other. This may be perceived in terms of hypocrisy on the part of senior managers, or a perverse desire to hang on to power. While each of these may contain glimmers of truth, there is something going on which is rather more structural: that is, a contradictory pull to centralize some forms of power and decentralize others.

The tensions between different discourses are not the only tensions we are concerned with. In a previous section we suggested that, rather than managerialism having displaced bureau-professionalism, it has operated alongside it in 'multiple and interacting regimes'. Managerial power may have become more dominant, but, as we have seen in the case of the NHS, it has not displaced professional power. Political accountability (achieved through the rules and decision-making hierarchies of bureaucracy) has continued to operate alongside managerial account-ability (which emphasizes greater transparency in decision-making and a shift towards power to the consumer). Organizations have to respond to multiple sets of pressures from the different stakeholders who have some influence over their goals and objectives. For example, they have to satisfy the requirements of central government, and attempt to meet the performance targets that are set by government bodies and agencies such as the Audit Commission. They have to pursue business goals in order to secure organizational survival in an increasingly uncertain environment. They have to meet the needs of different sets of customers and users. They have to work in partnership with other agencies in the increasingly dispersed field of welfare service. At the same time, they have to demonstrate their accountability and to ensure probity in their use of public resources.

The combined effect of these multiple pressures is to produce a field of tensions which operate at different levels and in different ways. Some of the key tensions that arise are those between centralization and decentralization;

between flexibility and standardization; between empowerment and control; between managerial and political forms of accountability; between management and politics. [. . .]

Centralization and decentralization

Devolution and decentralization have been key themes in the new public management. Both involve a dispersal of power away from the centre to the managers of particular business units or service providers. This has multiplied the number of points at which financial decisions are made and has sharpened accountability for performance within organizations. Although devolution and decentralization are potent sources of efficiency, they bring some dilemmas for the centre: for instance, how is it possible to retain control while at the same time giving power away? The answer to this tricky question lies in the way in which the dispersal of power contains a double movement of centralization and decentralization.

[. . .]

The key issues are the distribution of powers between centre and periphery (what decisions the centre wishes to retain) and the nature of the control systems put in place by the centre. In terms of the former, it is important to look at the kinds of decision-making power held at different levels: professional decisions, resource decisions, staffing decisions, decisions about what services should be provided, decisions about which service users are to be targeted, decisions about where and how to involve service users or citizens in decision-making, and so on.

Flexibility and standardization

The pull towards centralization means that organizations need to structure and manage themselves in a way that will enable them to meet centrally determined goals. This in turn often results in a standardization of management styles and practices, and reduced flexibility of the system as a whole. However, there is still considerable discretion for many organizations to set their own goals and organize their work in the way they think best. One expression of the potential tension between these imperatives lies in the relationship between central government or national agencies on the one hand, and local government on the other. [. . .]

Tensions between flexibility and standardization can also be seen in the changing role which voluntary, community-based and other 'not-for-profit' organizations play in the delivery of social welfare. Voluntary organizations have always had an important role in filling gaps in state provision, and in acting as advisers or advocates for individuals seeking to gain access to welfare services provided by statutory bodies. Their relative autonomy and high degree of flexibility meant that they were well placed to innovate by experimenting with new forms of provision, many of which were later incorporated into state agencies. However, the flexibility of voluntary organizations was threatened as cash-strapped local authorities became less able to provide funding to voluntary organizations to use as they wished, but instead began to set up contracts with them to provide core services [. . .]. Voluntary organizations found themselves having to sacrifice some of their autonomy and responsiveness in order to win and manage contracts. This required very different management arrangements in which the work of individual members of staff became more tightly controlled, supervised and standardized. Many voluntary organizations found that these 'neo-Taylorist' management arrangements sat rather uncomfortably with their ethos and purpose, and reduced their ability to attract volunteers.

Empowerment and control

Neo-Taylorism, as we know, is only one strand of managerialism. Others focus on diffusing responsibility and fostering self-control (through, for example, the 'discipline of the market' combined with the discipline of centrally set performance targets) rather than enforcing external controls. However, this rationale works rather imperfectly in the political context in which welfare services operate, where probity in the spending of public money is an important political requirement which may conflict with the entrepreneurial imperative of managerialism. The requirement that welfare organizations become more 'businesslike' implies a shift in culture: away from the values of stewardship and conservation to the more entrepreneurial and dynamic culture of the business world; from a culture which emphasizes the importance of the probity of process (accounting for the way we do things) to one which focuses on the achievement of results (being held to account for our success or failure).

[. . .]

Tensions between multiple cultures, and the potentially conflicting values and practices which they embody, have to be negotiated every day. Many of them stem from the interaction of the worlds of politics and management. While managerialism requires 'hands off' control in order to allow managers to use their delegated powers to maximum advantage, politicians seeking to win popular support, or to respond to sudden crises or scandals in the media, continue to intervene in what the managers might view as day-to-day operational decisions. [. . .]

Management, policy and politics

The relationship between politics and management has always been clouded with ambiguities. While in formal terms a clear distinction has been drawn between 'policy' (the realm of politics) and 'administration', in practice it has been difficult to sustain a clear boundary between them. Administrators have a role in advising on policy as well as delivering it, and the process of delivery involves a multiplicity of decisions about how policy is to be interpreted.

Many of the reforms attempted to create a stronger separation between policy and delivery by devolving responsibility for operations to agencies and other bodies working within some form of contract or framework document. Such a separation brought many potential benefits: it encouraged policy-makers to clarify their goals and to identify the outcomes they wanted, and to specify them in performance standards or targets. Managers could then be left to get on with the job, finding the best and most efficient ways of meeting their targets without undue interference, while being held to account for what they delivered. Such a separation addressed many of the presumed failings of bureaucracy identified by public choice theorists. There were also less explicit benefits. Decentralization provided a response to the potential political problems arising from the containment of welfare expenditure by distancing resource allocation and rationing decisions from the political realm. [. . .]

However, the struggle to shift issues and problems from one domain to another (and indeed from one organization to another) provided a point of instability in the new order: what we might term an unsettled aspect of the struggle to create a new organizational settlement. Many issues stubbornly refused to be de-politicized in this way, and became the ready stuff of parliamentary question times and political campaigns. [. . .] Decentralization, even with rigorous central controls and stringent performance targets, has remained inherently unstable in the politicized context of social policy. This is because however much power is decentralized, political accountability means that the exercise of that power, even at low levels of decision-making, remains open to public scrutiny and political debate. [. . .]

This section has placed particular stress on the difficulty of identifying clearly the boundaries between politics, policy and management for a number of reasons. First, this is a key site of tensions and instabilities. Despite the injunctions of managerialism, managers in the public domain do not have an unfettered 'right to manage', free from political interference, because of the nature of political accountability. Secondly, we are not just concerned with tensions between management and politics: many of the dilemmas which organizations have to work with stem from oscillations between different government departments. Given the paradoxes and tensions outlined in this section, how well does managerialism deliver on its promises? Furthermore, are there other criteria that should be used in evaluating its impact? [. . .]

Conclusion

Managerialism is likely to continue to be seen as a solution to economic problems of high welfare expenditure. It helps to deliver economies by bringing decisions about how to meet welfare needs closer to decisions about resource availability and the best use of scarce resources. Managerialism prioritizes particular sets of goals which are concerned with organizational survival and success alongside the professional goals of meeting needs or solving problems. It invokes particular ways of thinking about how activities should be carried out, based on notions of efficiency. It lays claim to particular types of expertise which underpin the exercise of discretion and judgement. As such, managerialism serves as the 'glue' which integrates and co-ordinates an increasingly fragmented field of social welfare delivery across the public, private and voluntary sectors. However, [. . .] there is no single managerialism, but a number of different discourses and practices. These have different sorts of consequences for decision-making, and reshape relationships in different ways. As a consequence, managerialism embodies a number of internal tensions and paradoxes [. . .]. These mean that change has been complex and uneven. Social actors have tried to find ways of resolving contradictions on the ground, working with multiple goals and success criteria, or reshaping the managerial agenda around other sets of values and goals – for example around professional goals or in the interests of staff, users or communities.

All of this means that evaluating managerialism is not an easy task. [. . .] The aim has not been to come up with a single conclusion, but to enable you to assess the arguments of others or develop arguments of your own. This is important because of the central role that managerialism seems to have played in the shaping of a new political settlement between 'neo-liberalism' and 'New Labour'. While the post-war project of building the welfare state looked to a mix of professional expertise and bureaucratic rationality, the project of containing welfare growth and reshaping the welfare order was seen to require a new form of co-ordination and control. The logic of efficiency has become the dominant ethos in this new managerial regime. However, efficiency may not be sufficient as either a single tool for evaluation or as a single imperative to be pursued in developing new policy agendas to meet the requirements of a complex and diverse society. The unravelling of the old social settlement raises critical questions about the effectiveness of managerialized and fragmented organizations in creating effective relationships between policy-makers and service users, and ultimately between state and citizen. [. . .]

References

Clarke, J. and Newman, J. (1997) *The Managerial State: Power, Politics and Ideology in the Remaking of Social Welfare*. London: Sage.

du Gay, P. (1994) 'Colossal immodesties and hopeful monsters: pluralism and organizational conduct'. *Organization*. 1(1): 125–48.

Hughes, G. (ed.) (1998) *Imagining Welfare Futures*. London: Routledge in association with The Open University.

Langan, M. (1998) 'The contested concept of need', in M. Langan (ed.), *Welfare: Needs, Rights and Risks*. London: Routledge in association with The Open University.

Lentell, H. (1998) 'Families of meaning: contemporary discourses of the family', in G. Lewis (ed.), *Forming Nation, Framing Welfare*. London: Routledge in association with The Open University.

Lowndes, V. (1996) 'Change in public service management: new institutions and management regimes', *La Journée d'Etude Local Governance*. February, Paris.

Mackintosh, M. (1995) *Putting Words into People's Mouths? Economic Culture and Its Implications for Local Governance*. Open Discussion Papers in Economics. no.9. Faculty of Social Sciences. The Open University.

Metcalfe, L. and Richards, S. (1990) *Improving Public Management*, 2nd edn. London: Sage.

Niskanen, W.A. (1971) *Bureaucracy and Representative Government*. New York: Aldine-Atherton.

Osborne, D. and Gaebler, T. (1992) *Reinventing Government: How the Entrepreneurial Spirit is Transforming the Public Sector*. Wokingham: Addison-Wesley.

Parker, H. (1982) *The Moral Hazard of Social Insurance*. London: Institute of Economic Affairs.

Peters, J. and Waterman, R.H. (1982) *In Search of Excellence: Lessons from America's Best Run Companies*. New York: Harper & Row.

Pollitt, C. (1993) *Managerialism and the Public Services*, 2nd edn, Oxford: Blackwell.

Taylor, G. (1993) 'Challenges from the margins', in J. Clarke (ed.), *A Crisis in Care? Challenges to Social Work*. London: Sage.

Walsh, K. (1995) *Public Services and Market Mechanisms: Competition, Contracting and the New Public Management*. Basingstoke: Macmillan.

Williams, F. (1996) 'Post-modernism, feminism and the question of difference', in N. Parton (ed.), *Social Theory, Social Change and Social Work*. London: Routledge.

From Decision to Action in Organizations: Decision-making as a Social Representation

HERVÉ LAROCHE*

[. . .]

The limits of the decision-making perspective

The lost object of decision-making

The decision-making perspective developed, at least partially, to challenge the rational, prescriptive, problem-solving approach to the making of choices in organizations, building on the idea that the rational model does not provide a realistic description of what happens in organizations. It highlighted the influence of concrete processes on the substance of choices: process does matter. Through many empirical studies, researchers tried to describe the decision-making process in a realistic manner. They identified numerous and very significant differences between observations and the rational model, revealing bureaucratic processes [. . .], political processes [. . .], psychological processes [. . .] etc. They constructed process typologies, both theoretic [. . .] and empirical [. . .] and established the ways these processes interact [. . .].

So far, the decision-making perspective has proven to be very fruitful. These works show evidence that decision-making is not easily controllable, that the decision-maker is merely one actor among others, and that the decision-making process is far from being neutral in regard to final choices. The evaluation that follows does not deny the contribution of this perspective; rather, it aims at questioning its implicit bases.

* From Laroche, H. 'From decision to action in organizations', *Organizational Science*, 6(1) (1995).

The decision-making perspective is not particularly concerned with the definition of decision (Meyer, 1990). It generally takes the point of view of an external observer. The observer analyses the process starting from what he points out as a choice and, working his way backwards, he reconstructs the process that led to this choice (generally through a case study). The decision is looked upon from the point of view of the completed process. It apprehends the object by the only part that a researcher can easily locate, that is to say, the conclusion of the process, the choice that has been made. In order to reconstruct the process, researchers isolate a case through time and space. They locate the decision between the identified result and a beginning yet to be discovered. They restrict the decision to what happened around this outcome, around the 'matter', to take the word used in the Bradford Studies (Hickson et al., 1986; this research is considered here as typical of the second perspective). This creates a 'slice' of organizational life, inside which the activities of the identified actors are interpreted in relation to the assumed 'matter.'

Such a decision is in fact a framing similar to the one a photographer chooses to compose his picture. It provides a window on a reality that is actually much more continuous. Actors, or participants, simultaneously engage in activities other than the decision in question. The nature of these activities, as well as the stakes involved, may quite differ (Cohen et al., 1972). Several different problems often link different actions together [. . .]. Research on the organizational and strategic agenda [. . .] suggests that problems accompany decision-making processes more than they initiate them; thus, it seems imprudent to assess a particular problem as the starting point of a decision. Moreover, problems are interdependent especially because of the decision-maker's limited capacity to deal with several issues simultaneously (Dutton, 1988).

Focusing on case studies in this way induces a methodological bias that cannot be neglected. The question here is not the arbitrary cutout of the process in itself. Rather it lies in the fact that this cutout is not thought to be arbitrary. The unit of analysis is not discussed. It is understood as self-evident. In doing as such, the decision-making perspective ends up as a prisoner of its unit of analysis: cases of decision-making. On one hand, it tends to dissolve the notion of decision-making (as an organizational activity) by an empirical and critical approach. It destroys the very idea of decision, because decision-making no longer refers to an identifiable behavior such as problem-solving. On the other hand, it maintains the idea that units of decision-making actually exist, even if research strongly suggests that inside these units reigns a good deal of confusion. The notion of decision is reproduced by the fact that, through a methodological bias, the research program constructs an arbitrary object called the decision.

Managers as decision-makers

In the midst of these decisions cases are decision-makers. Decision-making theorists scarcely question the status of the manager as a decision-maker. The rational model of decision-making (Allison, 1971) naturally places an isolated decision-maker at the heart of his assertions, to such a point that one could have renamed this model 'model of the lone actor' (Nioche, 1985).

In the alternative, realistic view of decision-making, the decision-maker is certainly not always a central character. The political school redefines the decision-making as an actor among other actors (Crozier and Friedberg, 1977). The idea of actors introduces a distance between the decision and the individuals involved: distance in strategic terms, in the way that actors approach the decision in relation to their interests and positions in the system; distance in terms of power and control, since the actor is only one of the forces that influence the process. Bureaucratic, organizational or behavioral theories of decision-making (Cyert and March, 1963; Carter, 1971) demonstrates that many decisions are produced without significant and deliberate intervention of human actors. Decision-makers frequently disappear behind routines and automatic processes.

But, even though both the scope and the power of decision-makers are seriously narrowed, managers remain decision-makers in the decision-making perspective. Their primary concern in organizational life is to make decisions; they are constantly trying to influence decision processes; they aim at building controlled choices. They may rely more or less consciously on automatic processes and routines, but it is only to concentrate on higher-order decisions. They may give up the idea of total control of the process, but doing so makes them more powerful (Quinn, 1980).

Research on the manager's activity seriously challenges the idea that managers primarily are decision-makers. Most of this research suggests that the making of decisions is not a central element of the manager's schedule [. . .]. In fact, managerial tasks reveal characteristics contrary to the idea of decision-making (Whitley, 1987). The problems managers handle are narrowly interdependent. Reproduction and change are not separated classes of managerial tasks, but are mixed in a continuous way. The outcomes of managerial tasks are not clearly isolable. These characteristics portray a manager rather different from the image of the decision-maker who eliminates a series of distinct problems by well-defined solutions. It even questions the idea of an actor, 'maker' of decisions.

How can we explain that decision-making theorists were so shy about challenging the identification of managers with decision-makers, when not reinforcing this idea? First, we must question the origins of the decision-making perspective. Secondly, we can suspect some form of ideological bias to have influenced students of decision-making.

The critical theory of decision-making developed, for a significant part, from the works of Simon (1957), March and Simon (1958), and Cyert and March (1963). The centrality of these works is undeniable in the academic field of decision-maker, even though this field is not very unified (Dery, 1990a). Simon's principle of bounded rationality implies looking at every organization member as a decision-maker, because as the individual encounters major limits in his ability to process information, the outcome of his cognitive processes can neither be predicted nor relied upon. The idea of the individual as an imperfect information-processing machine was meant to destroy the illusion of a well-oiled organizational machine that functions in a predictable manner, as intended by its designers. Since the individual information processing machine was a central assumption, it was very difficult for anything else to come out of this theory except an individual decision-maker. The success of the intellectual project encourages that its foundations are never questioned.

This theoretical bias converged with an ideological bias. The identification of managers and decision-makers is not neutral. It gives the managers a certain social identity. In our western societies, the human activity of decision-making carries with it an important symbolic weight. The decision-maker becomes a highly valued figure. It would be easy to enumerate all the positive connotations that the term decision-making evokes and to list the symbolic advantages, not only in the organization, but in society as a whole, from which 'decision-makers' benefit.

Management as a whole seems to be about decision-making. Most management books have the ambition to give the decision-maker the proper tools in order to prepare decisions, which are at the same time their responsibility and their prerogative. Managers cherish this image and favor theories that portray them in this heroic stance. Because theorists are also authors, lecturers, and/or consultants, they tend to stay 'in the neighborhood' of the practitioners' point of view (sometimes quite voluntarily; e.g. Schwenk, 1988a). Departing from this ideology is not only difficult, it is also costly.

Away from rationality and back

The debate on the rationality of human behavior in organizations seems to be inexhaustible. It is now common, following Allison (1971), to oppose other models to the rational one. These alternative models are supposed to throw a different light on decision-making processes. But these oppositions are sometimes more apparent than real. The attractiveness of the rational model is amazingly strong. Studying the empirical research may give the impression that the idea of rationality has pervaded the descriptive approaches of the decision-making process, even though they aspired to free themselves of this idea or at least not to presuppose it. We will use three examples.

First, works trying to describe the decision-making processes in an integrative manner (e.g. Mintzberg et al., 1976; Lyles, 1981) led to the cutting up of the process in successive phases: (1) problem awareness, (2) problem diagnosis, (3) development of solutions, (4) selection of a solution. This description bears a striking resemblance to the stages described in rationalistic approaches to decision-making (Johnson, 1987).

Secondly, after examining the so-called 'non-rational' processes, the empirical studies sometimes end up admitting the existence of a lesser form of rationality. In this way, the Bradford Studies conclude that decisions imply the meeting of three forms of rationality: problem-solving rationality, interest-accommodating rationality, and control rationality. The conclusion is that, after all, the blending of these different rationalities is usually 'reasonable' if not wholly rational (Hickson et al., 1986: 250).

Thirdly, the 'cognitive approach of strategic decision-making' (Schwenk, 1984, 1985, 1988b), developing a theory of strategic decision-making from concepts such as cognitive bias, causal maps, metaphor, and analogy, first seems to add cognitive processes to the list of 'non-rational' types of decision-making processes. Whereas, in fact, in this synthesis built upon Allison's typology (Schwenk, 1988a), its main sponsor puts cognitive processes in the category of the rational model, as an enrichment and revitalization of this model.

Thus, the critique frequently returns to the reassuring shelter of the rational model, or at least does not dare to venture too far from it. This leads one to question the impact of the critique. Looking backwards at the usual presentation of the field of decisionmaking, Huard (1980) and Sfez (1981) have shown that most of the works classed as concurrent analyses of the rational model can be interpreted as developments and extensions of this model. According to these authors, the result is not, as Allison suggests, the simultaneous presence of competing paradigms, but rather an extended domination of the rational model.

Overcoming the limits of the decision-making perspective means more than refining methodologies and concepts. It rather needs some kind of paradigm shift in our basic assumptions about organization processes.

From decision to action

Action first, decision later

An emerging trend, which could be labeled the 'action' perspective, strongly challenges the realistic decision-making perspective. Organizations are best understood as action generators (Starbuck, 1983). Automatic processes dominate by far explicit decision-making activities (Huard, 1980). Decision-making is the emerging part of an iceberg of unreflective action. This action is rationalized a posteriori through thinking (Starbuck, 1985). Decisions scarcely initiate actions in organizations. Furthermore, good decision-making contradicts good action, because good action needs strong commitment to a single course of action, whereas good decision-making implies carefully balancing several solutions before taking action (Brunsson, 1982, 1985). Rather than aiming at some explicit goal, managers are dealing with interactive 'management situations' where they have to react to demands (Girin, 1990). Managers are faced with contradictions and competing demands from internal and external stakeholders. They use decisions as instruments to satisfy these demands and legitimize their organization, but these decisions are decoupled from real action which goes on unchanged (Brunsson, 1989). In any case, managers' reflective thought is only a minor and powerless component in the flow of events and fortunes that forms action (Weick, 1983).

In these ideas, all is not quite new. The behavioral theory of the firm (Cyert and March, 1963) stressed that most choices did not proceed from a deliberate, explicit, conscious decision-making behavior. But higher-level, strategic choices were left out of this analysis and were believed to escape this fate. This is no longer true. The action perspective does not ignore strategic decision-making. In this view, there is more to strategy-making than an addition or a chain of decisions. The process of strategy formation cannot be analysed solely as a decision-making activity (Mintzberg and Waters, 1990).

In the action perspective, interpretation, not choice, is the core phenomena of organizational life (Weick, 1969; March, 1988). Cognitive structures shape cognitive processes, which in turn shape organizational action; action is followed by cognitive activities of sensemaking, rationalization and justification. Upstream from strategic decision processes, a central cognitive structure in the organization produces a representation of the world, of the organization, and of the organization in the world; it inspires strategic action and shapes strategy formation. Paradigms [. . .], belief systems [. . .], causal maps [. . .], strategic frame [. . .], dominant logic [. . .] are names given to this cognitive strategic action generators [. . .]. Beyond cognitive processes, the strength of organizational reproductive mechanisms, such as organizational culture [. . .] or identity [. . .] challenges the generally acknowledged idea of strategic decisions initiating ruptures and changes. Action theorists then tend to exclude decisions from explanations of both continuity and discontinuity in organizations. Decision-making is thus relegated to a restricted, local, punctual, and/or symbolic role.

Towards a theory of action in organizations

The emerging action perspective pictures organizational life as a flow of intertwined processes, rather than a sum of juxtaposed decisions. Managers lose their decision-making status and become merely participants immersed in processes they do not control and often even do not understand. The sequential order of decision-making steps, culminating in a choice, gives way to a continuous flow of action punctuated with moments of interpretation and evaluation. Decisions are constructs built either by the observer for his or her research purposes, or by organization members for symbolic purposes.

Theory of action could then be the basis of a renewed approach to organizational processes. Still, authors who promote the concept (Brunsson, 1985, 1989; Starbuck, 1983; Weick, 1987) may give the feeling that they are more about challenging the dominant idea of decision-making than actually setting the foundations for a theory of organizational action. The idea of action is still poorly defined, except as opposed to decision (Brunsson) or to problem-solving (Starbuck). This systematic opposition should give way to a self-sufficient definition on one hand, and, on the other hand, as we will argue later, to a redefinition of decision-making in the field of organizational action, rather than merely setting it aside.

This paper does not have the ambition of building a definition of organizational action. Still, we would like to suggest some ideas for that purpose.

First, setting the grounds for a theory of action should acknowledge a few basic postulates. As a starting point, we propose the following two:

1 Action processes determine, in part, outcomes; in other words, the way things happen matters; this point has been empirically tested by the realistic decision-making perspective, and is not questioned by the limits and biases discussed above.

2 Neither the organization's features (as structure, culture, system, function, etc.), nor those of the environment strictly determine action processes, though the latter are certainly influenced by the surrounding context in a variety of ways; processes unfold largely on their own dynamics, through mixed phases of renewal and change.

Such a theory of action is basically 'indeterministic' (Grandori, 1987): it acknowledges that no accurate prediction of outcomes and processes can be done, neither by organizational participants nor by external observers. Research can isolate recurring patterns, forms or figures of action, but the blending of content, context and process produces a unique outcome (Pettigrew, 1987).

Secondly, in the decision-making perspective, decision-making processes are motivated by objectives, preferences, missions, interests, etc. What motivates organizational action from a participant's point of view? Organizations are full of devices designed to control their members, so that action can be initiated and co-ordinated to some extent. How do participants 'interact' with these action generators? This raises the question of the participants' intentions and more generally, of the link between the individual and the organization.

Thirdly, a theory of action should fill in the wide gap between unreflective action and decision-making, the temple of reason. Administrative sciences tend to reproduce this opposition (Dery, 1990b). Conceiving of action as intimately intertwined with thought seems more fruitful. Thought shapes action because it is closely tied to action (Weick, 1983). Self-fulfilling prophecies are common and important phenomena in organizations. These phenomena should be fully acknowledged by an action perspective. As Weick states:

> A manager's preoccupation with rationality may be significant, less for its power as a problem-solving heuristic than for its power to induce action that implants the rationality that was presumed. (Weick, 1983: 235)

In other words, the belief in rationality guides an individual's action in such a way that, a posteriori, this action reveals to him a rationality in 'what happened'.

Fourthly, evaluation of action is an important and complex process in an action perspective. Action flows but is punctuated by moments of interpretation and evaluation. Conceiving evaluation processes is relatively simple if one assumes the existence of exogeneous objectives or norms and external evaluators. The classical decision-making perspective attributes this function to staff and/or hierarchy managers conducting evaluation through planning, monitoring and control systems, or through cultural norms and values. It is less easy if one views organizational action, as it unfolds, as moving the reference points which could be used in action evaluation. In fact, evaluation is not exterior to organizational action. Evaluation is in itself part of action processes. It is an endogeneous process, created by action and creating action in return.

Lastly, should we be content with a theory of action free of the idea of decision-making? The sharp decoupling of decisions and actions by sponsors of the action perspective (e.g. Starbuck, 1983; Brunsson, 1989, 1990) suggests that decision-making is a marginal phenomenon, an artifact built by conventional researchers, and/or a rhetoric device serving symbolic functions. The latter part of this paper argues that there is no reason to completely dissociate decisions and action and to limit decision-making to one or more symbolic functions. Decision-making is a real and important part of organizational life and should be included in a theory of action. Rather than dissociation or decoupling, we should think of some form of loose coupling, or even variable coupling. Decision-making should not be understood in a realistic way as in the decision-making perspective, but rather as a social representation.

From decision to 'decisions': Decision-making as a social representation

Recoupling decision and action

A striking characteristic of organizational life is that there is a lot of talk about decisions, decisions that have been made, are to be made, will be made, should be made, will never be made; talk about who makes decisions, when, how, why and with what results. Organization members interpret a significant part of activities around them in terms of decisions. Numerous organizational devices (planning systems, committees, assemblies, votes, etc.) are developed, implemented and operated for the purpose of producing decisions. Managers look at themselves as decision-makers.

There is a wide gap between theoretical descriptions of organizational life proposed by the action perspective and representations of participants and actors in organizations. This of course does not question in itself the relevance of theories, as theorizing is precisely about going beyond ordinary knowledge. Still, it raises some questions that the action perspective has not really addressed: to what extent do organizational participants misunderstand their environment and their own acts? To what point is decision-making a cosmetic ideology for managers to protect their heroic status as decision-makers in the eyes of lower-rank members and in their own (Laroche and Nioche, 1992)? Is decision-making a mere illusion and can we ignore the managers' understanding of their own action, as if this understanding has no effect on action?

Mintzberg and Waters (1990) argue that, because it turns out to be an 'artificial construct' (except in bureaucratic contexts), decision 'gets in the way' of researcher's understanding of action. Understanding organizational behavior in terms of decisions systematically 'imputes commitment to action,' whereas action can occur without explicit commitment. In order to avoid such a bias – which is consistent with the ones we analysed above – they simply propose to do without the concept of decision. We agree with Mintzberg and Waters (1990) about the concept of decision 'getting in the way' of organizational analysis. From a researcher's point of view, with his or her own frames of reference, a concept may seem relevant or not; if not, it becomes a source of 'misunderstandings.' But they do not pay attention to the fact that participants themselves believe in decision-making, just as researchers do. Does it 'get in their way' too? Should they do without it? How would they do without it? Participants' belief in decision-making is not a methodological stance. It is not an 'artificial construct,' but a part of their 'natural' understanding of their own world. The question then shifts to the functions served by such a construct. And the very reason why decision is not a suitable concept in the eyes of Mintzberg and Waters may give a clue to why managers use the concept: systematically imputing commitment to actions is a way of understanding the organizational world which is consistent with a manager's point of view.

March (1981) goes nearer to our point when he sees the decision process as 'a ritual by which we recognize saints, socialize the young, reassure the old, recite scripture, and come to understand the nature of our existence.' (1981: 232). Rituals convey meaning, and meaning is related to action in organizations. Managers are not helpless members of a primitive desert tribe, building idols and setting rituals to deal with the lack of control on their environments. Though they undoubtedly invent rituals and worship idols and fool themselves in a variety of ways, managers do try to take things in hand and control actions, events, themselves and others. Rituals and idols and even fooling oneself take place in this project of control and sensemaking. So do many management practices, and decision-makers. Managers see themselves as conscious decision-makers. This is false in some way, but yet the illusion is a 'fruitful error' (Saint-Sernin, 1989; Levy, 1990). Though observers may be tempted to point out the fallacies and illusions of their ambition, at the same time they have to account for the effective result it produces. For that purpose, organizational decision-making can be conceptualized as a phenomenon of social representation.

The social representation of decision-making

[. . .]

Social representations are 'modes of practical thinking oriented towards communication, understanding, and the mastering of the social, material and ideal environment' (Jodelet, 1984). As cognitive structures, social representations link a subject to an object. They are both the product of a construction of reality and the process by which this construction takes place in the individual's mind. But beyond their role in thinking and understanding, they convey normative implications as well as feelings, which regulate the individual's relationship with the world and with others, and which organize conducts and interactions (Jodelet, 1991).

Social representations are social phenomena in the sense that their objects are aspects of the social life. But most important is that the system producing and reproducing social representations is a social one. Social conditions – such as status, positions, roles, ideological and historical contexts – influence the cognitive contents and processes of social representations. The cognitive system of a representation is the product of a social metasystem (Doise, 1990). Social representations help people master the social world from their position in the social world. Thus, social representation can be studied from a psychological or from a sociological perspective as well.

Though they may have an ideological side, social representations are not closed ideologies impregnating the mind of passive individuals acting under influence. They rather look like 'explicit or implicit, more or less organized packages of ideas, judgements and images, which are used to describe, interpret or justify collective actions' (Padioleau, 1991). Through social representations, people are able to get a hand on the physical and social world around them, thus becoming actors of this world (Padioleau, 1986).

Conventionally, from here on in this chapter, the words 'decision' and 'decision-making' in quotes refer to the representation of the process in the organization members' minds; it is the label they use to describe the process. Outside quotes, decision and decision-making refer to other representations, for example scientific ones as in the realistic perspective described in the first part of the chapter.

Managers see themselves as decision-makers because making 'decisions' is a way of being an actor in the world of organizations.

Managers make 'decisions' because 'decisions' give meaning to the processes which surround and concern organization members. Organization members explain what they are participating in and what is happening around them in terms of 'decisions' which are made, which will be made, etc. 'Decisions' point out concrete and symbolic stakes. More precisely, organization members point out to themselves and to others what they consider to be the stakes. Through 'decision-making,' they discover a world made of problems, choices, decision-makers, and important times and places on all of which their fate of their interests may depend.

Which representation of decision-making?

The hypothesis of organizational decision-making as a social representation leads to the question of the contents of this representation. To our knowledge, this question has not been empirically investigated. We will have to draw ideas from research having a different focus.

The cultural and ideological context of western societies gives a central place to the rational model of decision-making. Representations of decision-making are likely to convey ideas and expectations of orderly, linear processes, where free and responsible individuals exercise their intellectual capacity through logical reasoning (Sfez, 1981). People tend to make organizations or groups into homogeneous actors, entities similar to the human being; they attribute acts, objectives and willpower to organizations, as they do to individuals. Thus, representations of decision-making are likely to underestimate social and interactive aspects of organizational processes.

This draws a general picture of 'decision-making.' Yet, the contents of social representations are marked by their conditions of emergence and of use (Jodelet, 1984). Thus, significant variations are to be expected. For example, managers of a higher rank seem to grant a larger place to politics in their perception of the processes (Madison et al., 1980). Internal differentiation is likely to be a source of variation in the content of decision-making representations. For example, the temporal horizon of action differs greatly between sub-groups in organizations (Lawrence and Lorsch, 1967). Speed, both as a perceived characteristic of processes, and as a normative expectation, is probably an important dimension of representations in the organization. [. . .] Decision styles can be pictured as an attribute of a manager, of a team (e.g. a top management team), or an organization as a whole (Bailey and Johnson, 1992). Though decision styles are not the direct expression of local representations of decision-making, they may well be related, and the variations of the former could be an indicator of the variations of the latter. At a higher level, we can expect cultural variations [. . .] though data is rare and evidence is not clear [. . .].

In other words, there would be not one, but numerous social representations of decision. Further research should identify significant dimensions and relate them to the bearers of these representations, as social groups in specific social positions.

But social representations are both content and process. Decision-making refers to the process by which decisions are made. In a similar way, 'decision-making' refers to the process by which 'decisions' are made. The process of 'decision-making' actualizes 'decision-making' in constructing a reality of 'decisions' and 'decision-makers'; simultaneously, such a reality confirms and reproduces the content of the representation. Thus, 'decision-making' is an active component of action. We will develop this idea around three points. First, 'decision-making,' far from being a mirage in managers' minds, influences the substance of organizational processes. Secondly, from a manager's point of view, 'decision-making' facilitates action in the messy world of organizations. Thirdly, still from a participant's perspective, 'decisions' help interpret what happened.

'Decision-making' in action

'Decisions' as self-fulfilling prophecies

Decision as a representation becomes a component part of what is happening around the participants: their activity will direct itself in relation to the 'decisions' they locate in the past, perceive in the present course of things, and sense for the future. They will have the feeling of taking part in or being witness to 'decisions,' and will act or react in relation to this feeling. Even more so, as there is a normative aspect in the social representation of decision, people expect that 'decisions' explain most actions clearly. Participants will then tend actively to build what they will prospectively and retrospectively call 'decisions.'

In this way, it is natural that bosses make 'decisions,' that meetings are devoted to the making of 'decisions,' that notes are written about 'decisions' which have just been made, that organization members behave as actors mobilizing themselves in relation to 'decisions,' that they demand to take part in 'decision-making,' that they defend their power of 'decision,' that they ask how such a 'decision' could possibly have been made, why a 'decision' has not yet been made, that they complain about the absence of 'decisions,' etc.

Decision as a representation tends to create concrete situations which concretely approach representations. In other terms, the effect of this representation is to actualize itself to some extent. For example, if a group of people think that there is a 'decision' to be made, a meeting takes place, at the end of which the participants think that a 'decision' has or has not been made. They are more likely to believe this since they came to the meeting with the idea that they were going to 'decide,' and since they believe that they are experiencing a decision-making process. They communicate between themselves in order to confirm their feelings: before the meeting to assure themselves of what is going to be 'decided,' and after the meeting to make sure of how it ended up (Sims, 1979, 1987). Those who do not participate in the meeting, but know it took place, think that a 'decision' was at stake. They look for information about the income by asking: 'what has been decided?' Those who are not in the picture will eventually find a reference to this meeting in a report, note or conversation; they will interpret this meeting as the time and place of the 'decision,' the results of which they can see today.

Looking ahead: 'decisions' as useful illusions

The strength of this process of self-fulfilling prophecies must not be overestimated. In spite of the limits that have been indicated, empirical research on organizational decision-making demonstrates that there are good reasons to believe that social representation of decision-making leads participants to 'invent' 'decisions' where an observer would be tempted to describe reality in completely different terms. The social representation of decision-making makes up artifacts which participants call 'decisions,' backing themselves up with numerous potential signs of 'decisions' such as speeches, notes, reports, meetings, agendas, deadlines, etc. 'Decisions' are constructs which use these elements as empty shells that they inhabit much like hermit crabs. This 'constructing' can be retrospective, through a process of rationalization. It can be prospective, as in a planning process. It can be both, in the way the decisions serve to establish a link between a past (realized) and a future (potential).

It is likely that this process (the making of a 'decision') is seldom fully accomplished. In other words, to say that people tend to interpret what is going on around them in terms of 'decisions' does not mean that they build coherent, solid and durable interpretations. The function of decision is not to explain the world with a strong degree of truth. Above all, decision enables people to act in this world. Consequently, it is likely that in constructing 'decisions,' organization members show incoherences; they more or less easily review their interpretations: they forget; they rewrite history, present or future. In fact, their constructions vary in 'quality' to a great extent.

The social representations of decision-making help participants make their way in the organizational mess. To some extent, it reduces the mess as co-ordinated expectations and behaviors stem naturally from sharing of these representations. But this self-fulfilling process is not powerful enough to completely overcome the organizational disorder. Evidence remains that things do not match with their representations. In short, 'decisions' are not quite the 'decisions' they should be. Participants are more or less conscious of this. A few of them become cynical. Many tell funny and/or bitter stories about flaws in the decision-making process. Yet, nobody really gives up: they all persist in trying to build 'decisions.' Though it is obviously a rather inaccurate description of real processes, the social representation of decision is not challenged, precisely because it is a social representation.

Feldman (1989) describes this paradox in the behavior of bureaucratic analysts in the US Department of Energy. The analysts work hard to produce information to help policy-makers solve problems. But they know policy-makers almost never use this information, so that their contribution to the decision-making process appears to them as almost nil. They nevertheless keep on producing reports and papers just as if they did not know it was hopeless. Feldman calls on several reasons to explain the paradox. First, it is their job to do so, and they are motivated by possible promotions and salary raises. Secondly, their work sometimes happens to be used by policy-makers, and such a glorious possibility is worth the ordinary frustrations. Thirdly, after all, doing their job the best they can is all they can do to help things go the way they think they ought to go.

In our view, these reasons are certainly relevant, but they would not persist in the long run if they did not benefit from the shelter of an idealistic representation of organizational action. Feldman herself depicts analysts as 'captive to the problem-solving or rational perspective' (1989: 106–14). This representation of decision-making is precisely the one that justifies analysts in organizations. It supports the analysts' social identity. As a social group, their representation of decision-making cannot be separated from what they are and what they do, and how they legitimize their existence in the organization and in the world as well.

As a consequence, analysts need to believe in problem-solving in order to do their job each time they have to do it. They work to make 'decisions': this vision of their role gives sense to what they do and confirms what they have learned to do. It is a useful illusion, and its first use is to allow them to act a priori, to get into the course of action. They do not need things to really happen the way they think they should, but they need to believe they will.

Continuity is the primary condition of such a process. 'Decisions' organize the flow of action in endless series of cycles. 'What's next?' is the main managerial concern. Being retrospective and focusing on final choices, classical empirical studies of decision-making completely obscured this phenomenon. Managers are primarily oriented towards the future. For them, the past matters only as a starting situation for action and future results. No choice is ever standing alone in the light of their detached judgement. The process of constructing 'decisions' through a social representation is not a process of constructing one 'decision;' it is a continuous movement of developing cycles of action.

Organizational routines play an important part in this respect, because they materialize the process. They form an underlying network of concrete motives, to which participants are able to attach their projects of 'decisions.' They are the solid ground on which the social representation can lean. In this sense, they are 'action generators' (Starbuck, 1983) or 'hidden technologies' (Berry, 1983).

The social representation of decision-making conveys a paradox. Because they think of organizational action through social representations, organization members are in a way disconnected from the 'real' processes. In this sense, we are right in naming them participants rather than actors. But as their representations help them to engage in action and interact with others in a productive way, they truly became actors rather than more or less absent participants.

Looking back: 'decisions' as rationalizations

Not being stupid, analysts (and organization members in general) easily understand that things did not follow their a priori model. Yet they do not question it deeply. Why is this? How do organizational participants accommodate the discrepancies they perceive between what they expected and engaged in, and what they understand that 'really' happened?

We have argued that as managers are primarily in a proactive stance, and tend to look forward rather than to look back, they are not likely to be as shocked as external observers might be. Thus, managers partly avoid or minimize this discrepancy. Realizing 'after the fact' is not so important. It may be in some cases, when the discrepancies are very obvious, when patent have been made or when people can see that they have been intentionaly fooled. But the ordinary flow of action takes away a good part of the cognitive dissonance.

The social division of work is another factor favoring the persistence of beliefs in decision-making. Feldman's (1989) analysts are a small part of the huge machine of policy-making, and they know it. This is why they have to believe in decision-making, to find their place in the machine. But when they are faced with how things really go, being so powerless allows them to think that they are not to blame. After all, they did their job properly. Because they truly believe in problem-solving as the correct way to handle policy-making, they cannot see why they should change their ways. Quite on the contrary, being an island of rationality in a messy world comforts them in their rationalistic behavior. In most cases in organizations it is not clear why things did not turn out the right way. People say that the 'system' is responsible for that. In any case, the participant himself is not to blame. We can hypothetize that the feeling of not having an active part in the flaws of the process allows participants to readily acknowledge these flaws, though, as Feldman shows, they may be quite bitter about it.

Other organizational participants – and especially managers who think of themselves or are regarded as central in the making of 'decisions' – may need greater coherence between their prospective expectations of what should happen and retrospective interpretation of what really happened. As visible discrepancies would require justifications in their eyes and to others, they have to adopt some sort of strategy.

The basic strategy is to interpret what happened according to the normative aspects of their social representation of decision-making. The rational model of decision-making offers many opportunities to do so. It is a remarkable explanatory garbage can. For instance, it easily:

- reframes violent political struggles as useful and normal debates – though maybe a little too passionate ones – that give more depth to collective deliberation;

- reinterprets heavy constraints put on participants by bureaucratic procedures as rational methods saving time and efforts and preventing actors from wandering in vain;

- legitimizes discretionary power of a single actor as the only way to integrate diverging opinions and interests.

Other strategies acknowledge the discrepancies, but minimize them greatly. Managers may pretend that the perceived gap is an exception. Things normally go right but happen to go wrong. Exception proves the rule. Or they may pretend that on the whole, in spite of a few marginal events, things went right.

Of course, double strategies are to be expected. There are ways of believing without believing. 'Distant familiarity' (Matheu, 1986) allows managers to partly dissociate what they do and what they think, what they really think and what they should think. Complete dissociation leads to unbearable stress, to bitter resignation or to plain cynicism. But partial dissociation helps organizational participants play the organizational games with more efficiency both for the organization and for themselves. Building a tolerance to discrepancies may be a distinctive competence, as organizations frequently distrust both innocents and cynics.

Looking back mobilizes the social representation of decision-making as well as looking ahead. We can hypothesize that participants construct 'decisions' as more or less isolated cases, thus becoming able to explain things and to attribute responsibilities to actors (including themselves or not). Doing this may imply reorganizing their initial ideas about the process. Normative aspects of the representation are likely to play a central role in these retrospective interpretations, as justification and legitimation are frequent issues in looking back. Discrepancies between the normative expectations and perceived realities are not likely to be fully acknowledged, as accurate descriptions of processes seldom make good post-decisional justifications (Crozier, 1989). In any case, acknowledging these discrepancies does not lead participants to seriously challenge their representation of decision-making. Thus, they engage in the ongoing course of action in the same way as they did before. Both the representation and the concrete forms of action are then left unchanged for the most part.

The idea of a social representation of decision-making may enrich existing models of organizational action. For instance, it suggests that 'action generators' may activate managers through their representations of decision-making rather than take them along in a passive, unconscious and mechanistic way. It could help develop the action view of the strategic process (e.g. Johnson, 1987): 'decision-making' plays a central role in the actualization of the organization strategic paradigm and, through dramatic episodes of 'strategic decision-making,' in the burst of strategic revolutions. Referring to 'strategic decision-making' is in itself a way of categorizing issues and actors, and thus, it may be an aspect of the 'strategic discourse' (Knights and Morgan, 1991).

Summary and conclusion

Students of decision-making tried to depart from what appeared as overly rational, normative and inaccurate descriptions of organizational choices, by empirically investigating many aspects of decision-making processes. This stance is 'realistic' in two ways: first, as intended, the decision-making perspective has tried to 'stick to the facts'; secondly, as not explicitly intended, it conveyed the idea that decisions themselves are facts. This paper argued that decision-making is best understood as a process of reality creation through organization members' representations of their own role and activity. Decision as a social representation is a part of a general, broader process of organizational action. Considering decision-making as a social representation phenomenon draws some kind of a missing link between the realistic decision-making perspective and the emerging action perspective. It is not meant to integrate the two at the same level, but to help the action perspective to reinterpret the realistic decision-making perspective rather than to oppose decision and action in an artificial and unfruitful manner.

Organizational researchers undoubtedly have to broaden their perspective and build descriptions and explanations of action processes, not of decision processes solely. But no theory of action can develop without integrating the fact that, to a significant extent, organizational members think and act in terms of decision-making. Decision-making is a relevant phenomenon for a theory of action, not a marginal one.

References

Allison, G. T. (1971) *The Essence of Decision*. Boston, MA: Little Brown.

Bailey, A. and Johnson, G. (1992) 'An integrated exploration of strategic decision-making', paper presented at the 12th SMS Conference on Strategic Renaissance. London, UK, 14–17 October.

Berry, M. (1983) *Une technologie invisible? L'impact des instruments de gestion sur l'évolution des systèmes humains*. Paris, France; Centre de Recherche en Gestion de l'Ecole Polytechnique.

Brunsson, N. (1982) 'The irrationality of action and action rationality: decisions, ideologies and organizational action', *Journal of Management Studies*, 19: 29–44.

Brunsson, N. (1985) *The Irrational Organization*. Chichester, UK: Wiley.

Brunsson, N. (1989) *The Organization of Hypocrisy*. Chichester, UK: Wiley.

Brunsson, N. (1990) 'Deciding for responsibility and legitimation: alternative interpretations of organizational decision-making', *Accounting, Organizations and Society*, 15: 47–59.

Carter, E. E. (1971) 'The behavioral theory of the firm and top level corporate decisions', *Administrative Science Quarterly*, 16: 412–28.

Cohen, M. D., March, J. G. and Olsen, J. P. (1972) 'A garbage can model of organizational choice', *Administrative Science Quarterly*, 17: 1–25.

Crozier, M. and Friedberg, E. (1977) *L'acteur et le système*. Paris, France; Seuil 1977.

Crozier, R. (1989) 'Postdecisional justification: the DeLorean case', in H. Montgomery and O. Svenson (eds), *Process and Structure in Human Decision-Making*. Chichester, UK: Wiley.

Cyert, R. M. and March, J. G. (1963) *A Behavioral Theory of the Firm*. Englewood Cliffs, NJ: Prentice Hall.

Dery, R. (1990a) *La multidisciplinarité des sciences de l'organisation du discours de l'unité au jeu des luttes et des alliances*. Cahier de recherche no. 90 18, HEC, Montréal Canada.

Dery, R. (1990b) *Action et connaissance dans les organisations*, Cahier de recherche no. 90–19, HEC, Montréal, Canada.

Doise, W. (1990) 'Les représentations sociales', in R. Ghiglione, C. Bonnet and J. F. Richard, *Traité de psychologie cognitive, Tom 3: cognition, représentation, communication*. Paris, France: Dunod.

Dutton, J. E. (1988) 'Understanding strategic agenda and its implications for managing change', in L. R. Pondy, R. T. Boland and H. Thomas (eds), *Managing Ambiguity and Change*. Chichester, UK: Wiley. pp. 127–44.

Feldman, M. S. (1989) *Order without Design: Information Production and Policy Making*. Stanford, CA: Stanford University Press.

Girin, J. (1990) 'Analyse empirique des situations de gestion: éléments de théorie et de méthode', in A. C. Martinet (ed.), *Epistémologie et sciences de gestion*. Paris, France: Economica.

Grandori, A. (1987) *Perspectives on Organization Theory*. Cambridge, MA: Ballinger.

Hickson, D. J., Butler, R. J., Cray, D., Mallory, G. R. and Wilson, D. (1986) *Top Decisions*. Oxford, UK: Blackwell.

Huard, P. (1980) 'Rationalité et identité,' *Revue Economique*, 3: 540–72.

Jodelet, D. (1984) 'Représentation sociale: phénomènes, concept et théorie', in S. Moscovici (ed.), *Psychologie Sociale*. Paris, France: PUF.

Jodelet, D. (1991) 'Représentations sociales: un domaine en expansion', in D. Jodelet (ed.), *Les représentations sociales* (2nd edn). Paris, France: PUF. pp. 31–61.

Johnson, G. (1987) *Strategic Change and the Management Process*. Oxford, UK: Blackwell.

Knights, D. and Morgan, G. (1991) 'Corporate strategy, organizations, and subjectivity: a critique', *Organization Studies*, 12 (2): 251–73.

Laroche, H. and Nioche, J. P. (1992) 'Pour une pédagogie de la métadécision', paper presented at the 1st International Colloquium 'La Pédagogie de la prise de décision,' ICN, Nancy, France, June.

Lawrence, P. R. and Lorsch, J. W. (1967) *Organization and Environment*. Boston, MA: Harvard.

Levy, P. (1990) *Les technologie de l'intelligence: l'avenir de la pensée à l'ère informatique*. Paris, France: La Découverte.

Lyles, M. A. (1981) 'Formulating strategic problem: empirical analysis and model development', *Strategic Management Journal*, 2: 61–75.

Madison, D. L., Allen, R. W., Porter, L. W., Renwick, P. A. and Mayes, B. T. (1980) 'Organizational politics: an exploration of managers' perceptions', *Human Relations*, 33: 79–100.

March, J. G. (1981) 'The decision-making perspective', in A. H. Van de Ven and W. F. Joyce (eds), *Perspectives on Organization Design and Behavior*: New York: Wiley.

March, J. G. (1988) 'Introduction: a chronicle of speculations about decision-making', in J. G. March (ed.), *Decisions and Organizations*. Oxford, UK: Blackwell. pp. 1–24.

March, J. G. and Simon, H. A. (1958) *Organizations*. New York: Wiley.

Matheu, M. (1986) 'La familiarité distante', *Annales des Mines, Gérer & Comprendre*, No. 2: 81–94.

Mintzberg, H., Raisinghani, D. and Theoret, A. (1976) 'The structure of unstructured' decision processes', *Administrative Science Quarterly*, 21: 247–75.

Mintzberg, H. and Waters, J. A. (1990) 'Does decision get in the way?', *Organization Studies*. 11: 1–16.

Nioche, J. P. (1985) 'La décision, ou l'action stratégique comme processus', in Anastassopoulos et al., *Pour une nouvelle politique d'entreprise*. Paris, France: PUF.

Padioleau, J. G. (1986) *L'ordre social*. Paris, France: L'Harmattan.

Padioleau, J. G. (1991) 'L'action publique moderniste', *Politiques et Management Public*, 9: 134–43.

Pettigrew, A. (1987) 'Context and Action in the Transformation of the Firm', *Journal of Management Studies*, 24 (6): 649–70.

Quinn, J. B. (1980) *Strategies for Change: Logical Incrementalism*. Homewood, IL: Irwin.

Saint-Sernin, B. (1989) *Genèse et unité de l'action*. Paris, France: Vrin.

Schwenk, C. R. (1984) 'Cognitive simplification processes in strategic decision-making', *Strategic Management Journal*, 5: 111–28.

Schwenk, C. R. (1985) 'Management illusions and biases: their impact on strategic decisions', *Long Range Planning*, 18: 74–80.

Schwenk, C. R. (1988a) *The Essence of Strategic Decision-Making*. Lexington, MA: Lexington Books.

Schwenk, C. R. (1988b) 'The cognitive perspective on strategic decision-making', *Journal of Management Studies*, 25: 41–55.

Sfez, L. (1981) *Critique de la décision* (3rd edn). Paris, France: Presses de la Fondations des Sciences Politiques.

Simon, H. A. (1957) *Administrative Behavior*. New York: The Free Press.

Sims, D. (1979) 'A Framework for Understanding the Definition and Formulation of Problems in Teams', *Human Relations*, 32: 909–21.

Sims, D. (1987) 'From harmony to counterpoint: reconstructing problems in an organization', in I. L. Mangham (ed.), *Organization Analysis and Development*. New York: Wiley.

Starbuck, W. H. (1983) 'Organizations as action generators', *American Sociological Review*, 48: 91–102.

Starbuck, W. H. (1985) 'Acting first and thinking later. Theory versus reality in strategic change', in J. M. Pennings (ed.), *Organizational Strategy and Change*. San Francisco, CA: Jossey Bass.

Weick, K. E. (1969) *The Social Psychology of Organizing*. Reading, MA: Addison Wesley.

Weick, K. E. (1983) 'Managerial Thought in the Context of Action', in S. Srivastva and Associates, *The Executive Mind*. San Francisco, CA: Jossey Bass.

Weick, K. E. (1987) 'Perspectives on action in organizations', in J. Lorsch (ed.), *Handbook of Organizational Behavior*. Englewood Cliffs, NJ: Prentice Hall.

Whitley, R. (1987) *On the Nature of Managerial Tasks and Skills: Their Distinguishing Characteristics and Organization*, Working Paper, Manchester Business School, Manchester, UK.

INDEX